Arthur Rackam

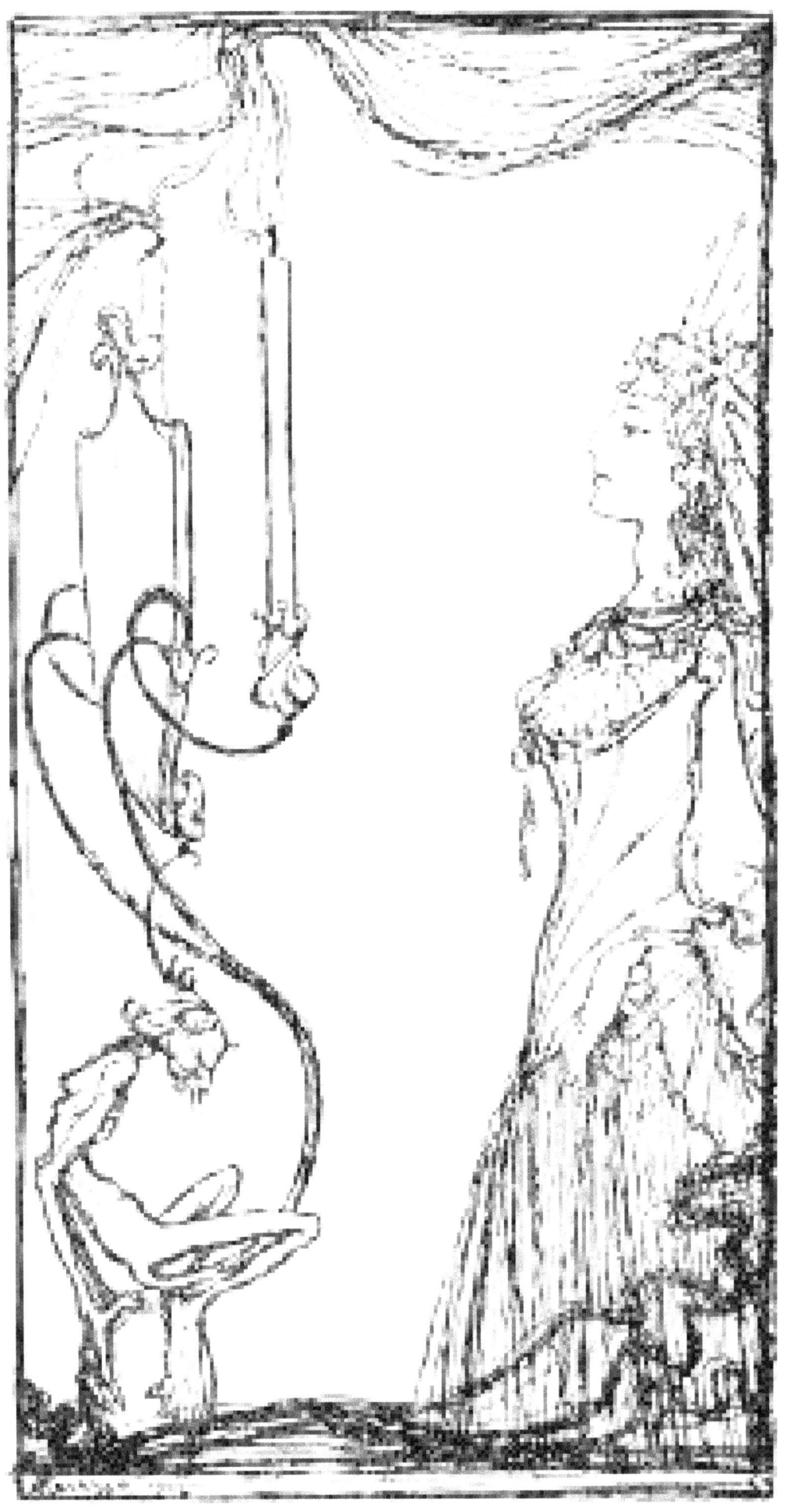

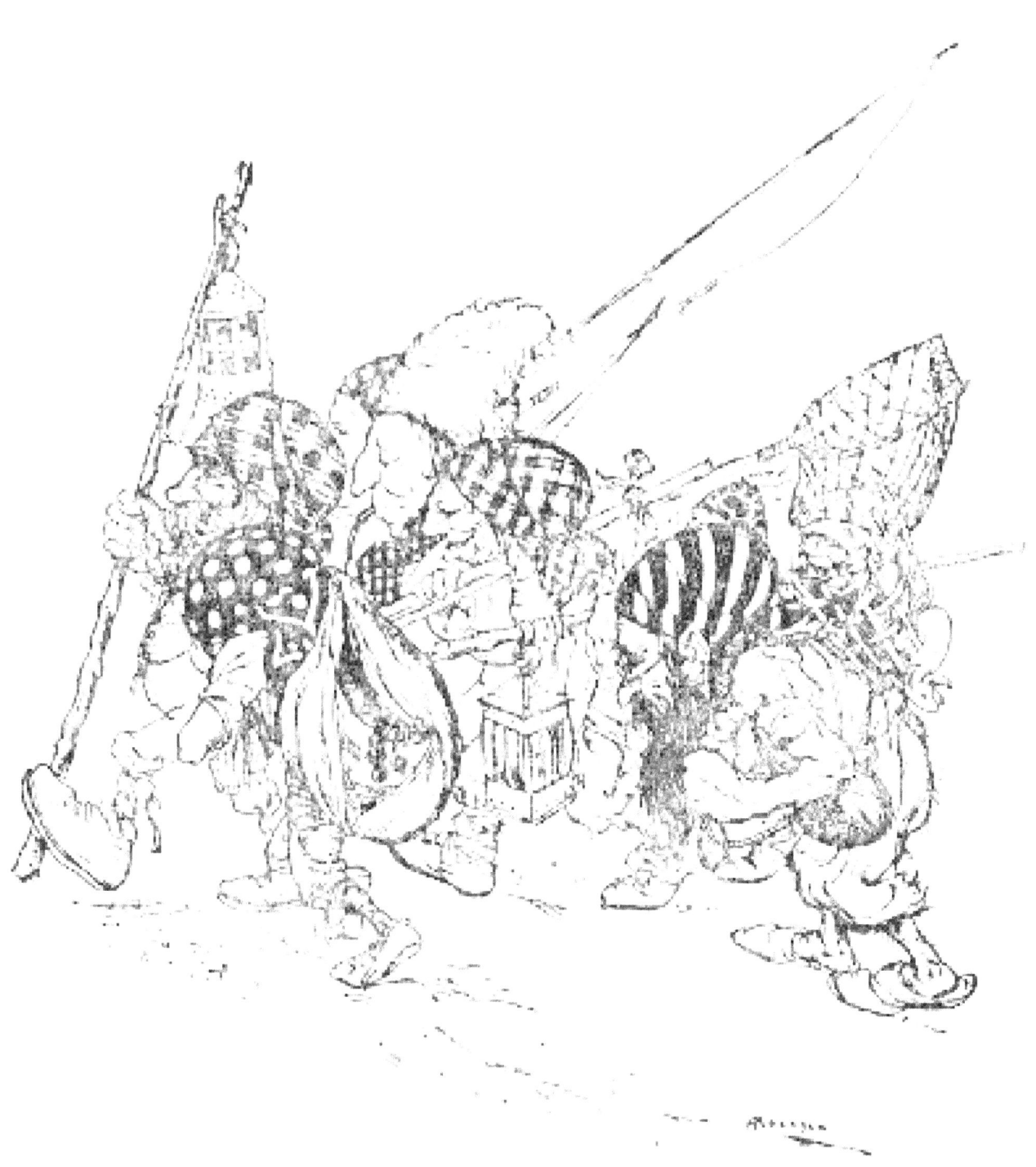

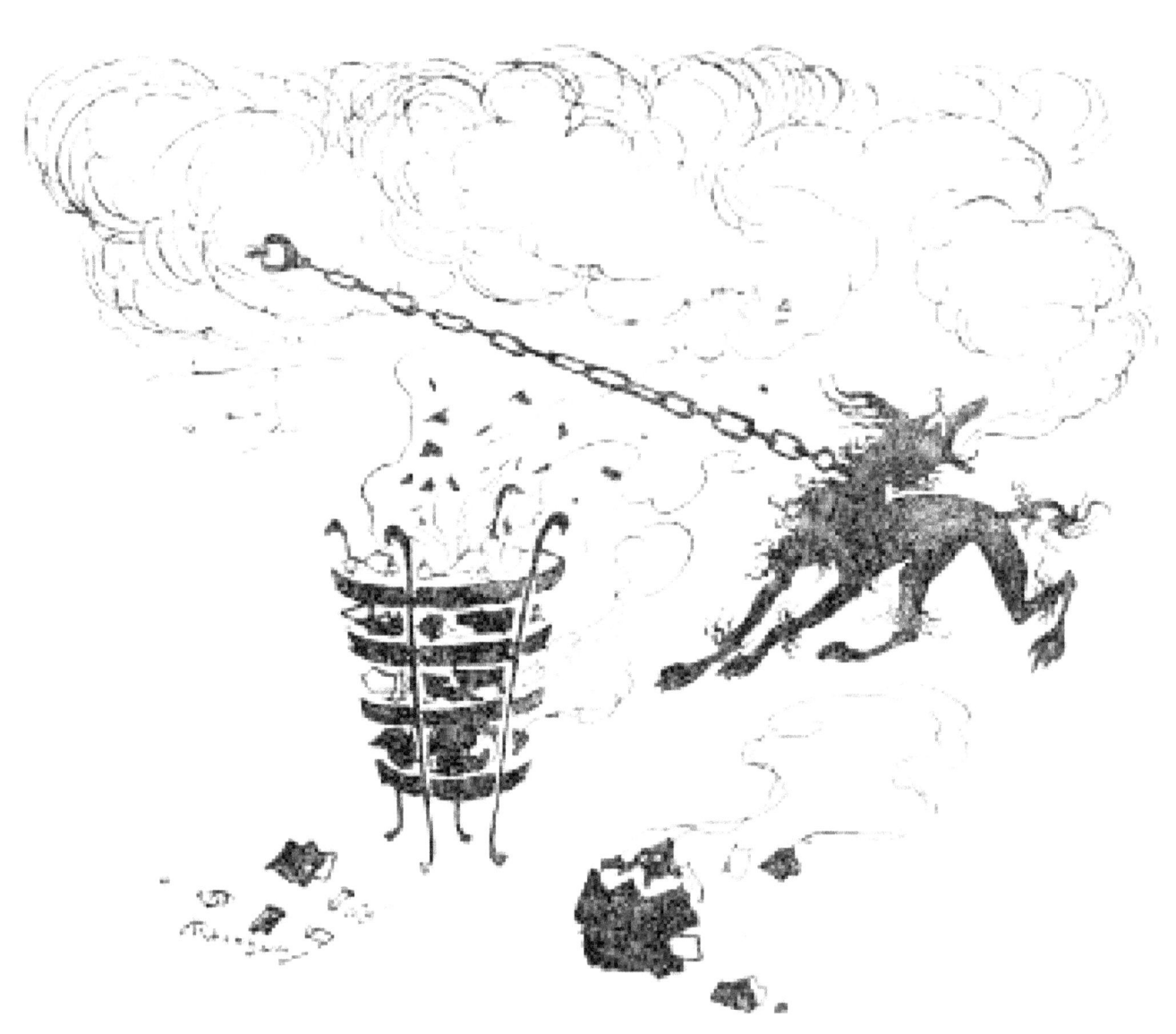

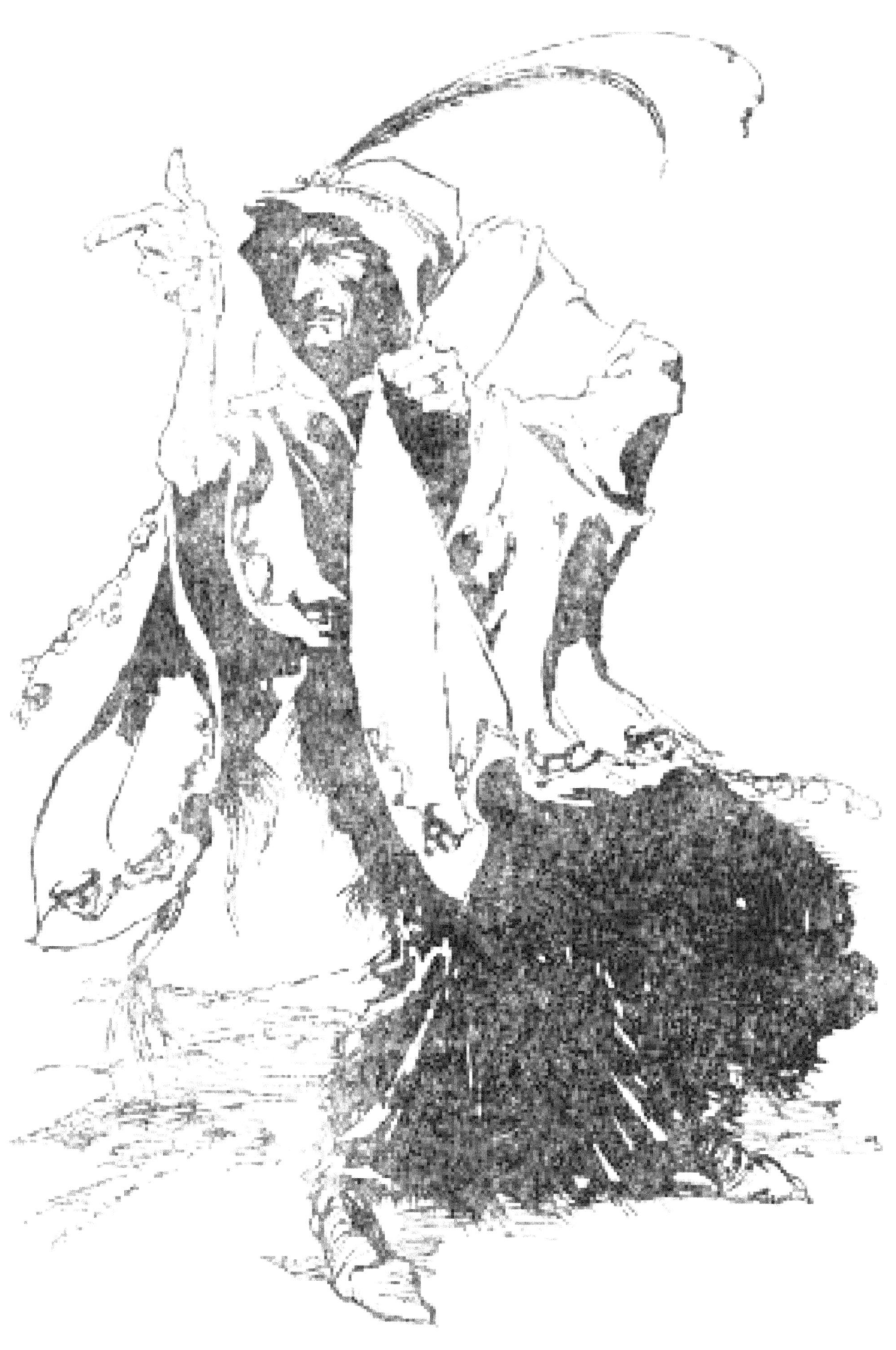

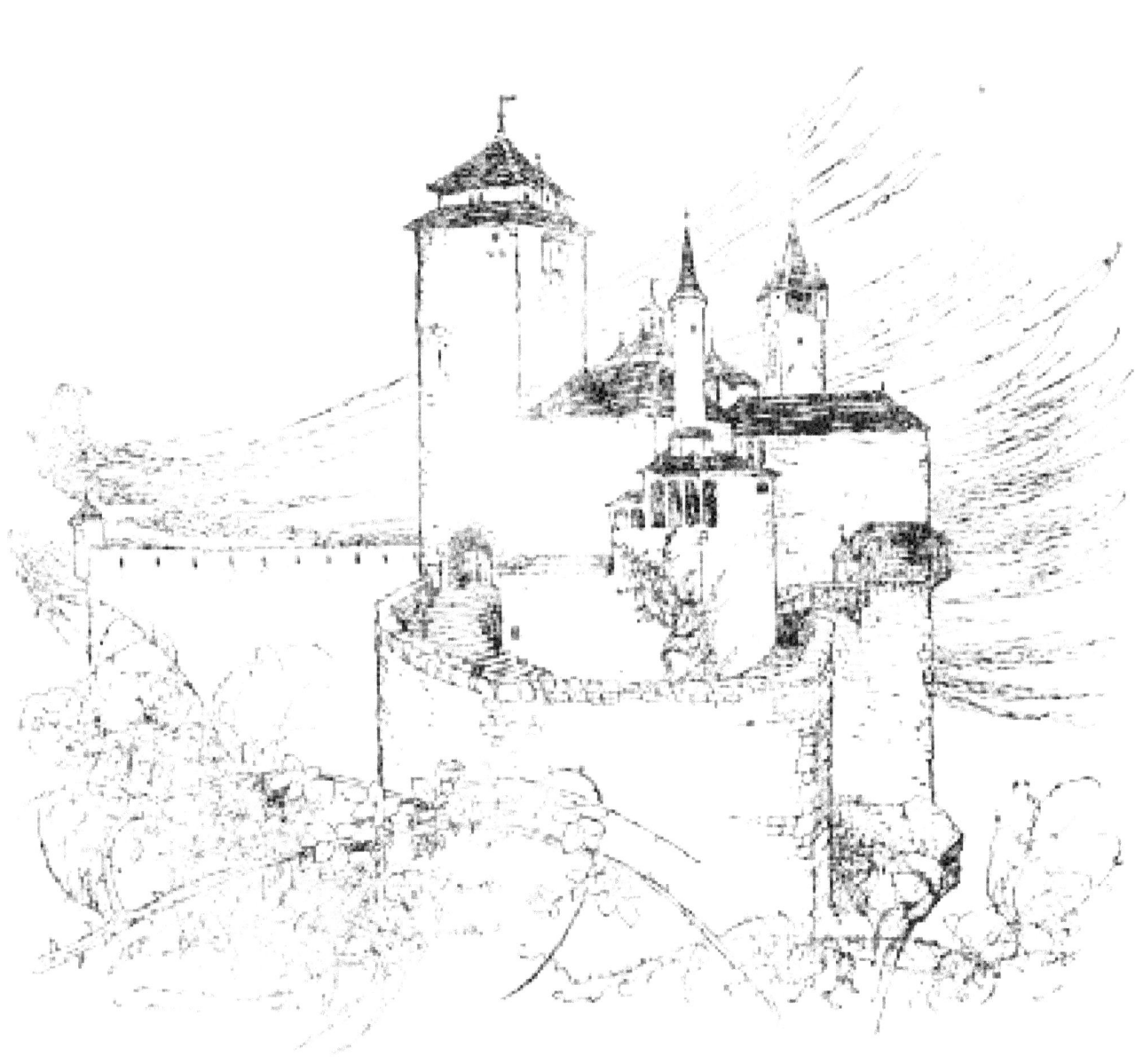

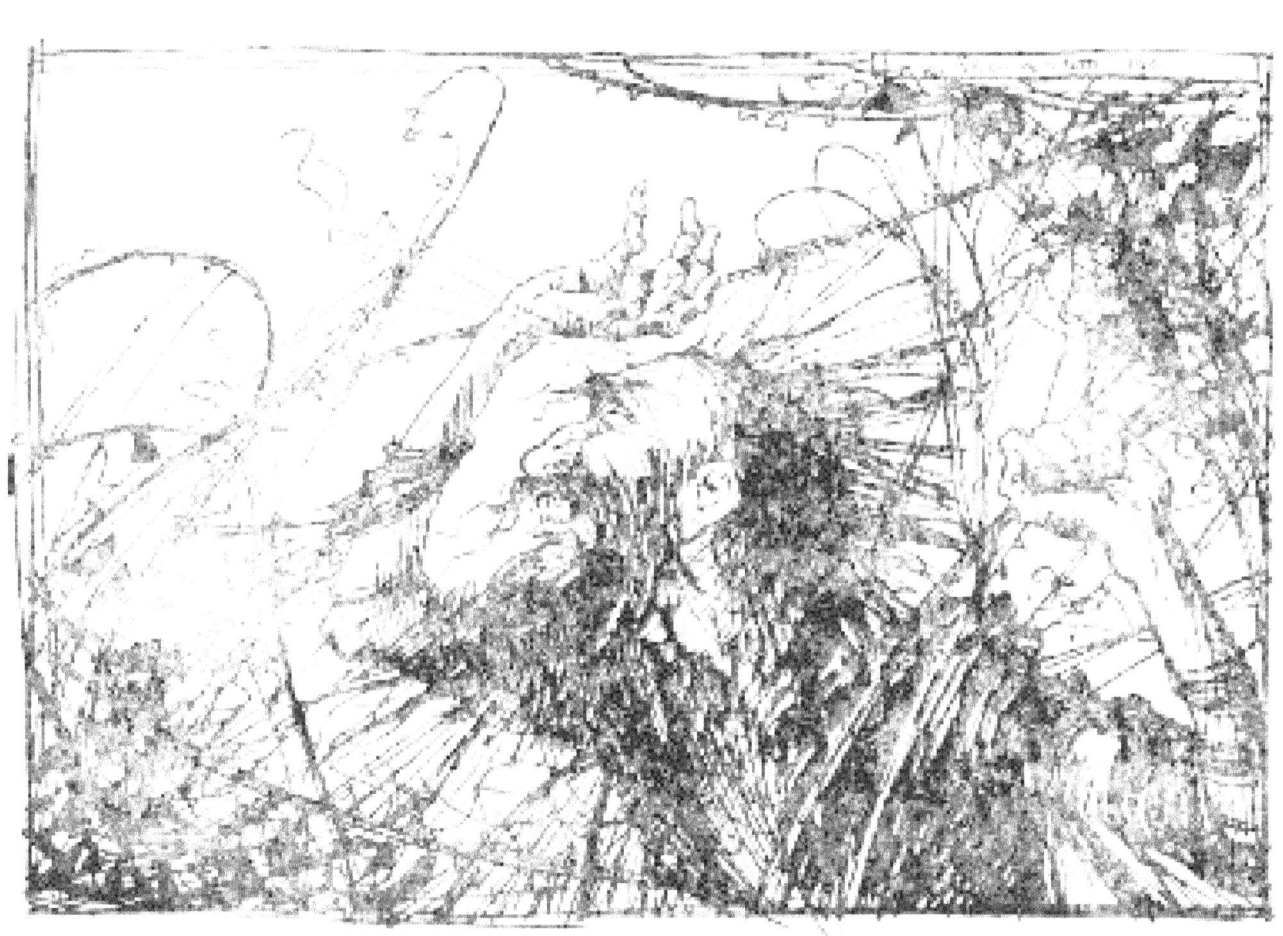

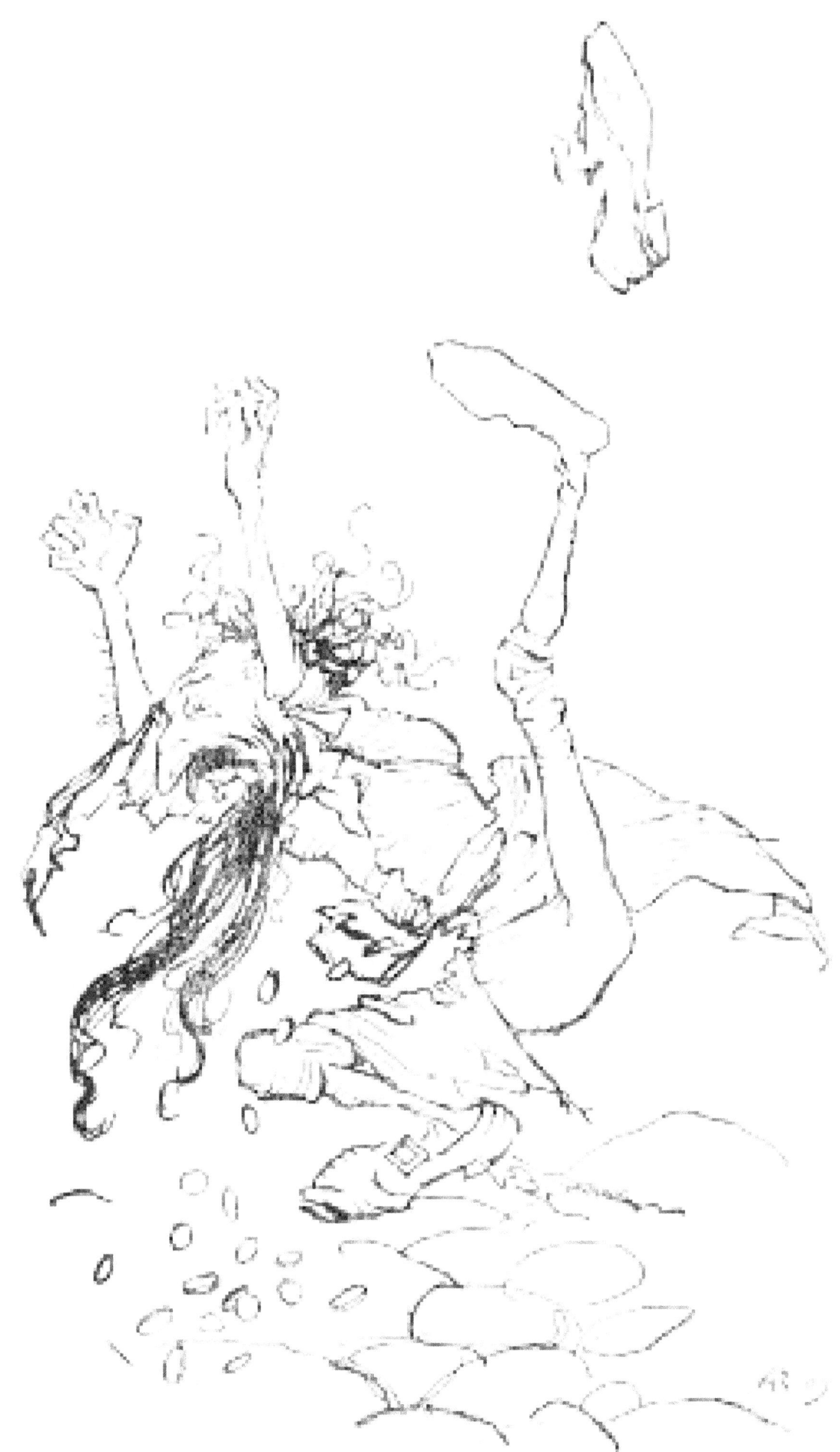

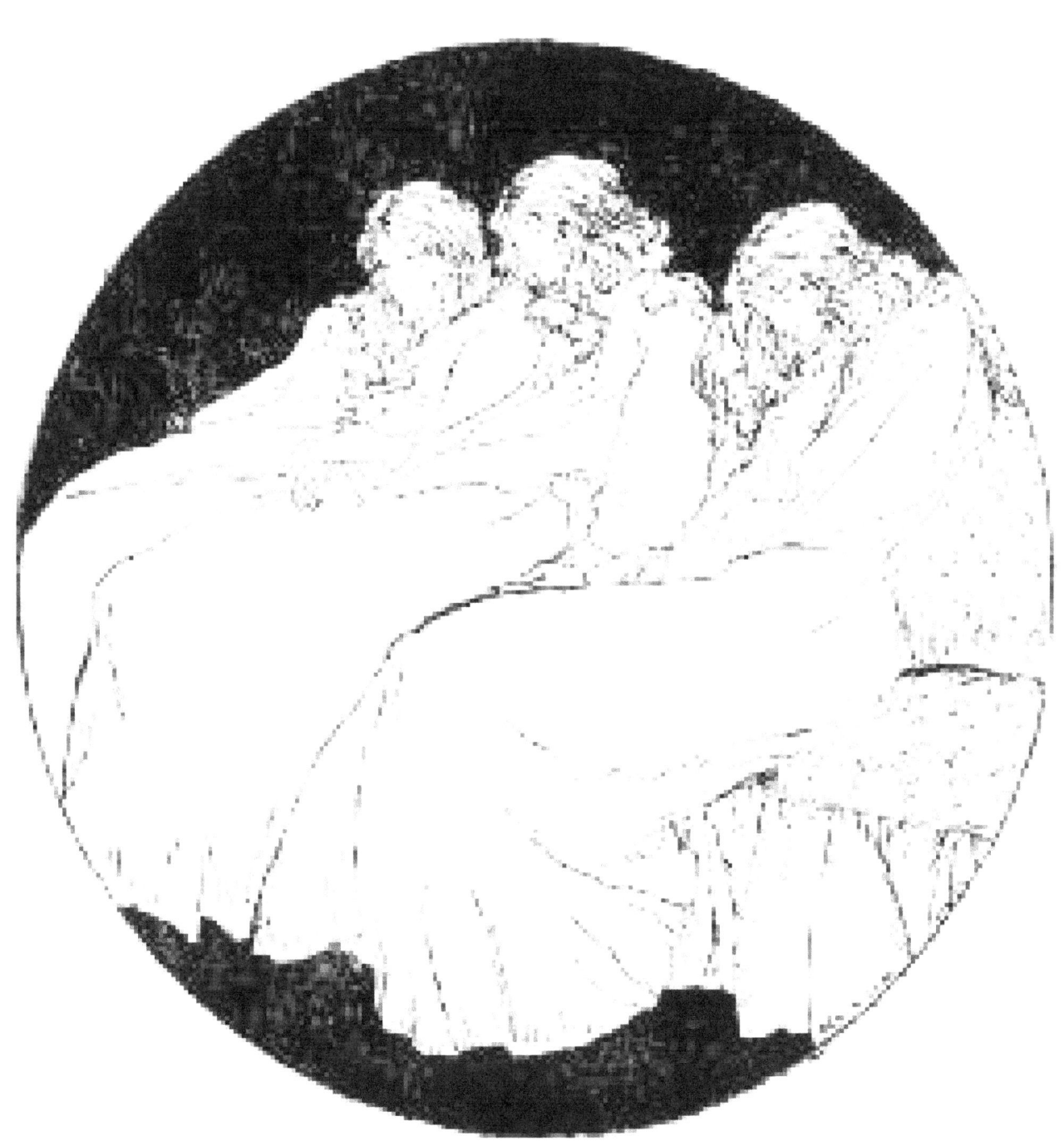

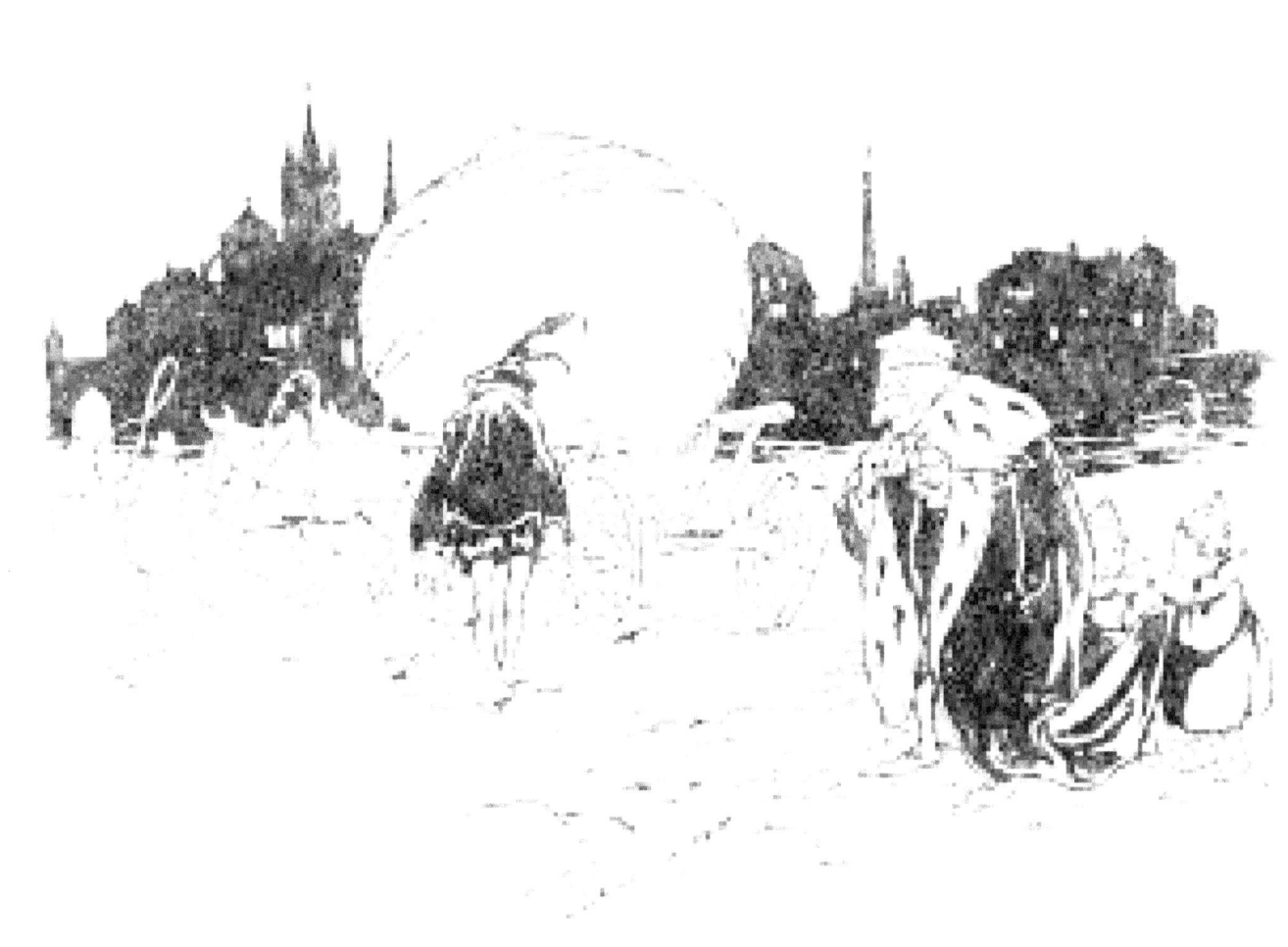

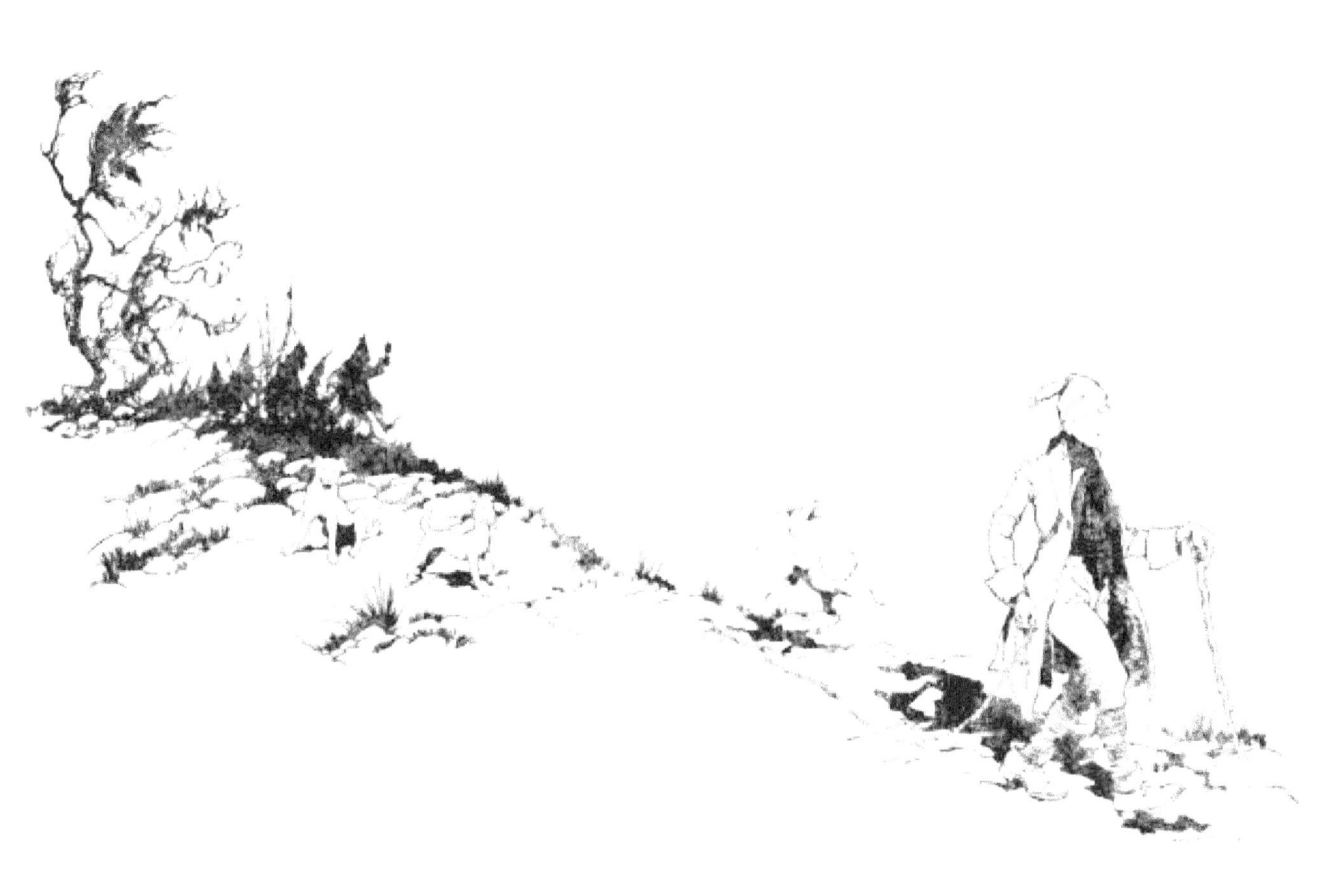

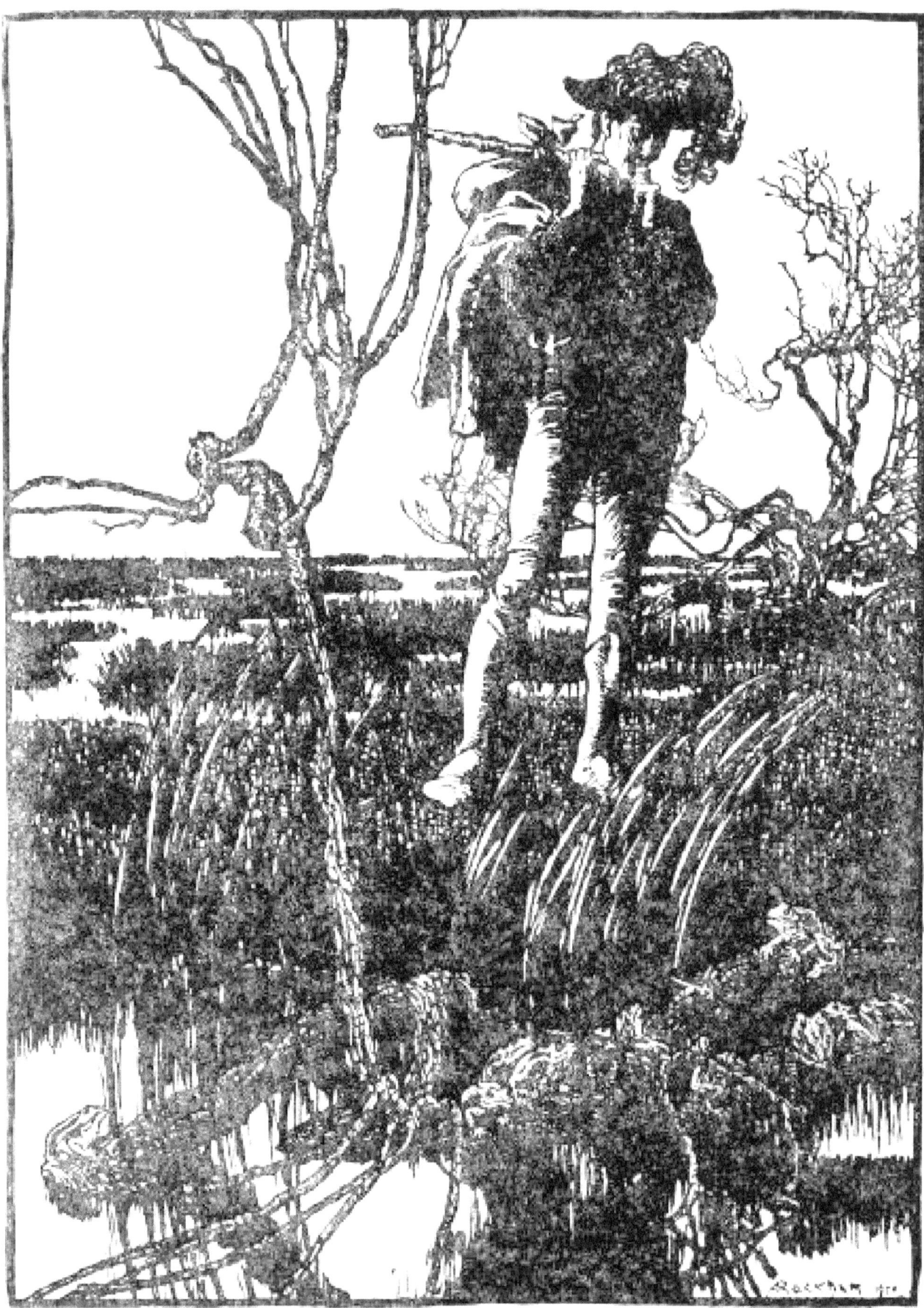

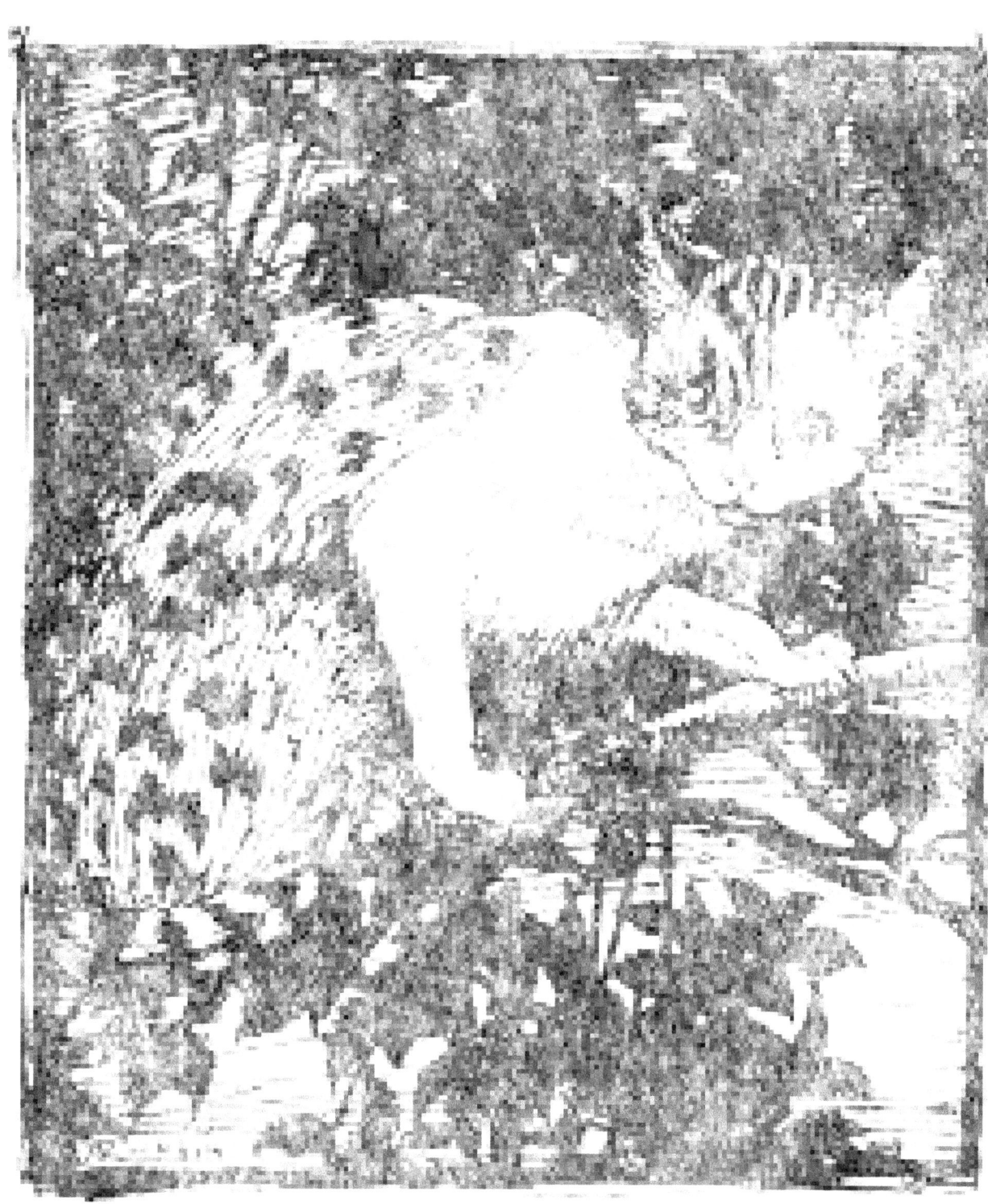

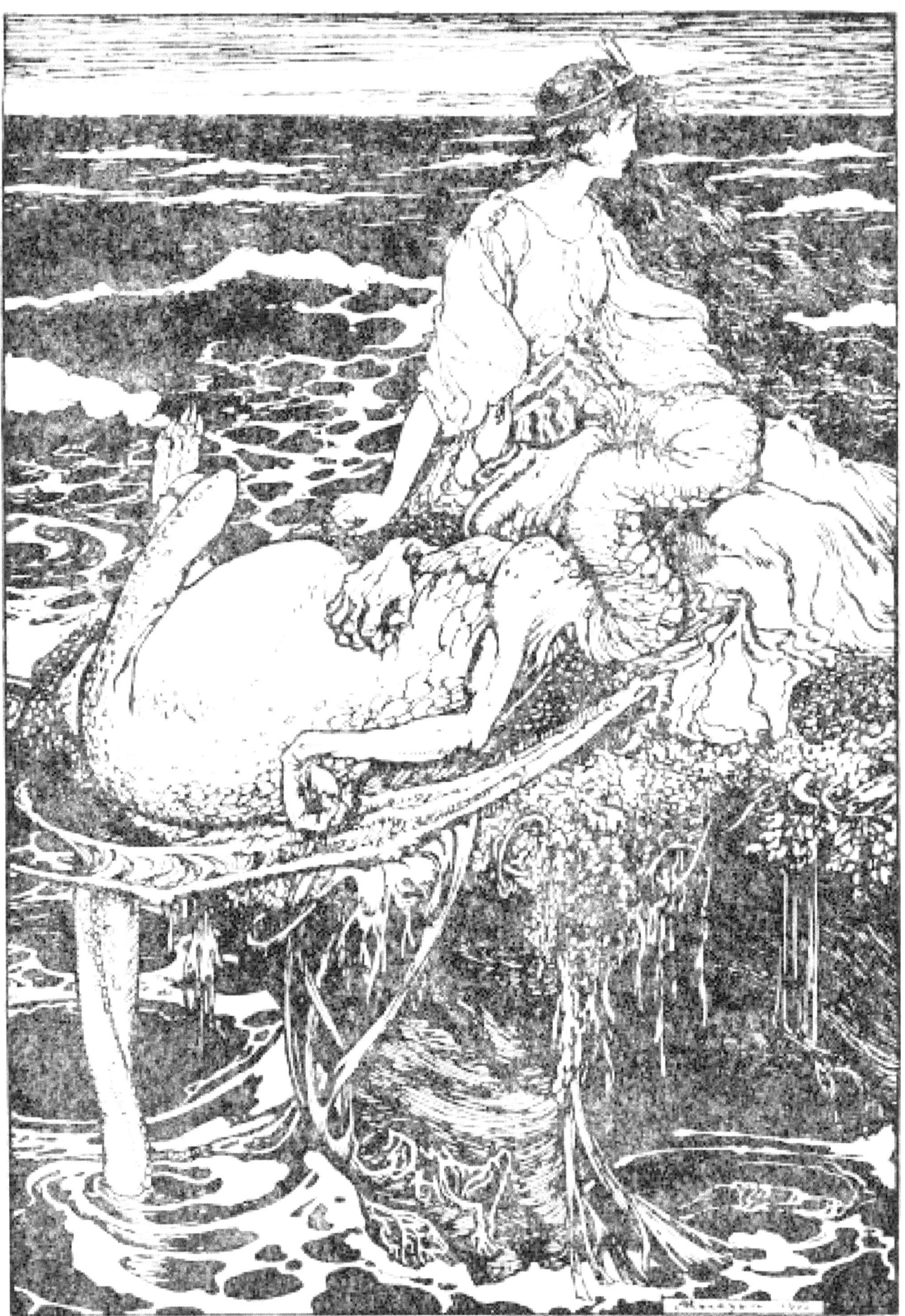

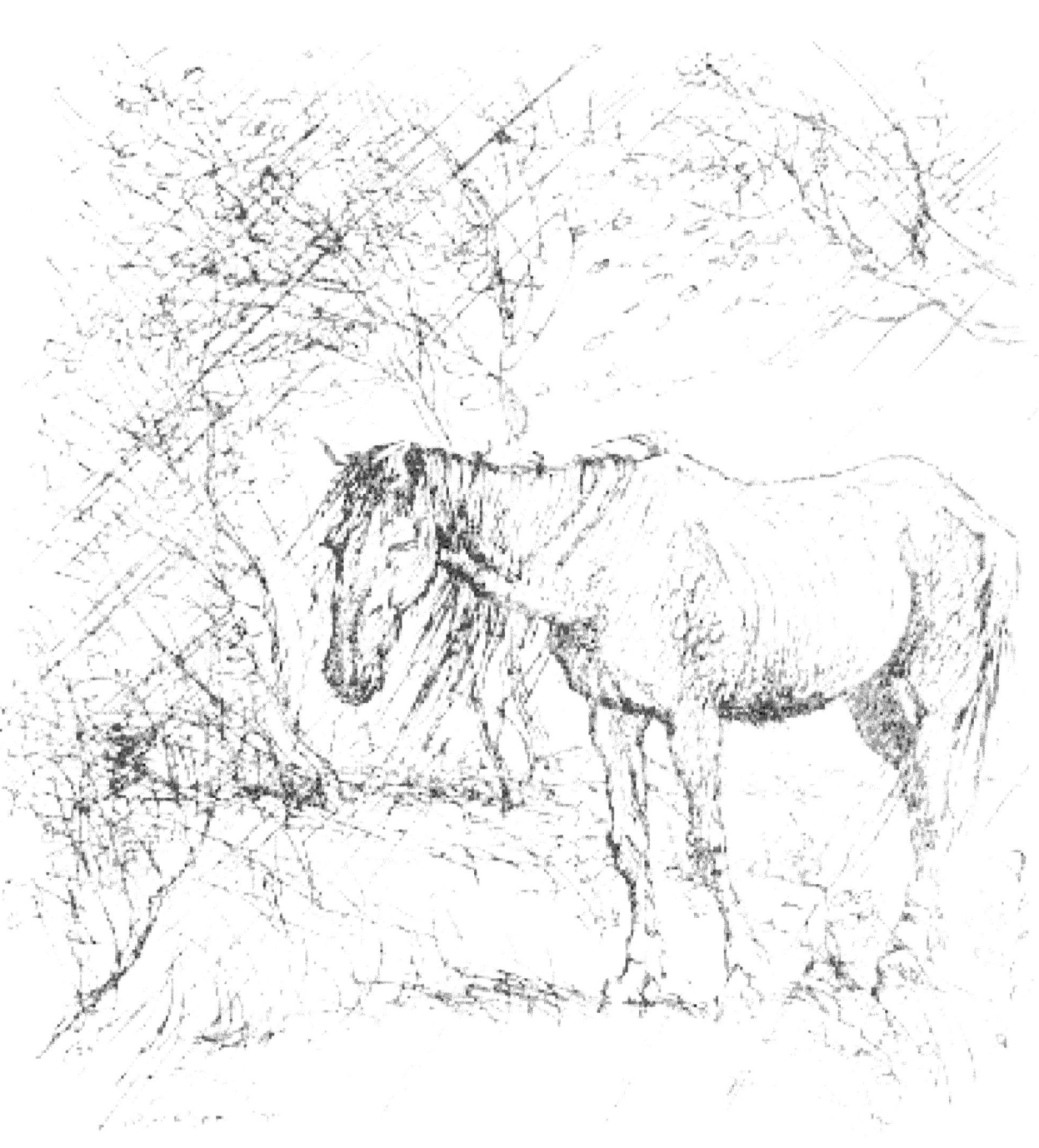

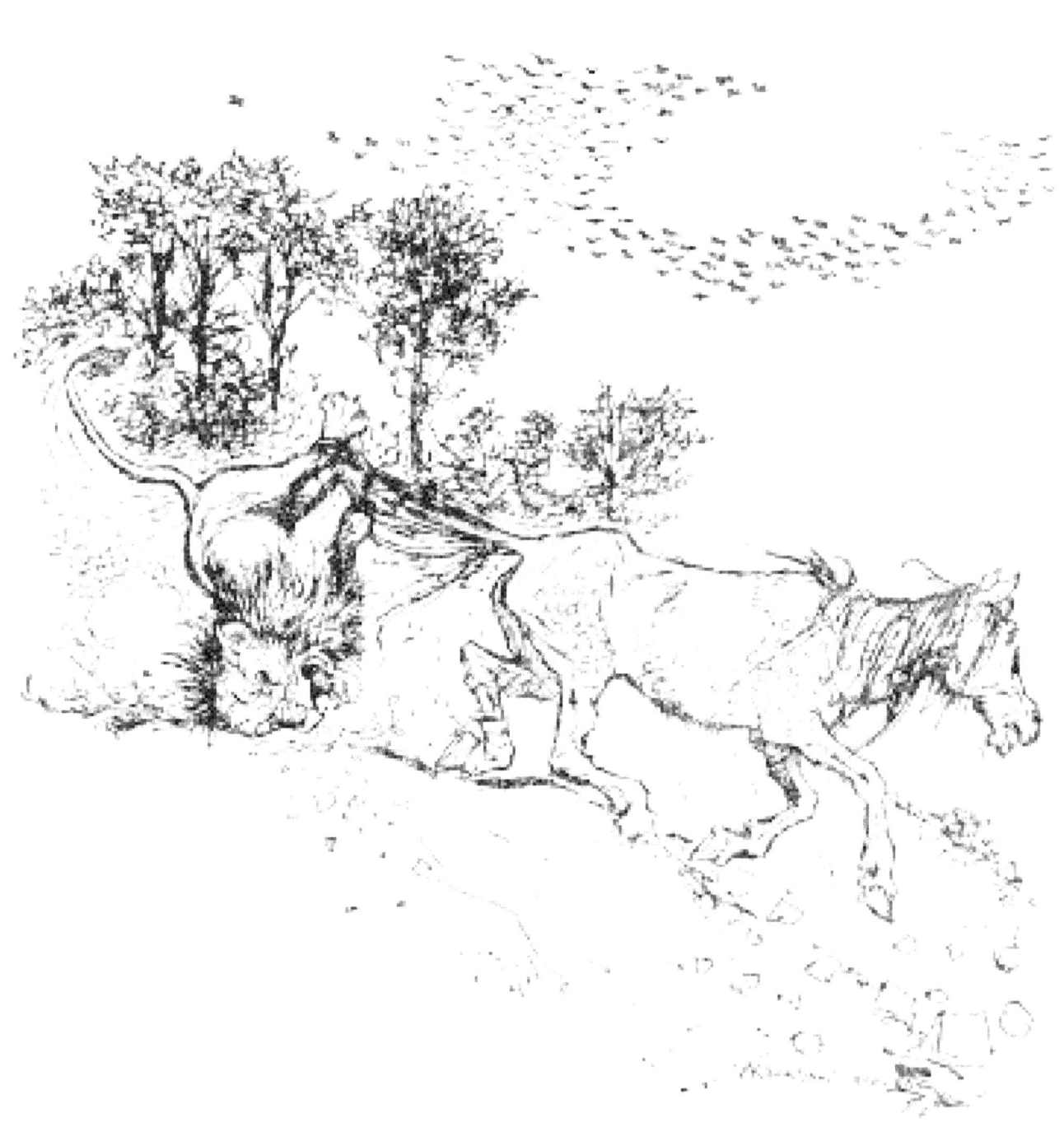

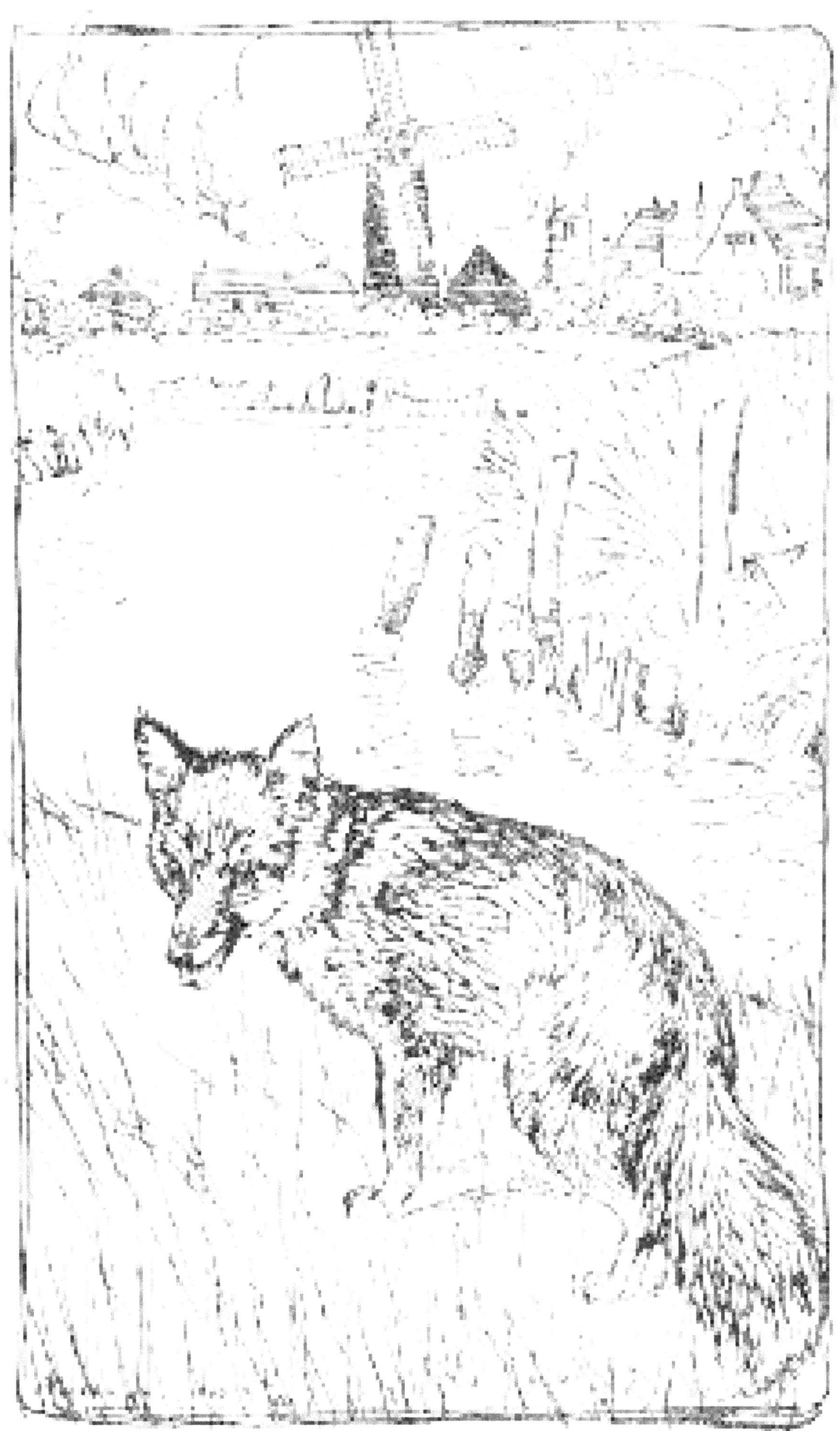

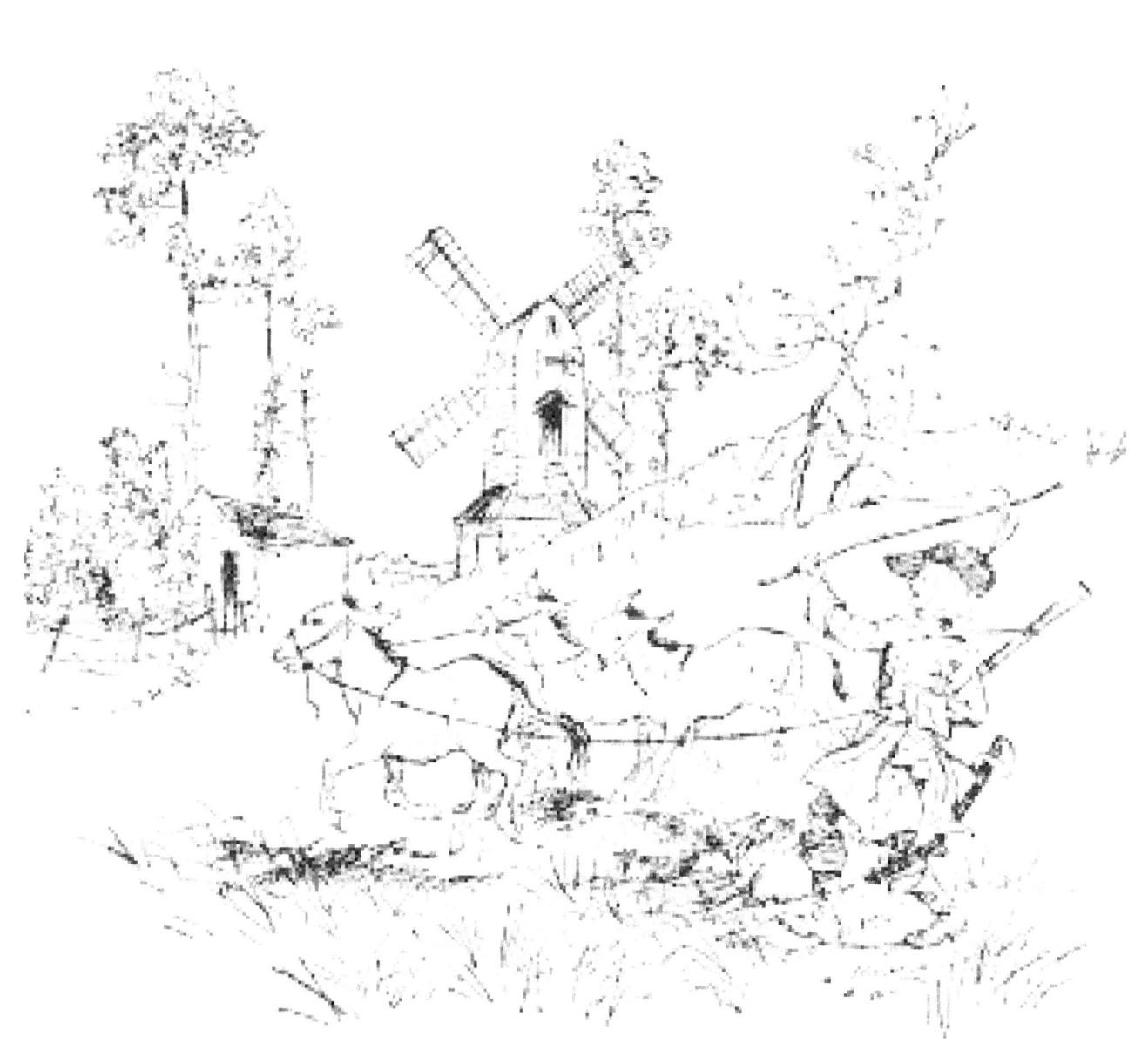

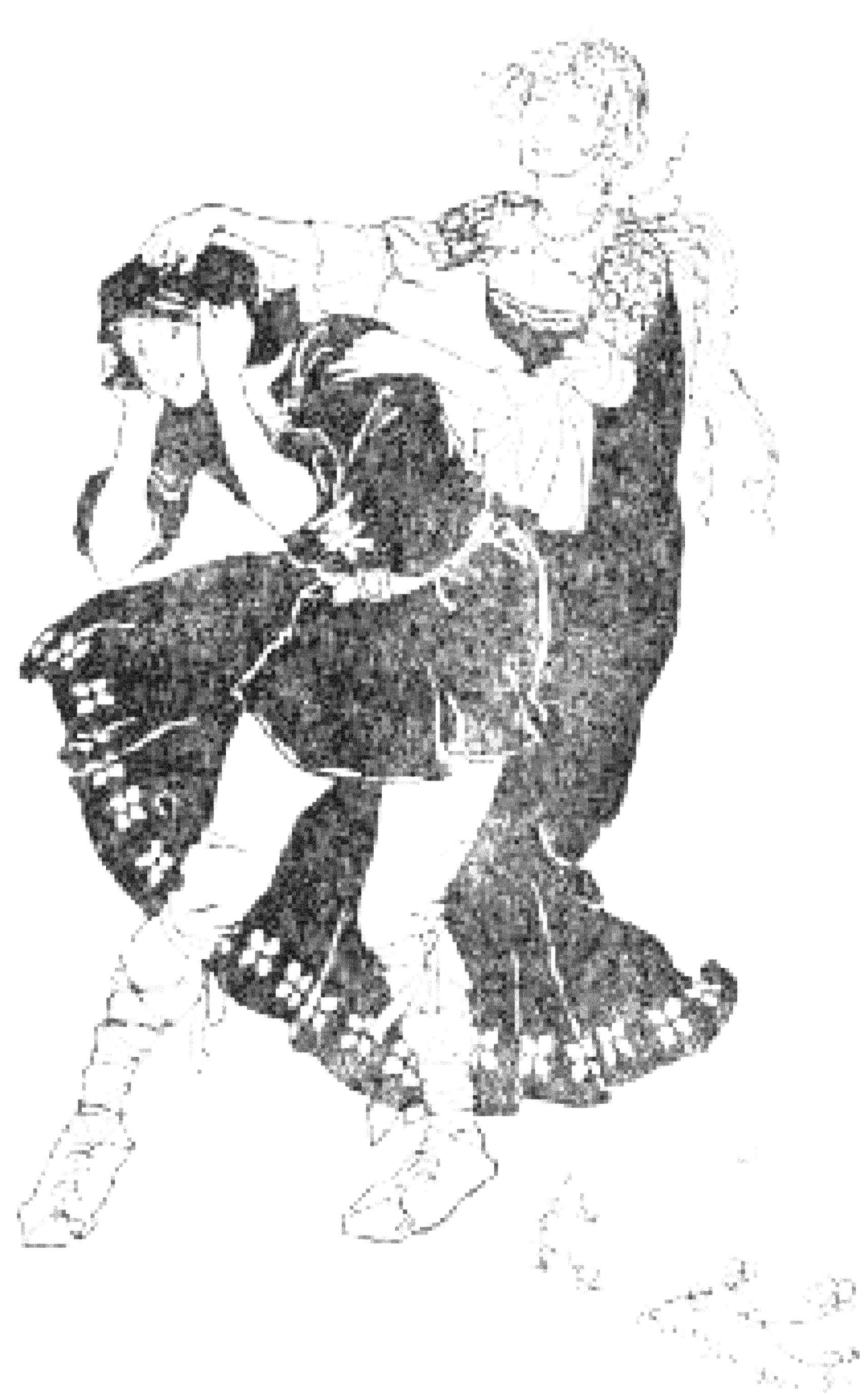

Walter Crane

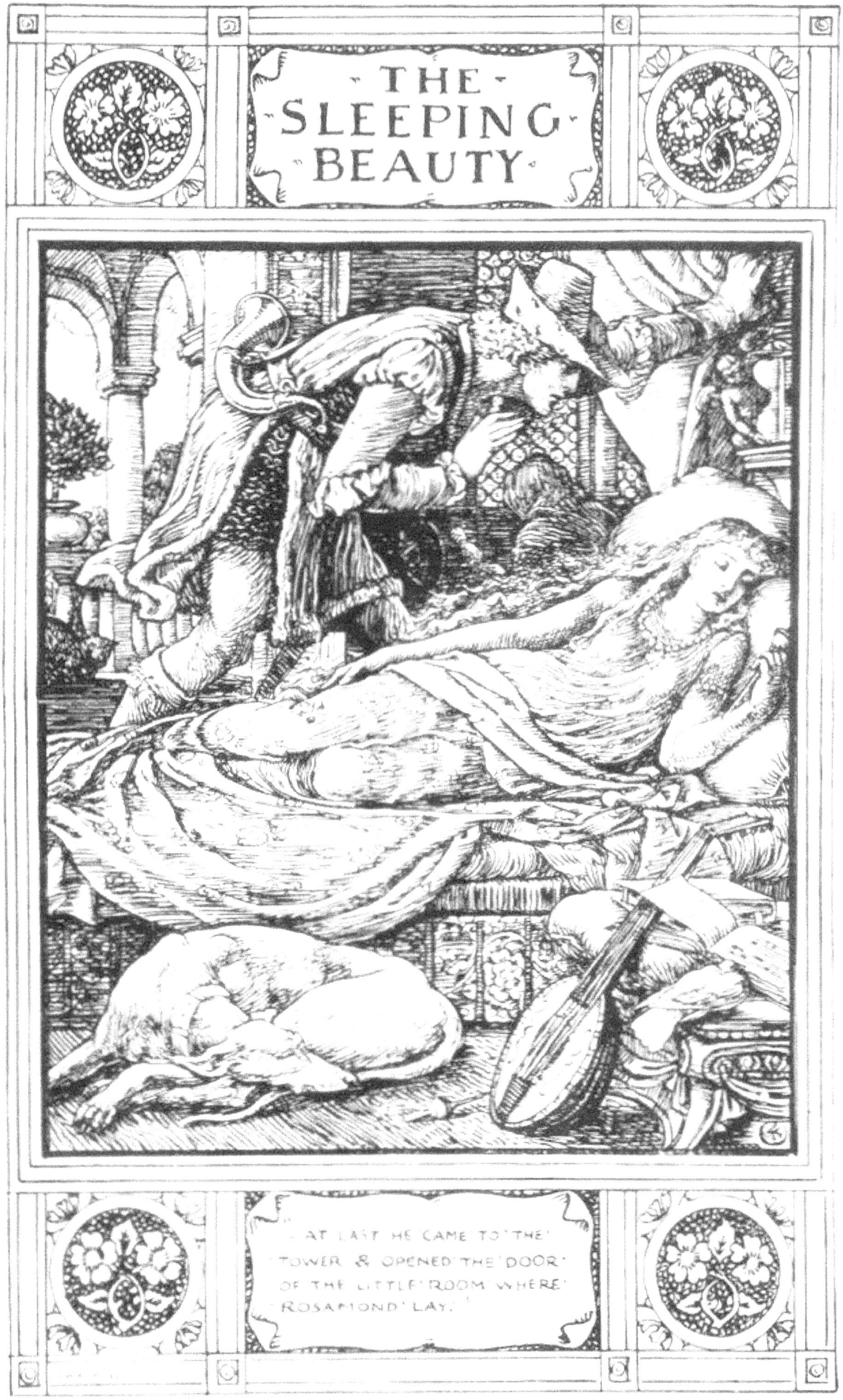

THE SLEEPING BEAUTY

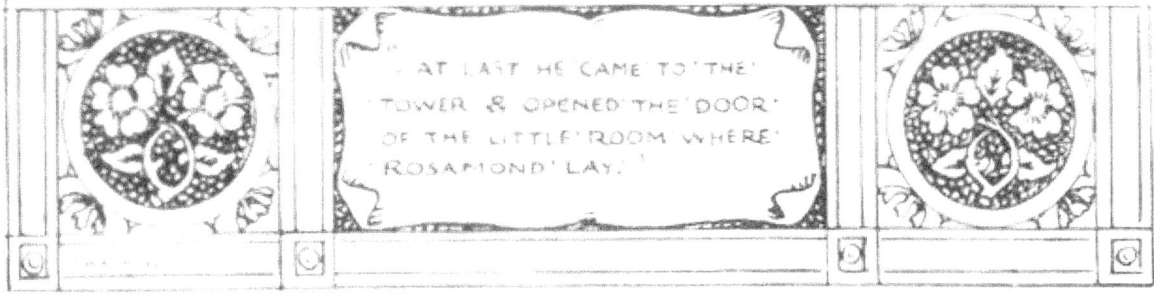

AT LAST HE CAME TO THE
TOWER & OPENED THE DOOR
OF THE LITTLE ROOM WHERE
ROSAMOND LAY.

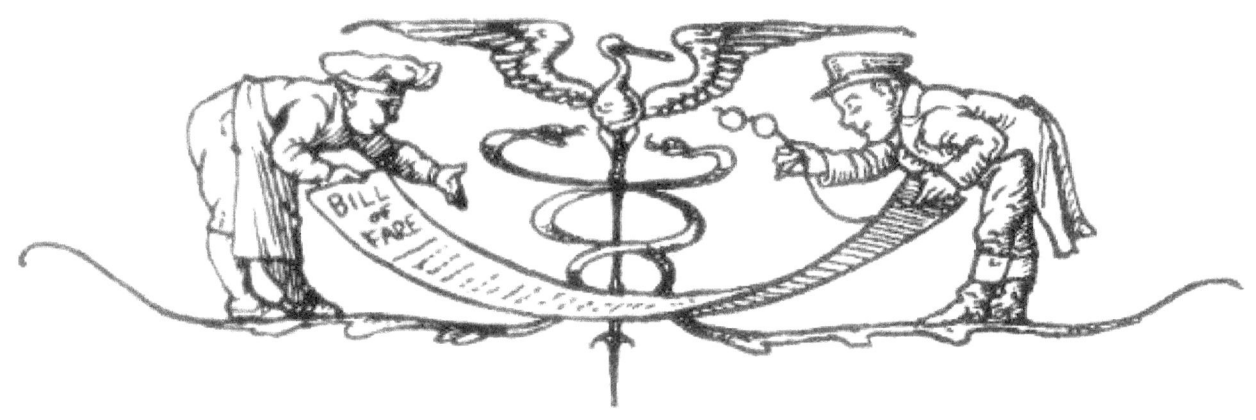

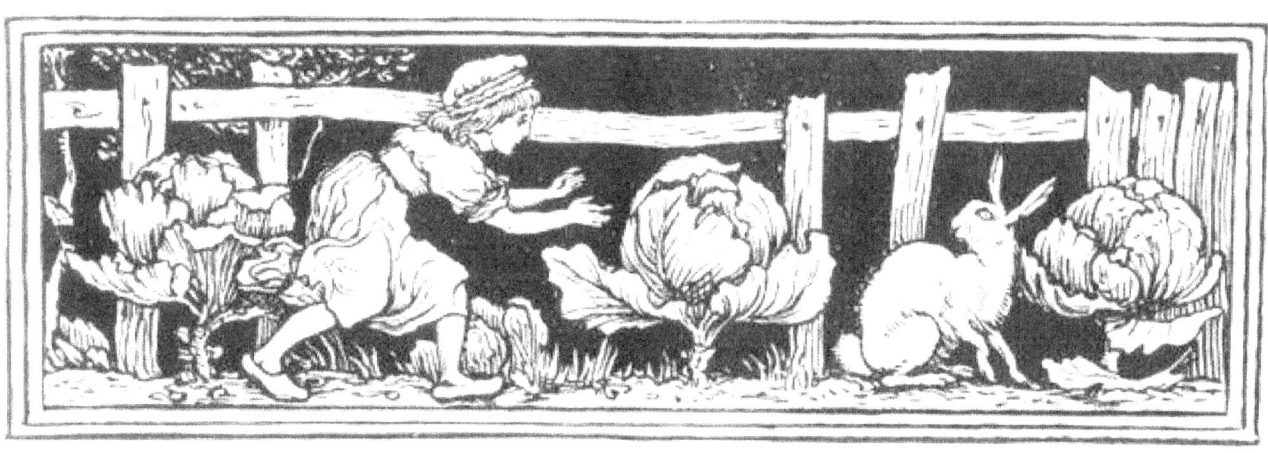

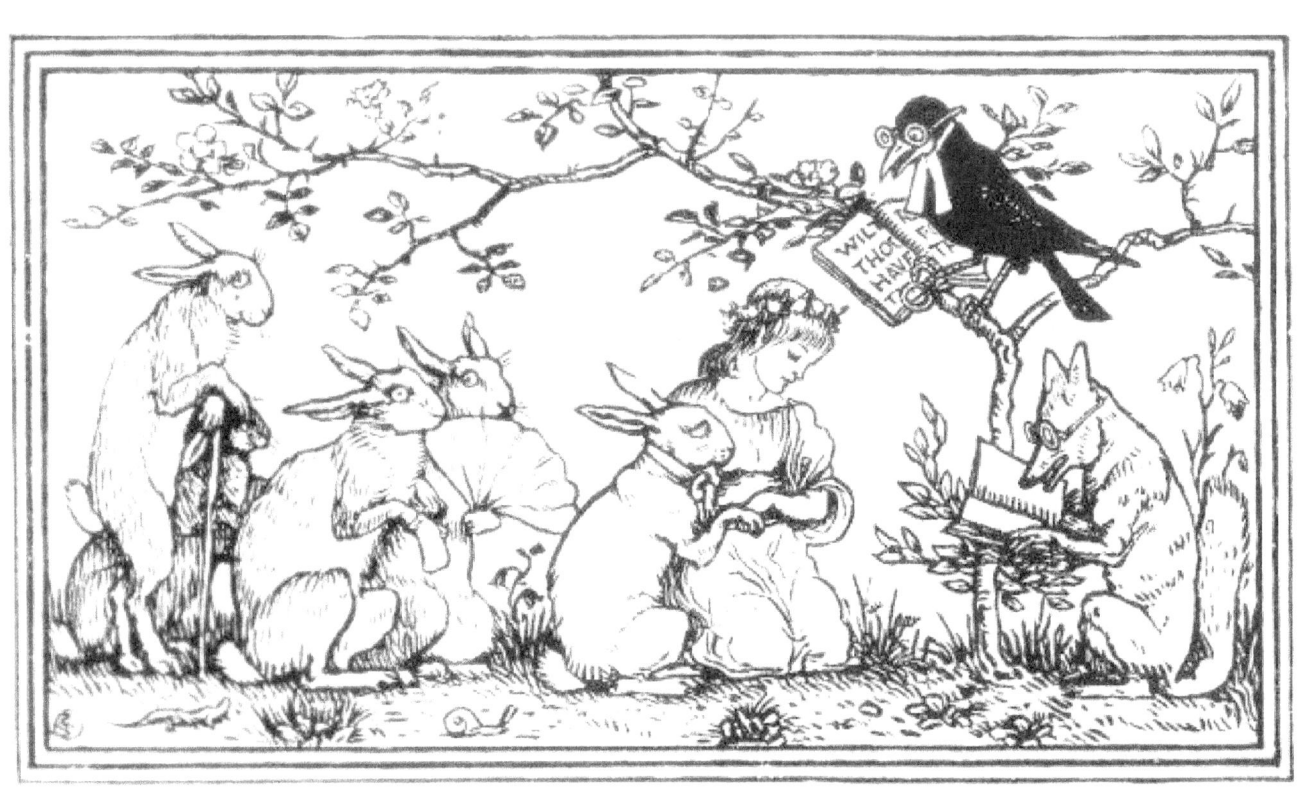

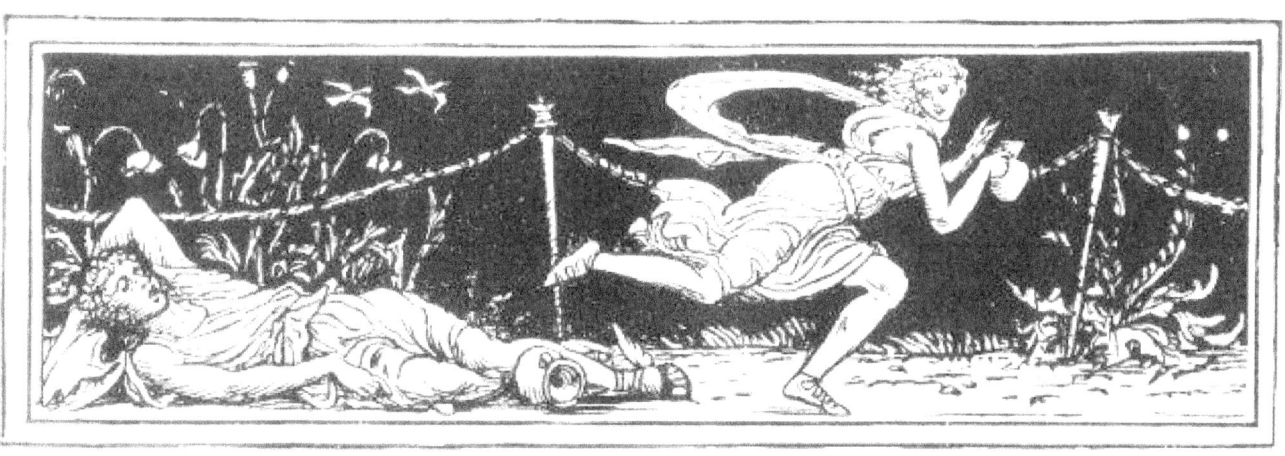

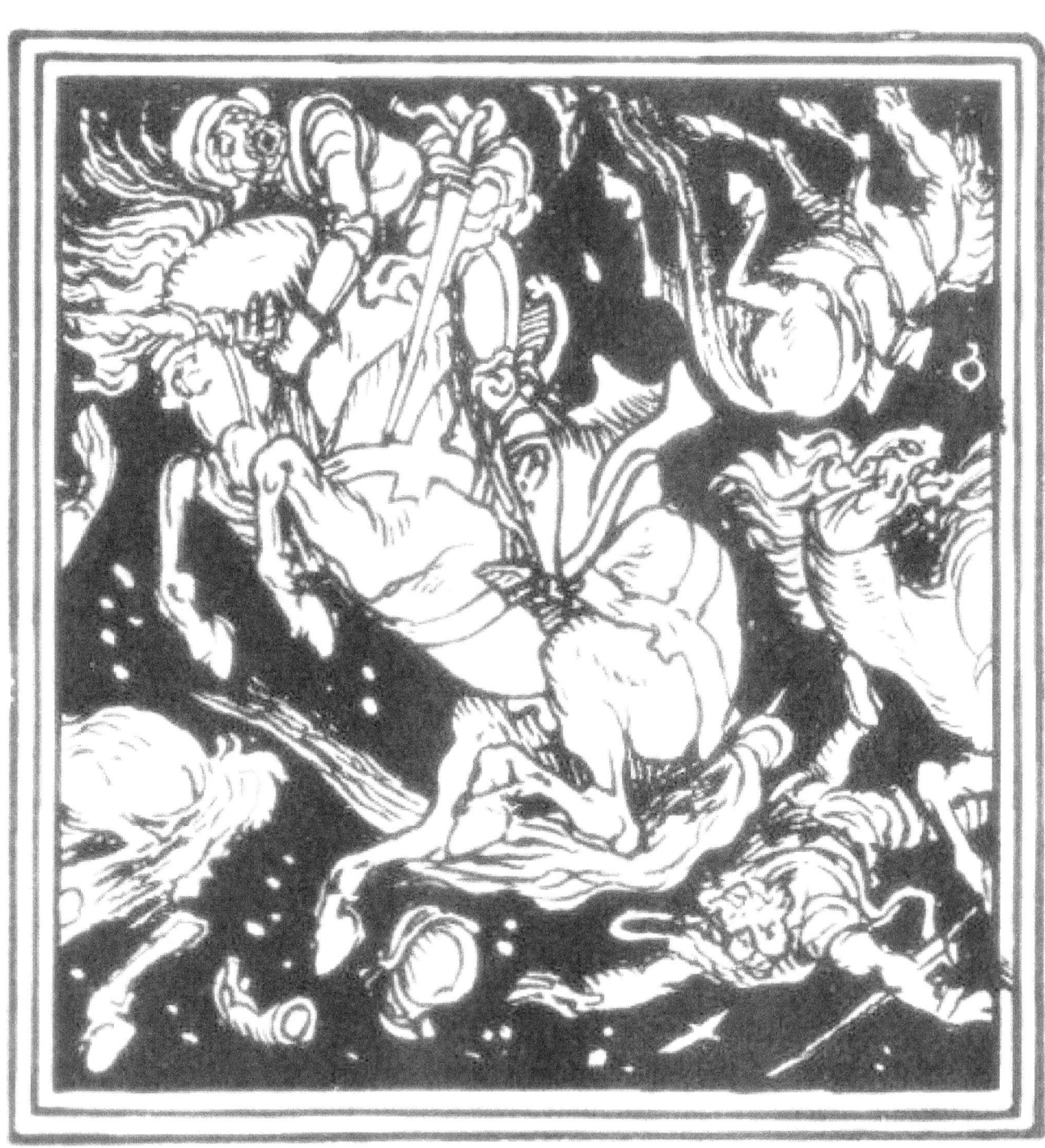

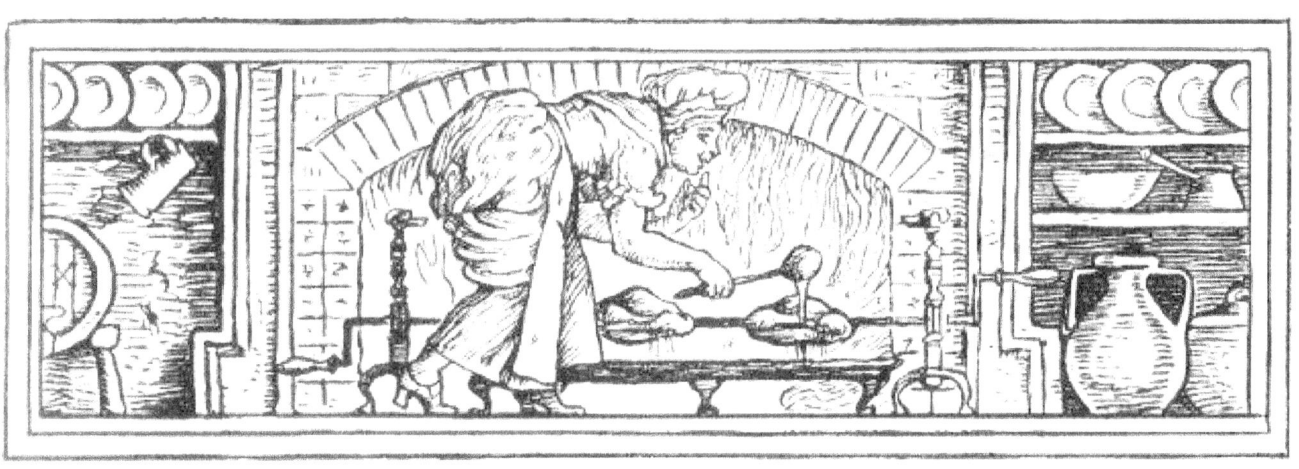

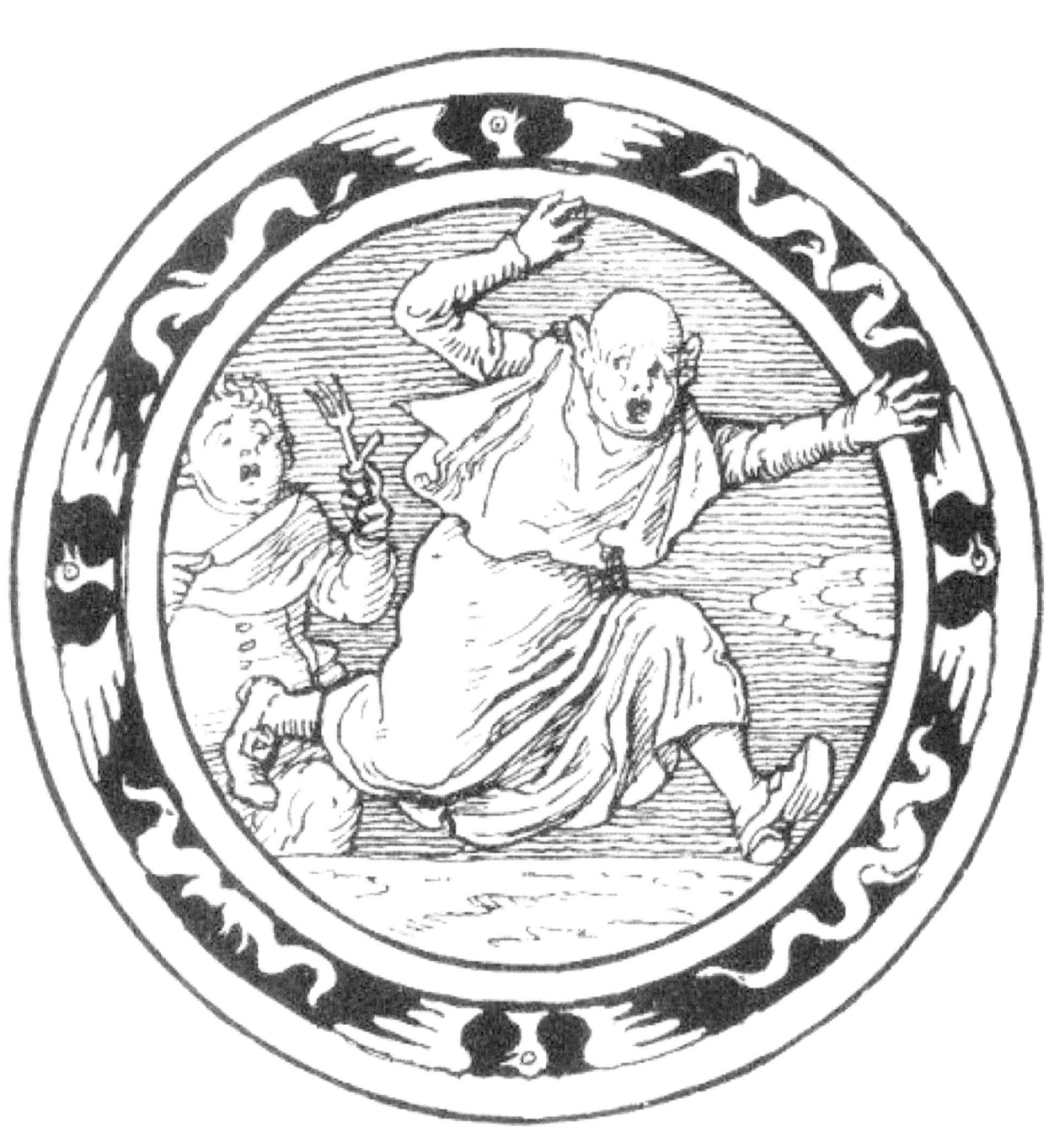

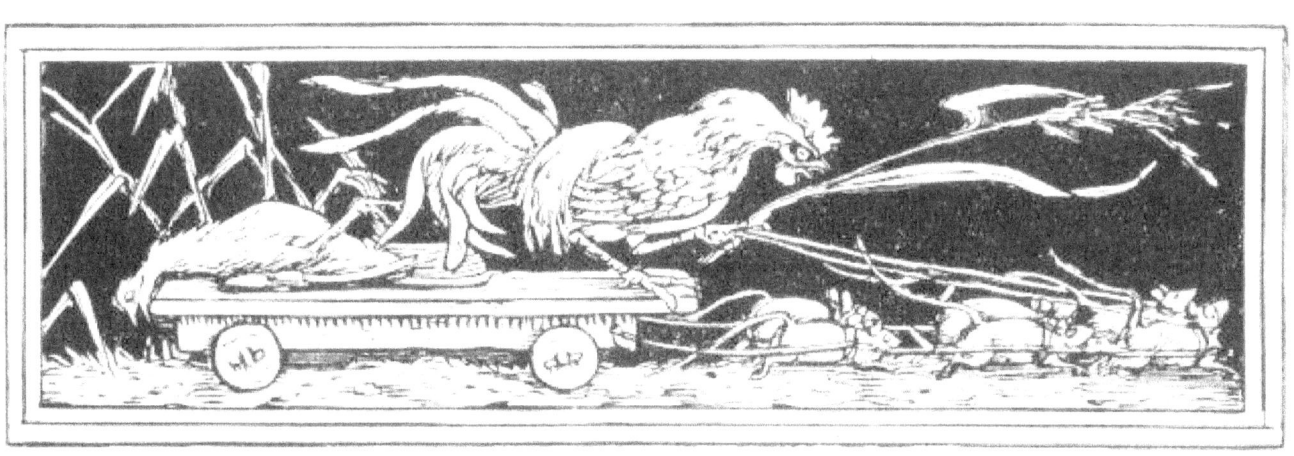

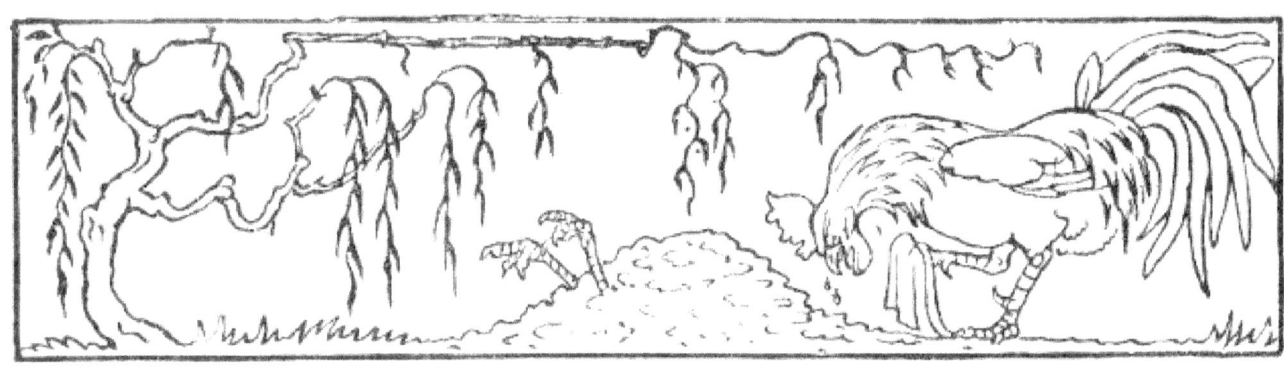

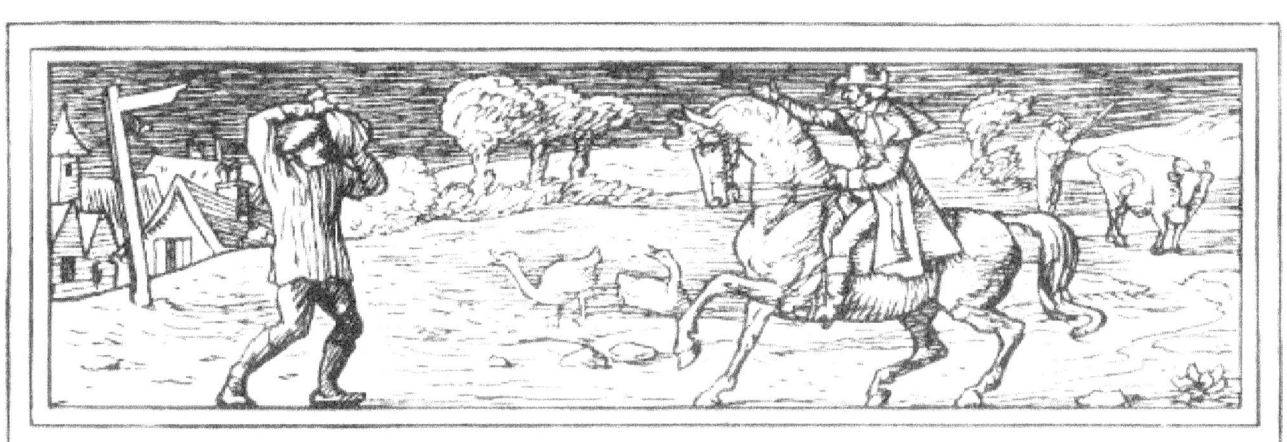

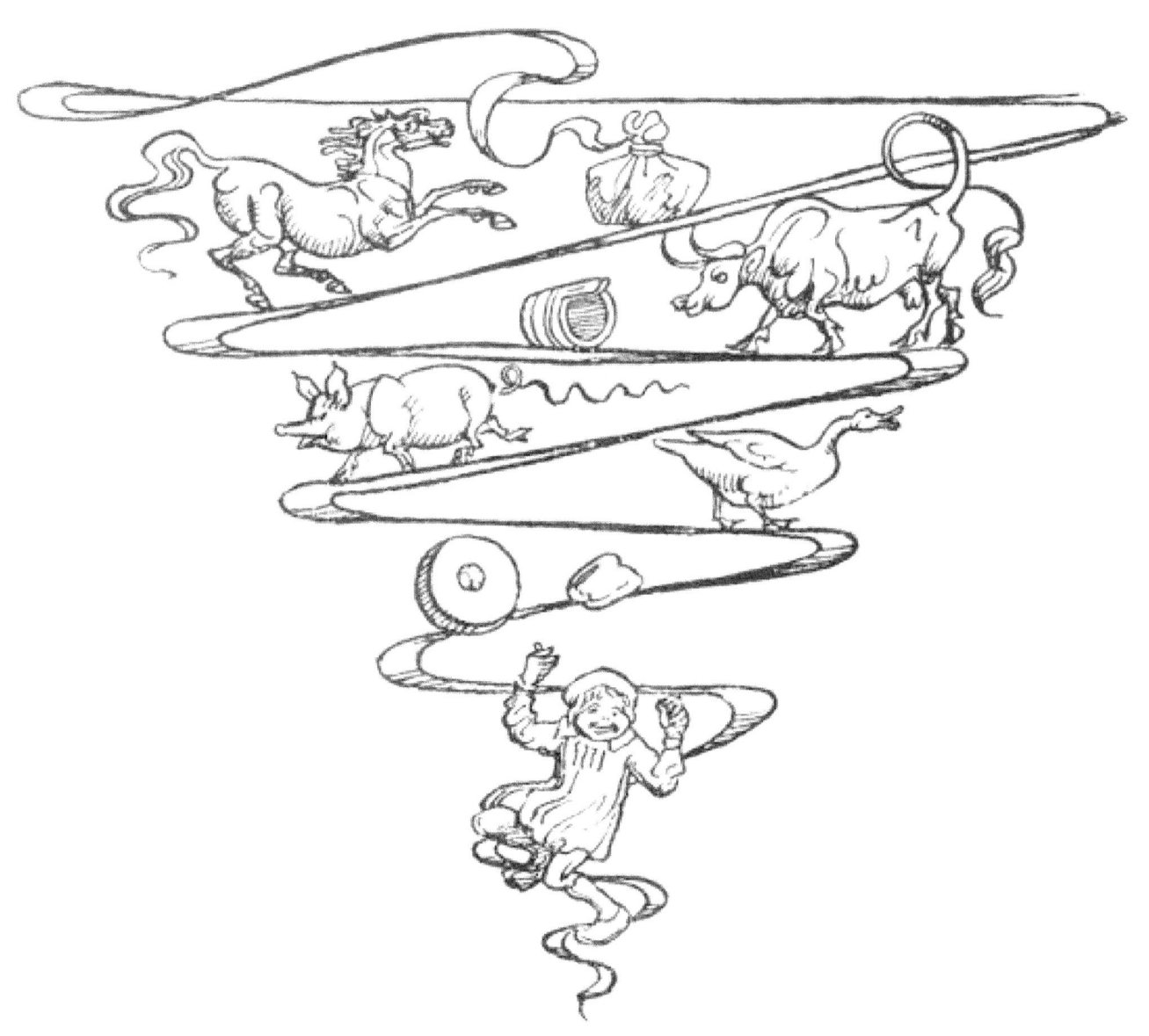

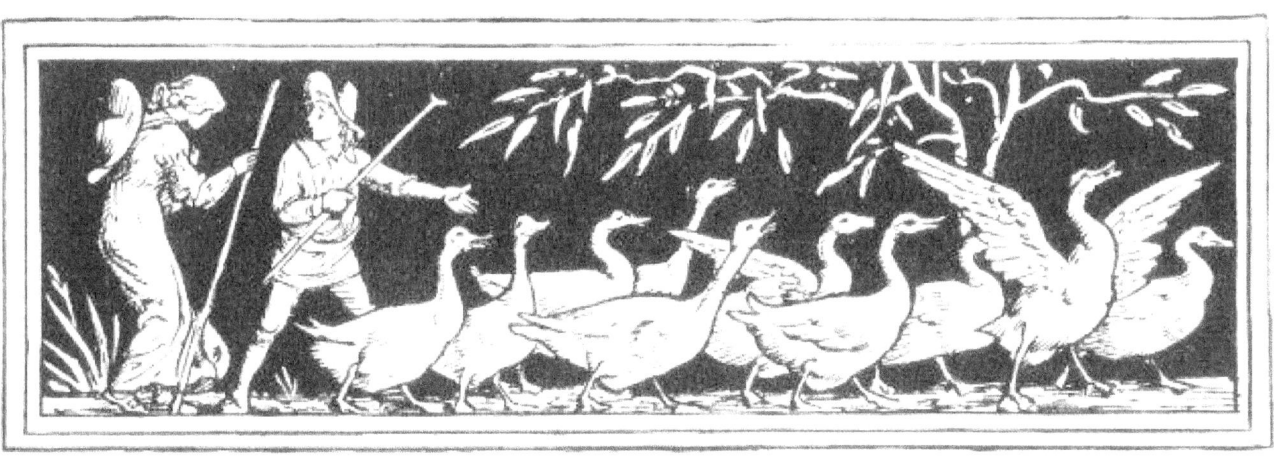

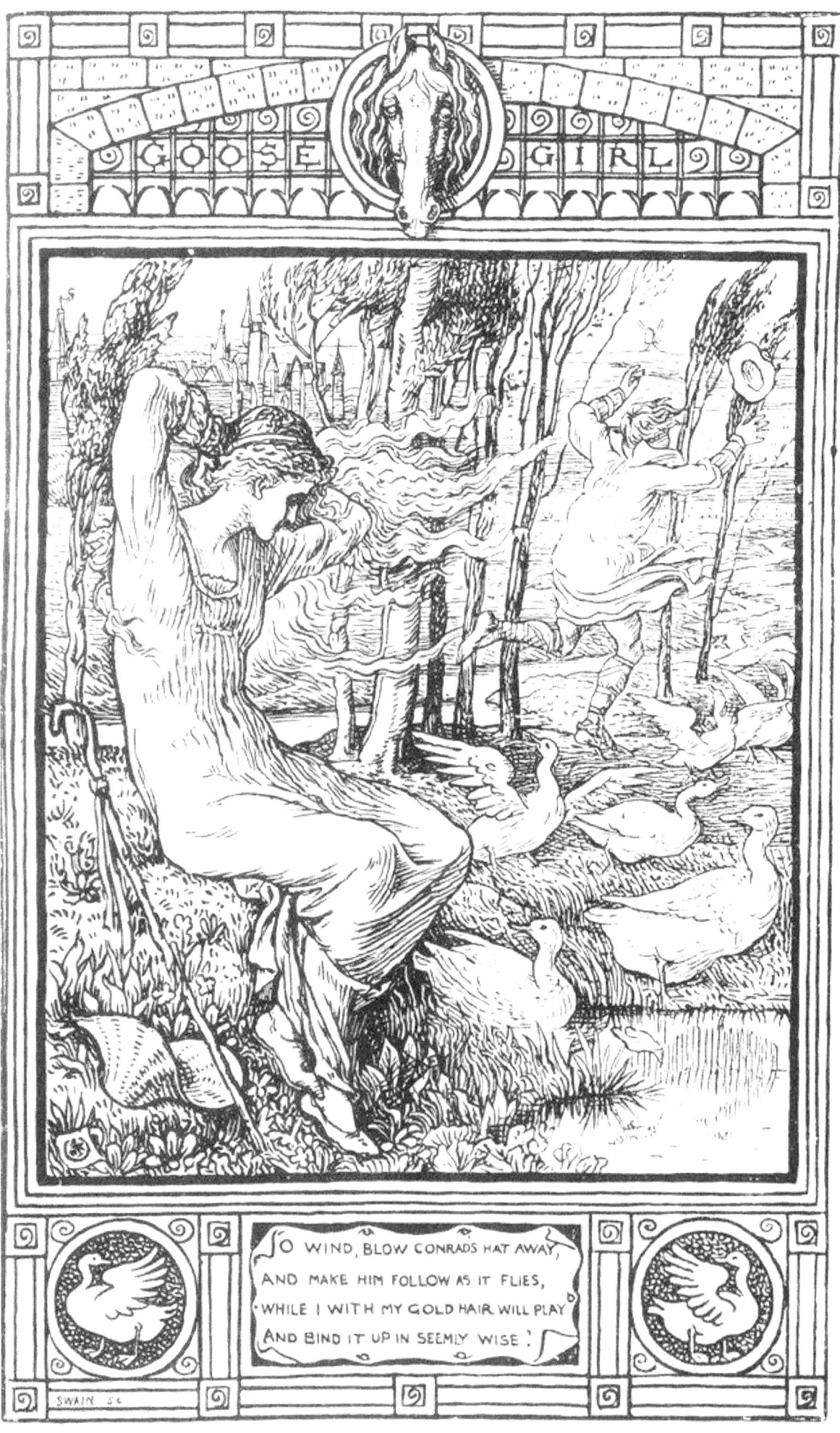

GOOSE GIRL

O WIND, BLOW CONRADS HAT AWAY,
AND MAKE HIM FOLLOW AS IT FLIES,
WHILE I WITH MY GOLD HAIR WILL PLAY
AND BIND IT UP IN SEEMLY WISE!

SWAIN SC

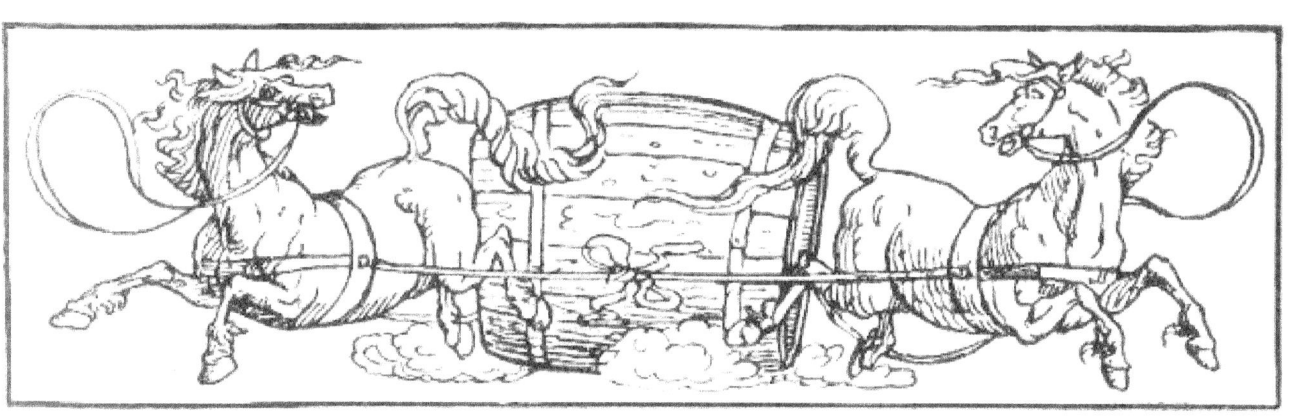

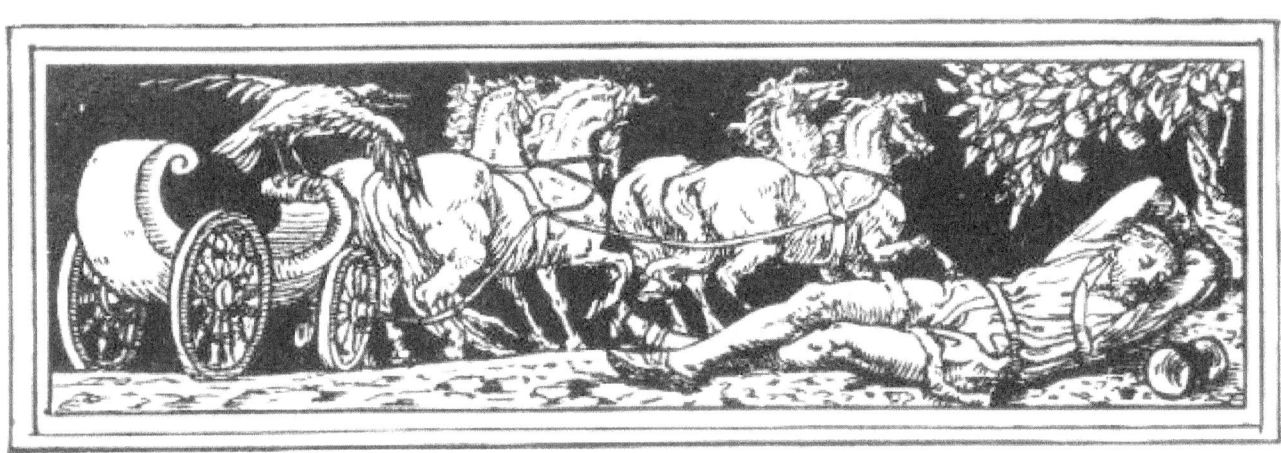

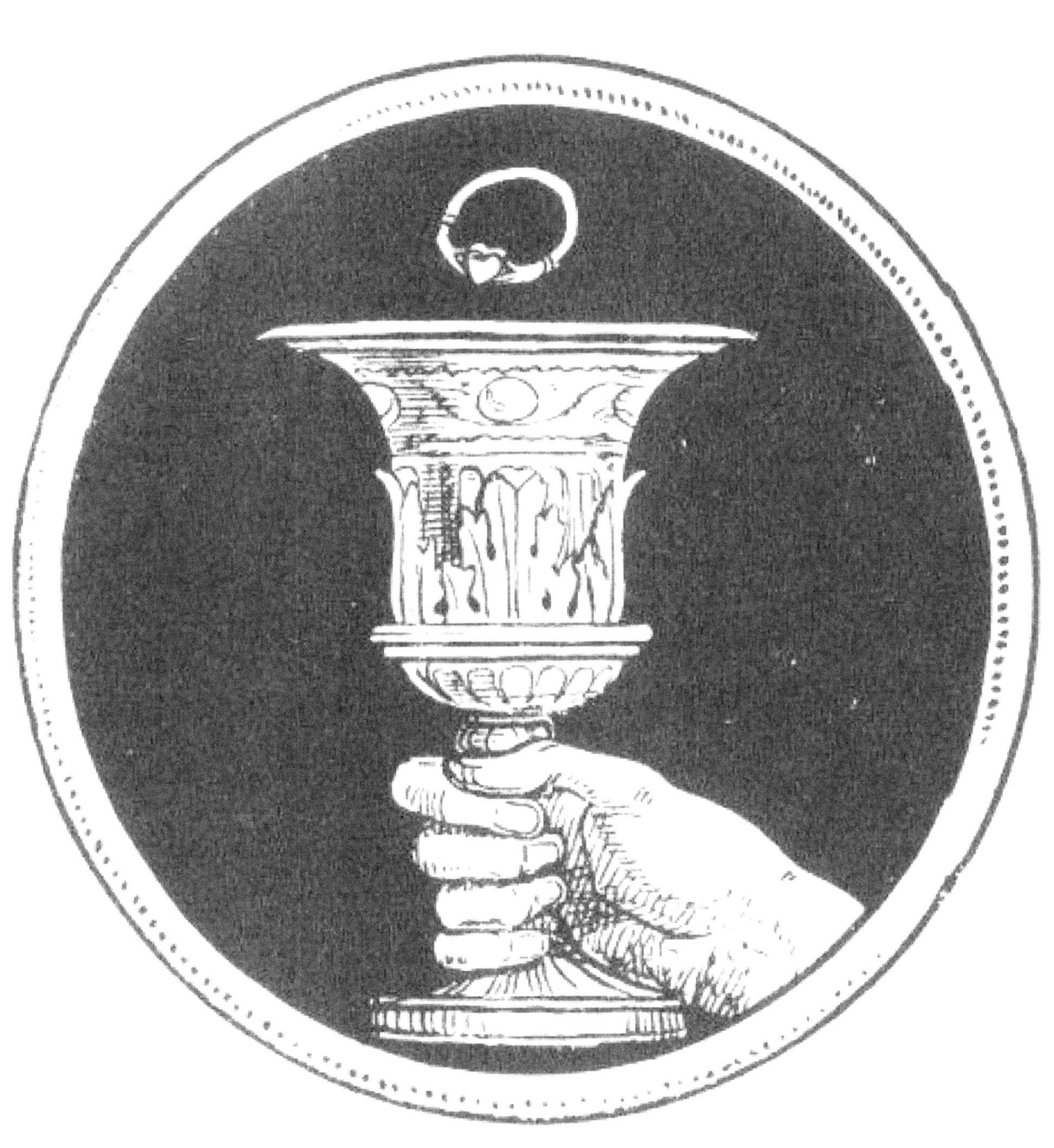

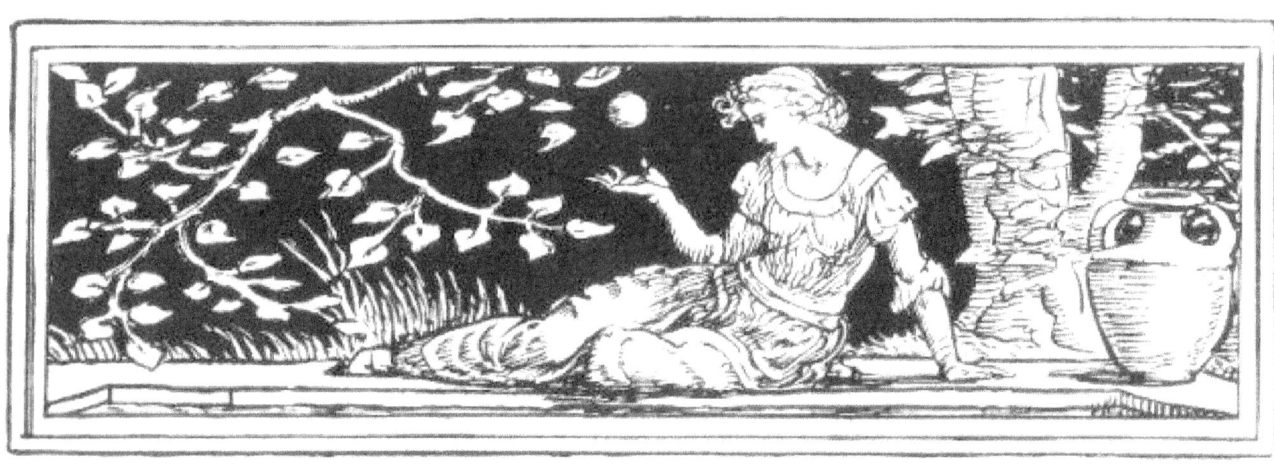

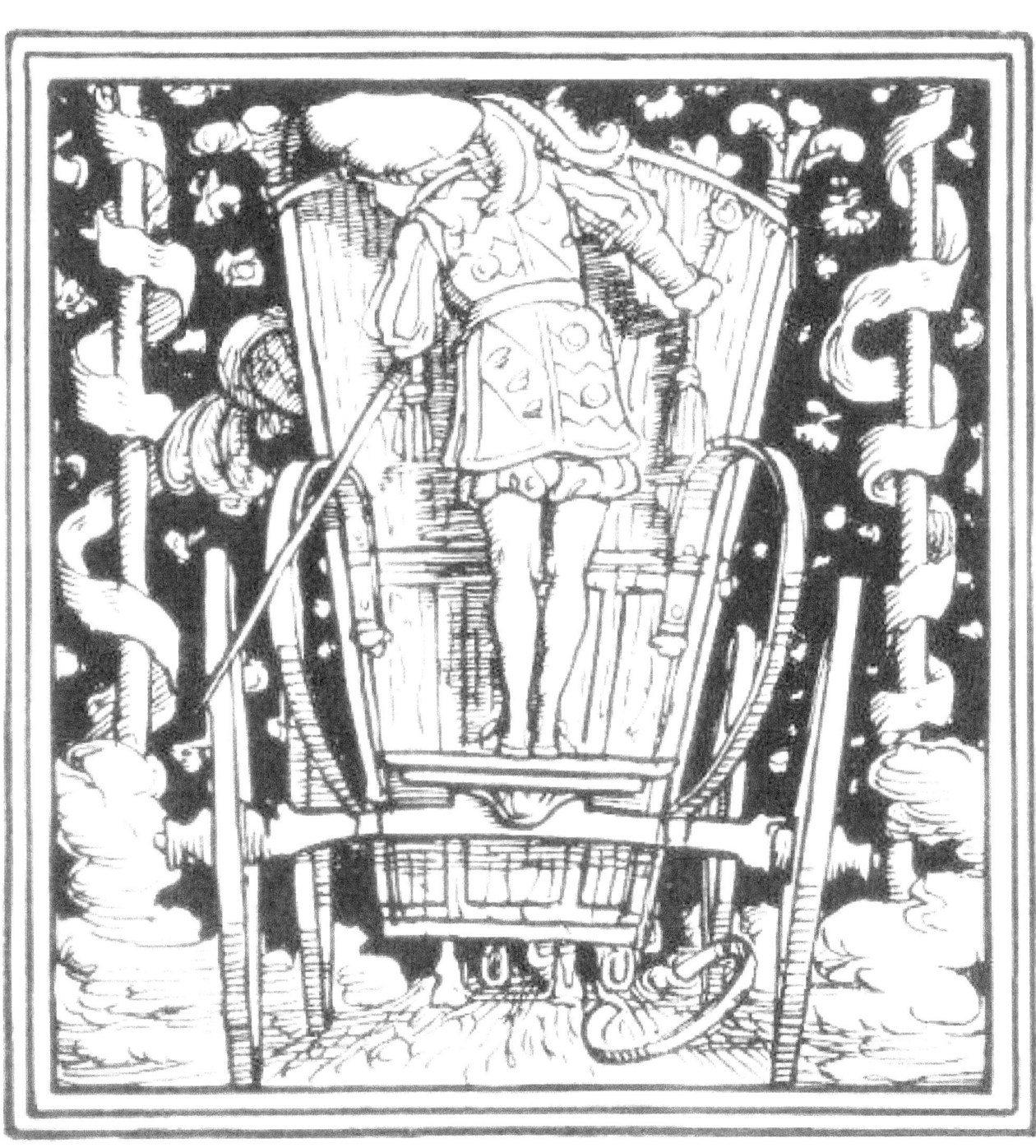

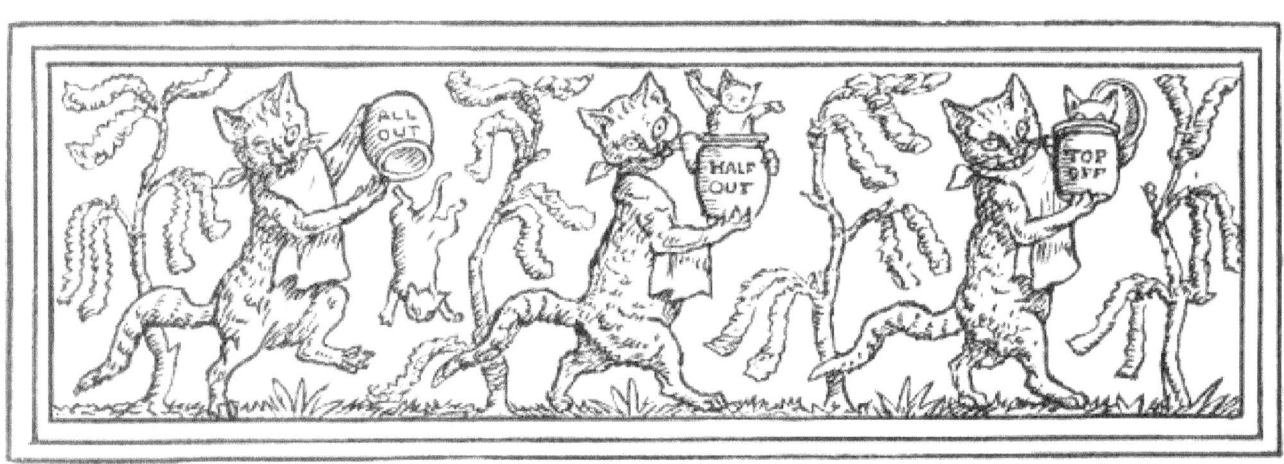

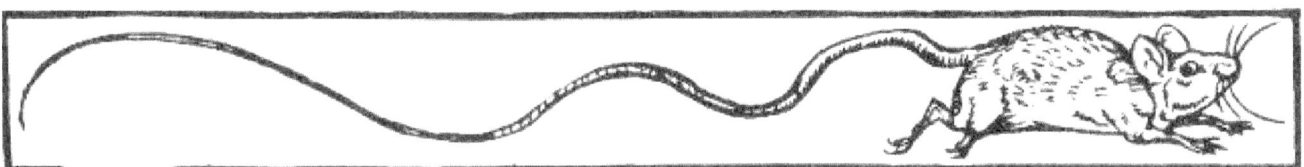

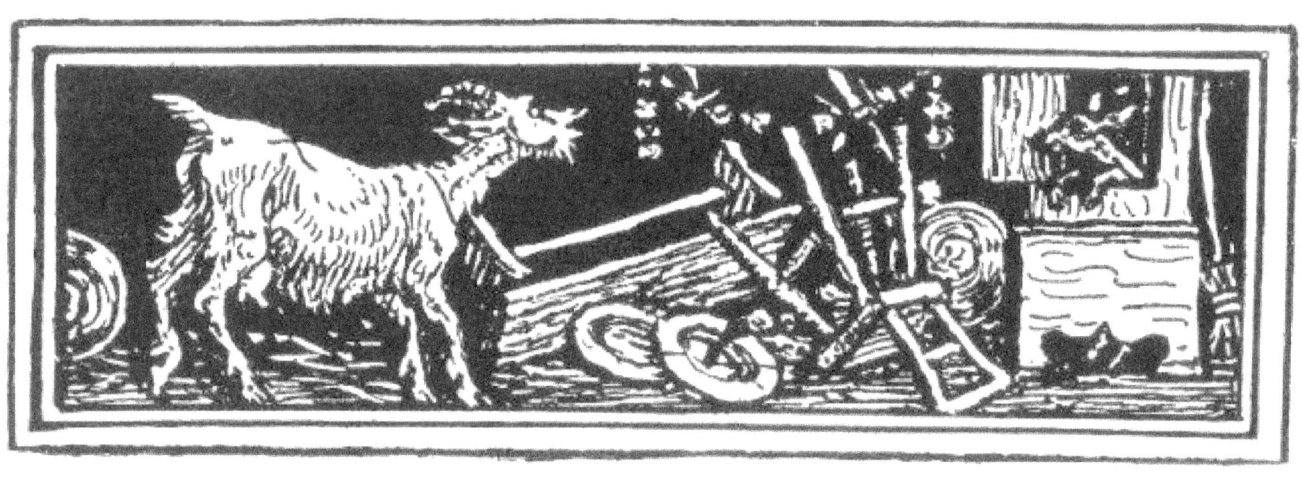

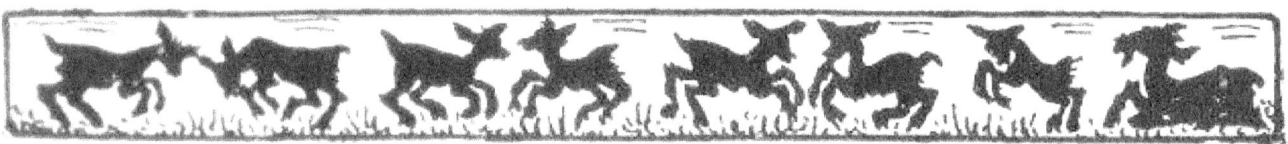

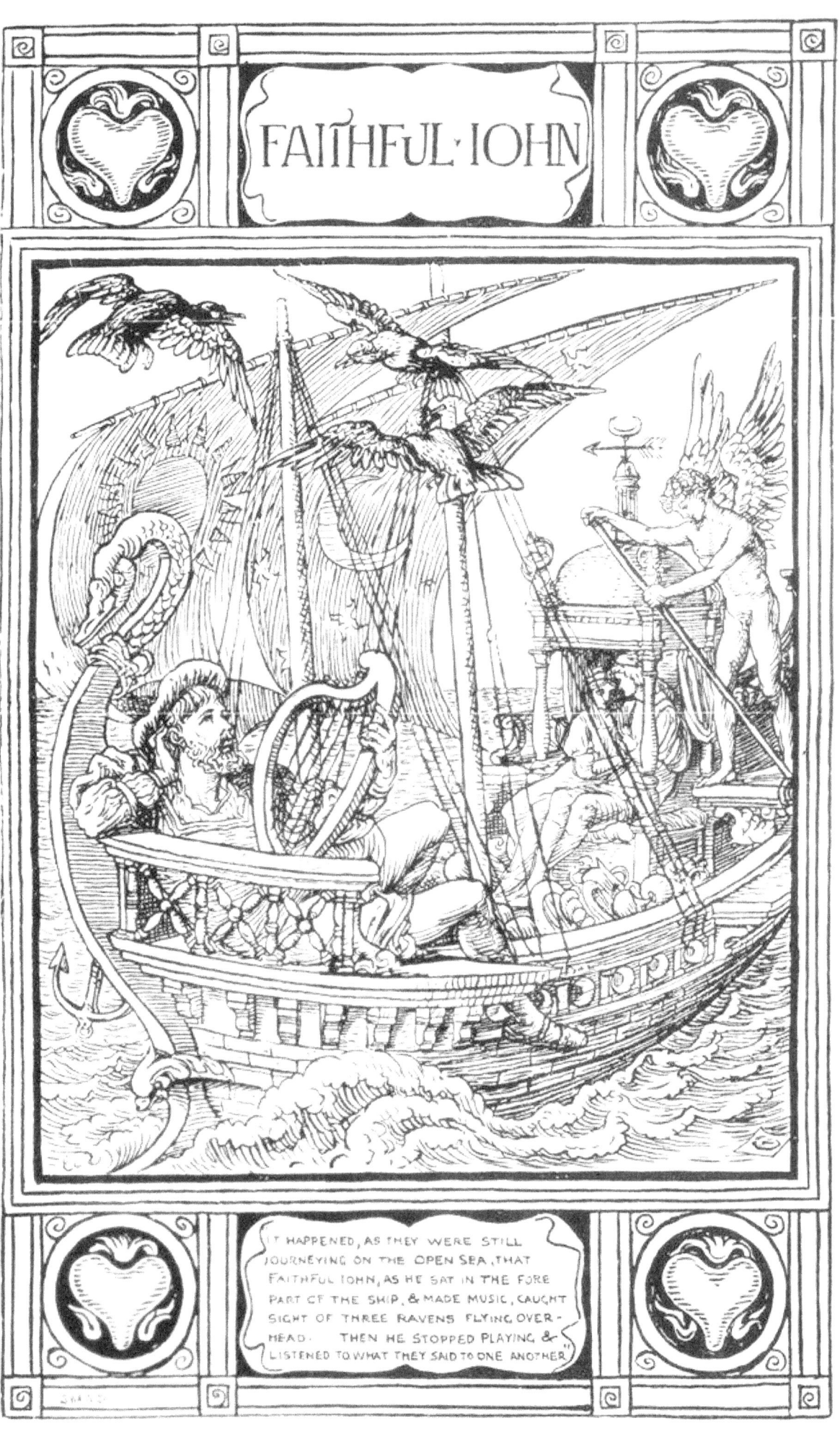

FAITHFUL·IOHN

IT HAPPENED, AS THEY WERE STILL
JOURNEYING ON THE OPEN SEA, THAT
FAITHFUL IOHN, AS HE SAT IN THE FORE
PART OF THE SHIP, & MADE MUSIC, CAUGHT
SIGHT OF THREE RAVENS FLYING OVER-
HEAD. THEN HE STOPPED PLAYING &
LISTENED TO WHAT THEY SAID TO ONE ANOTHER"

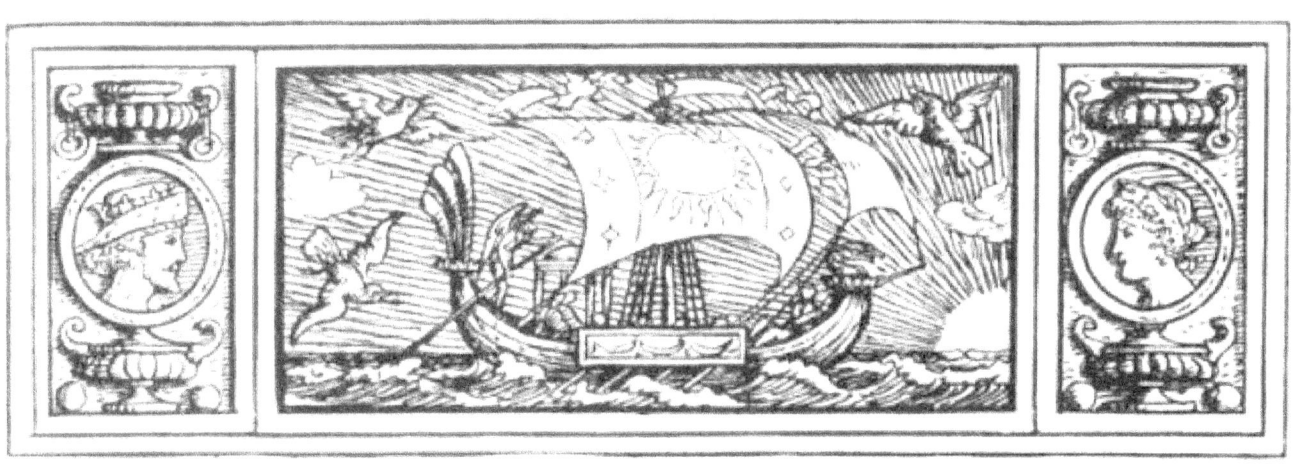

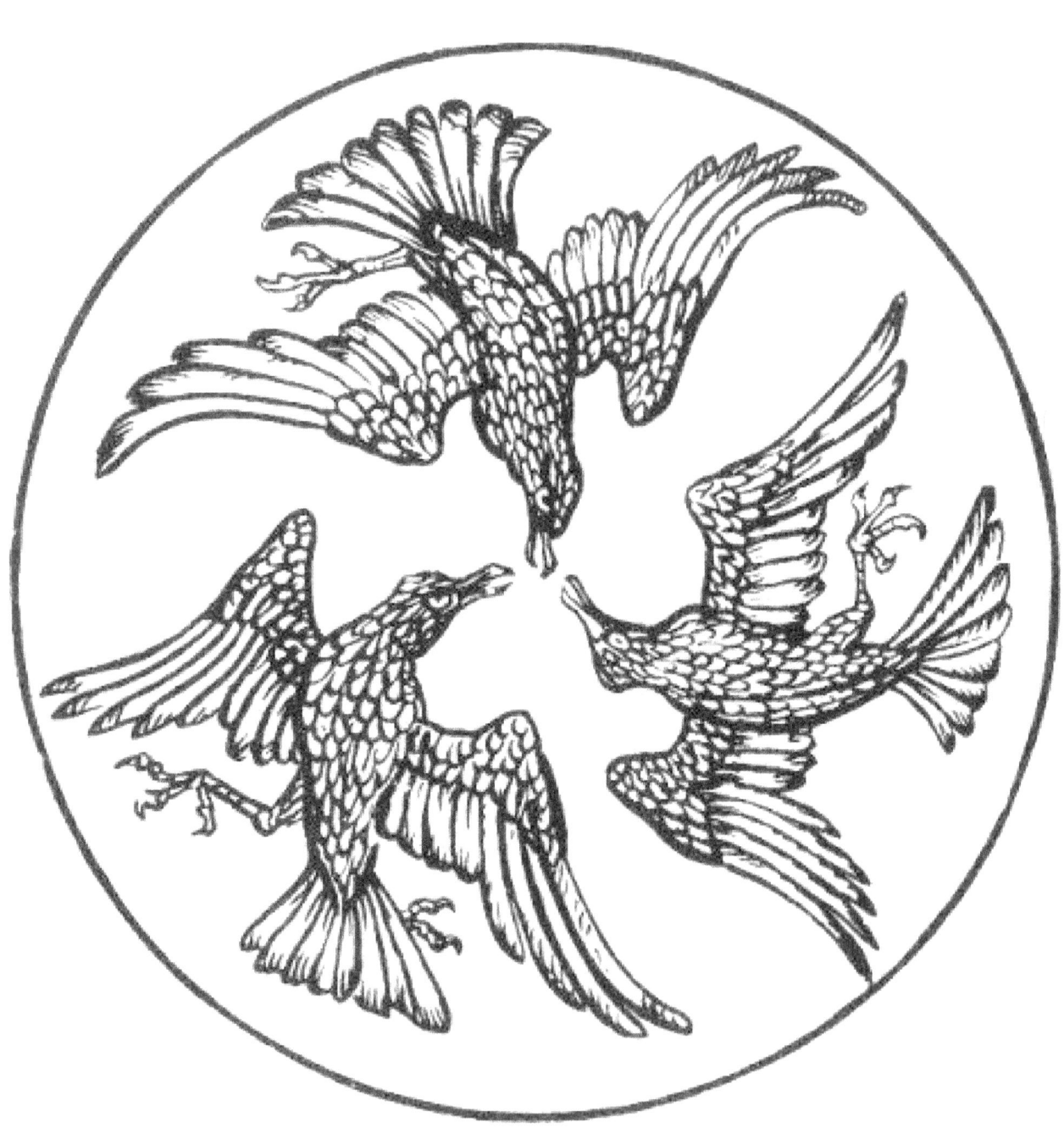

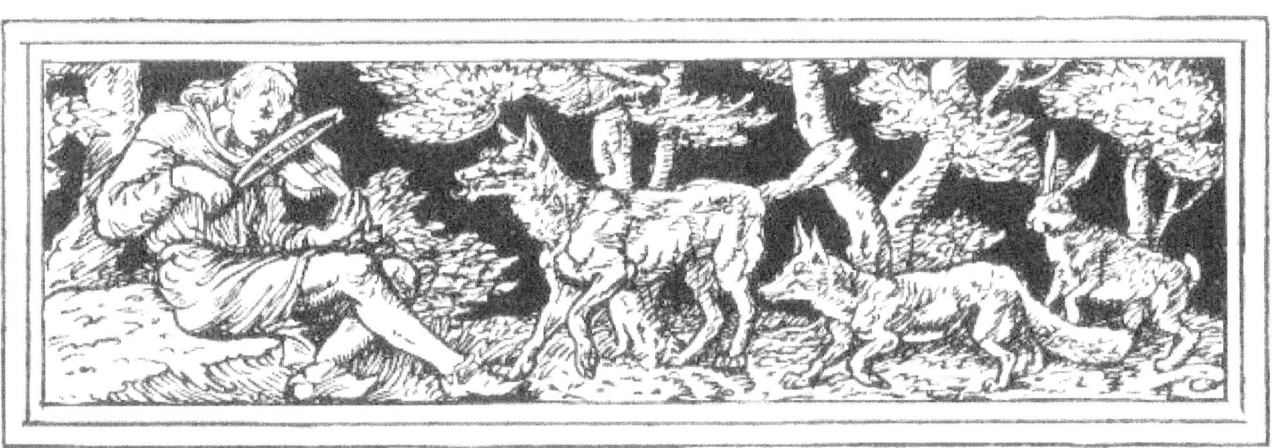

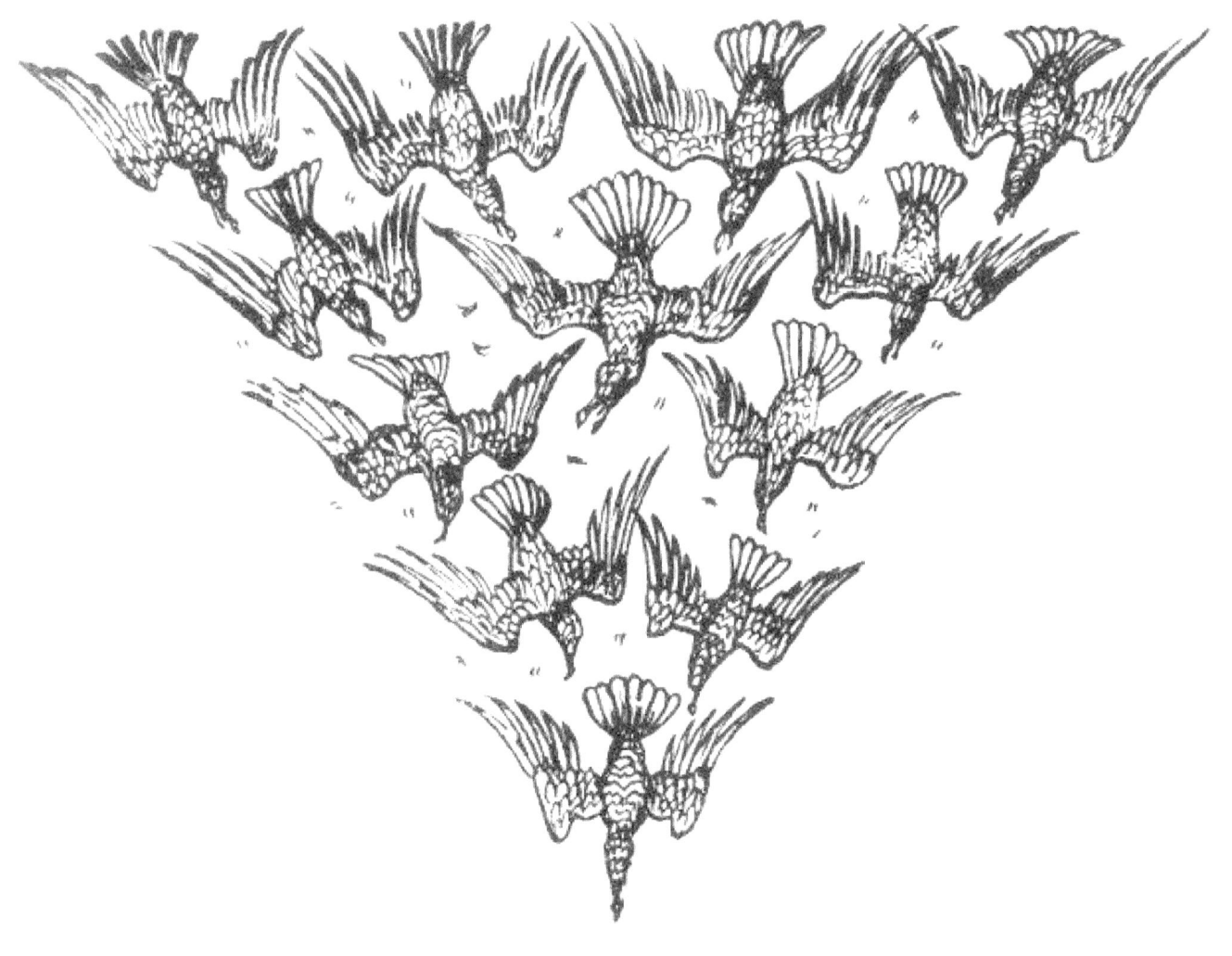

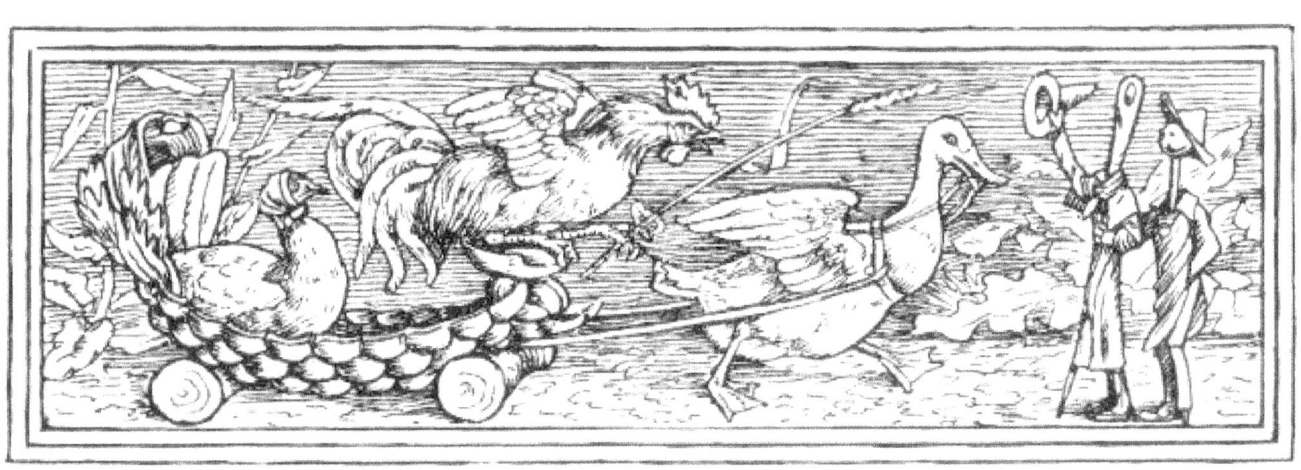

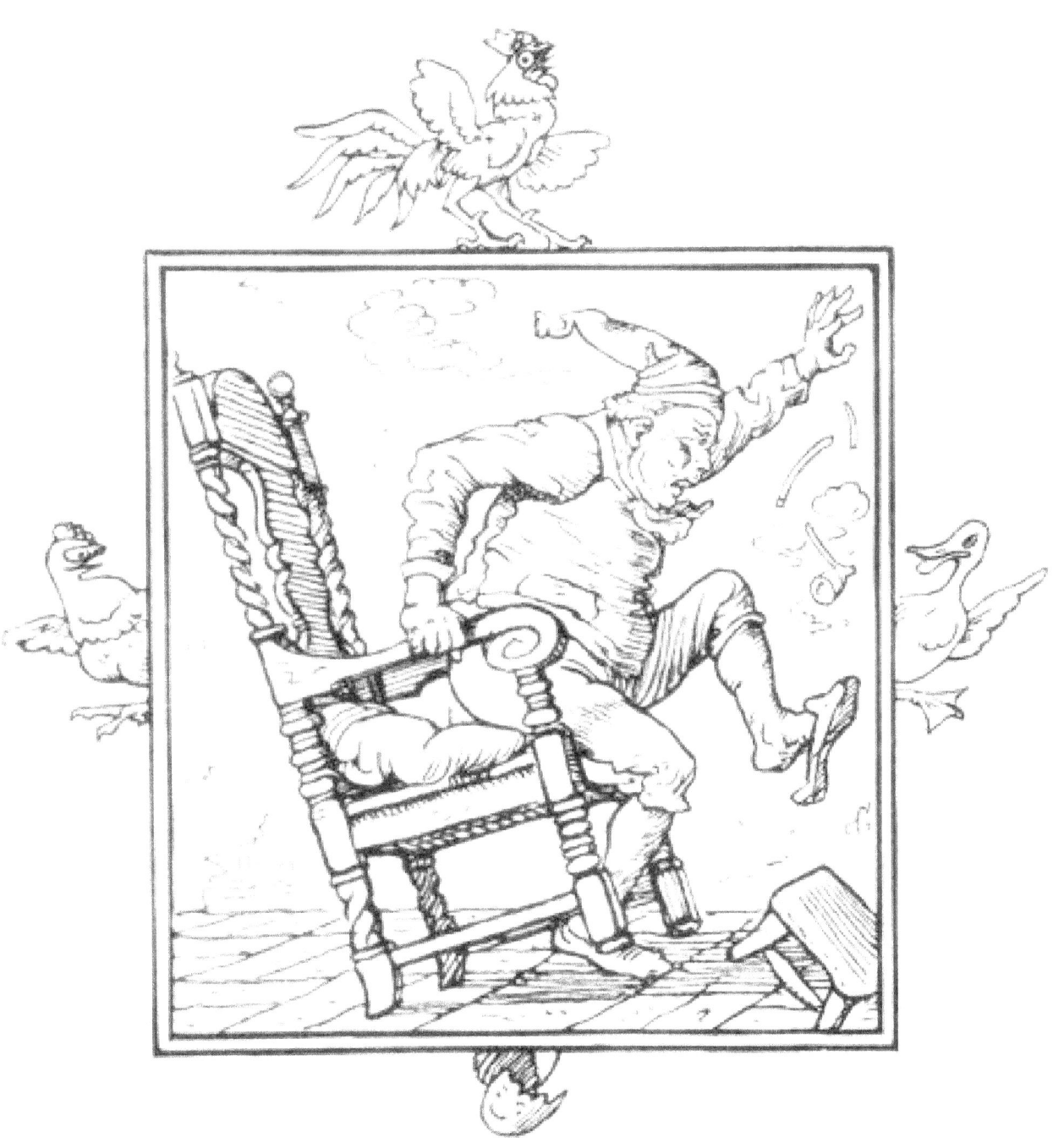

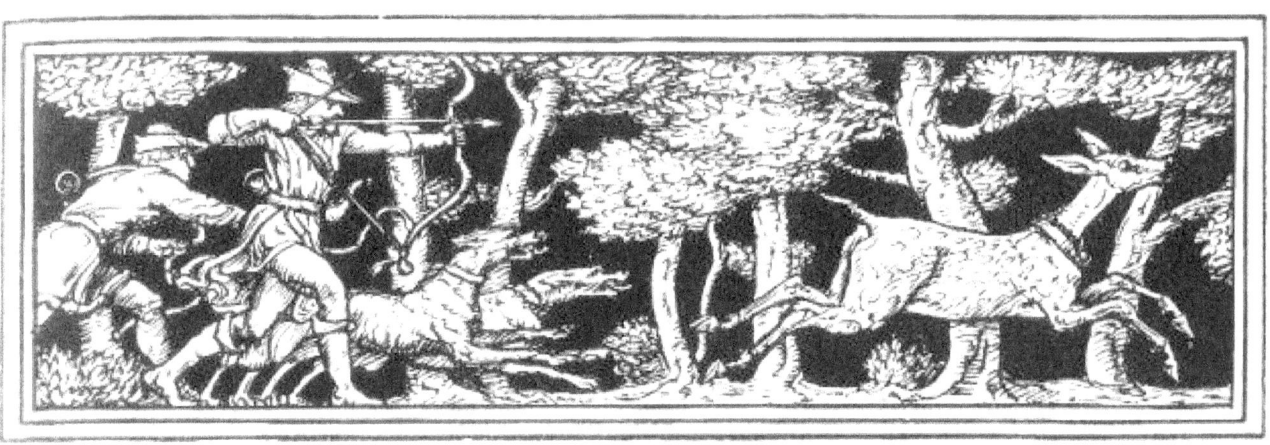

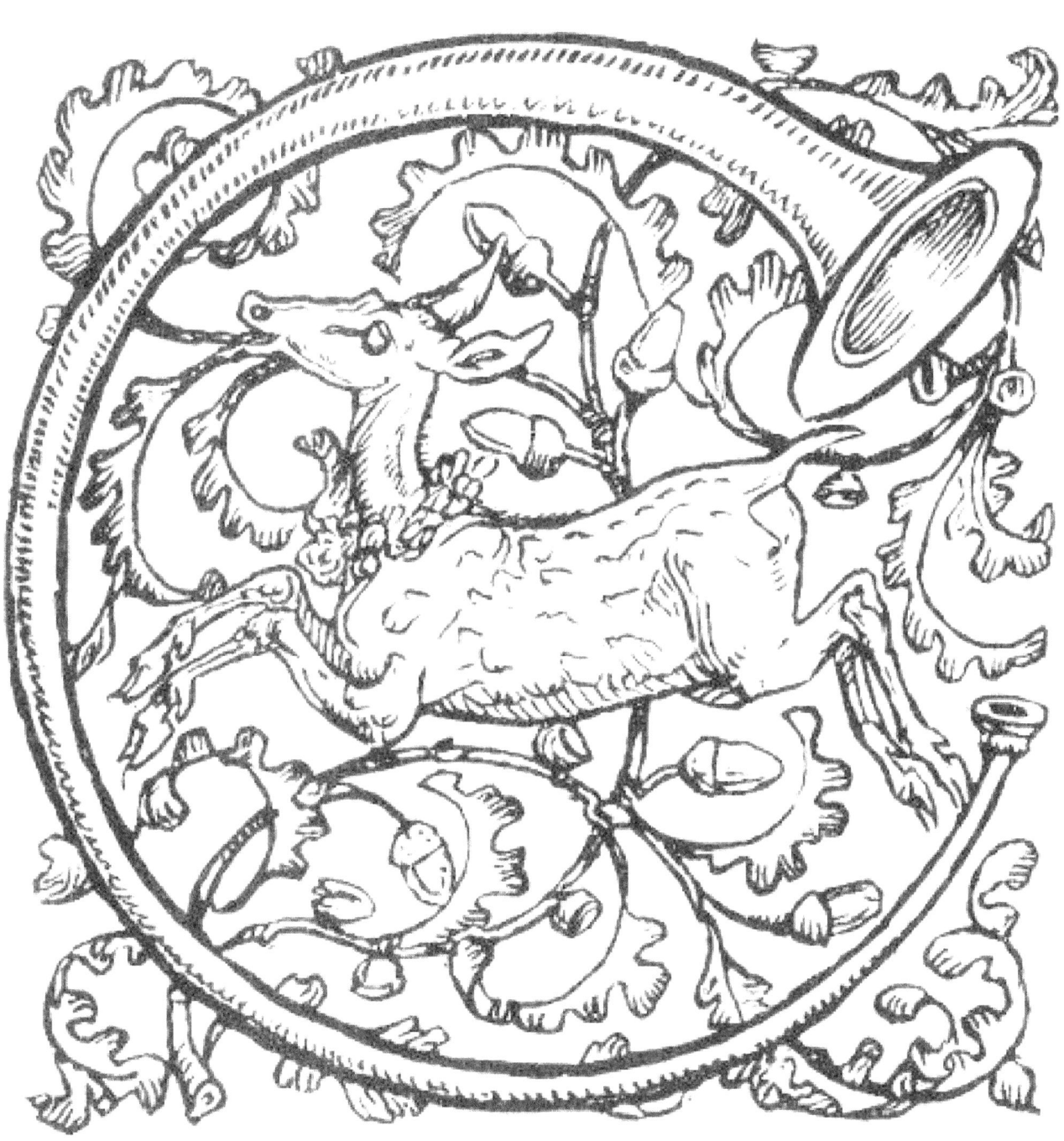

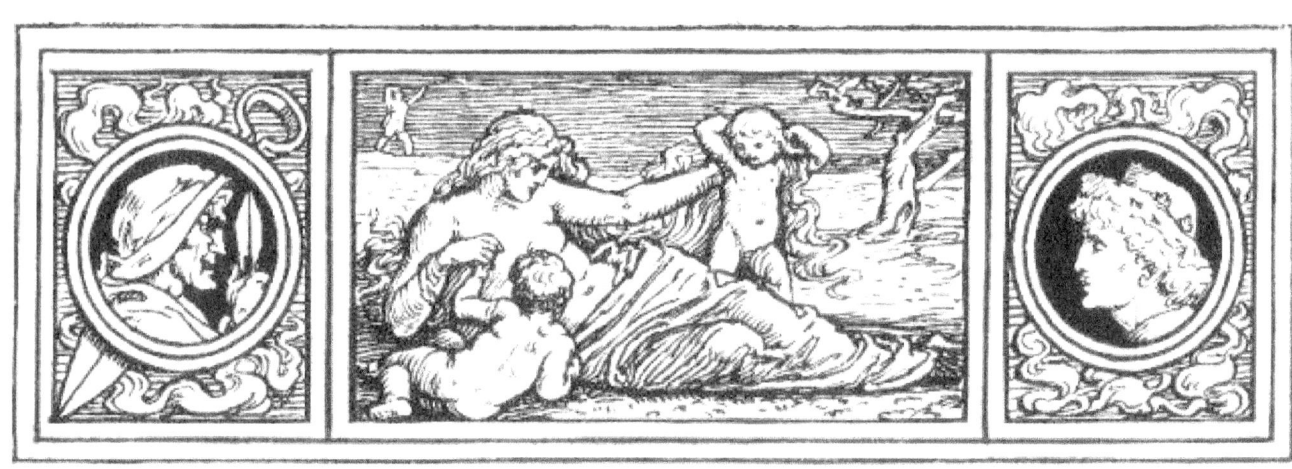

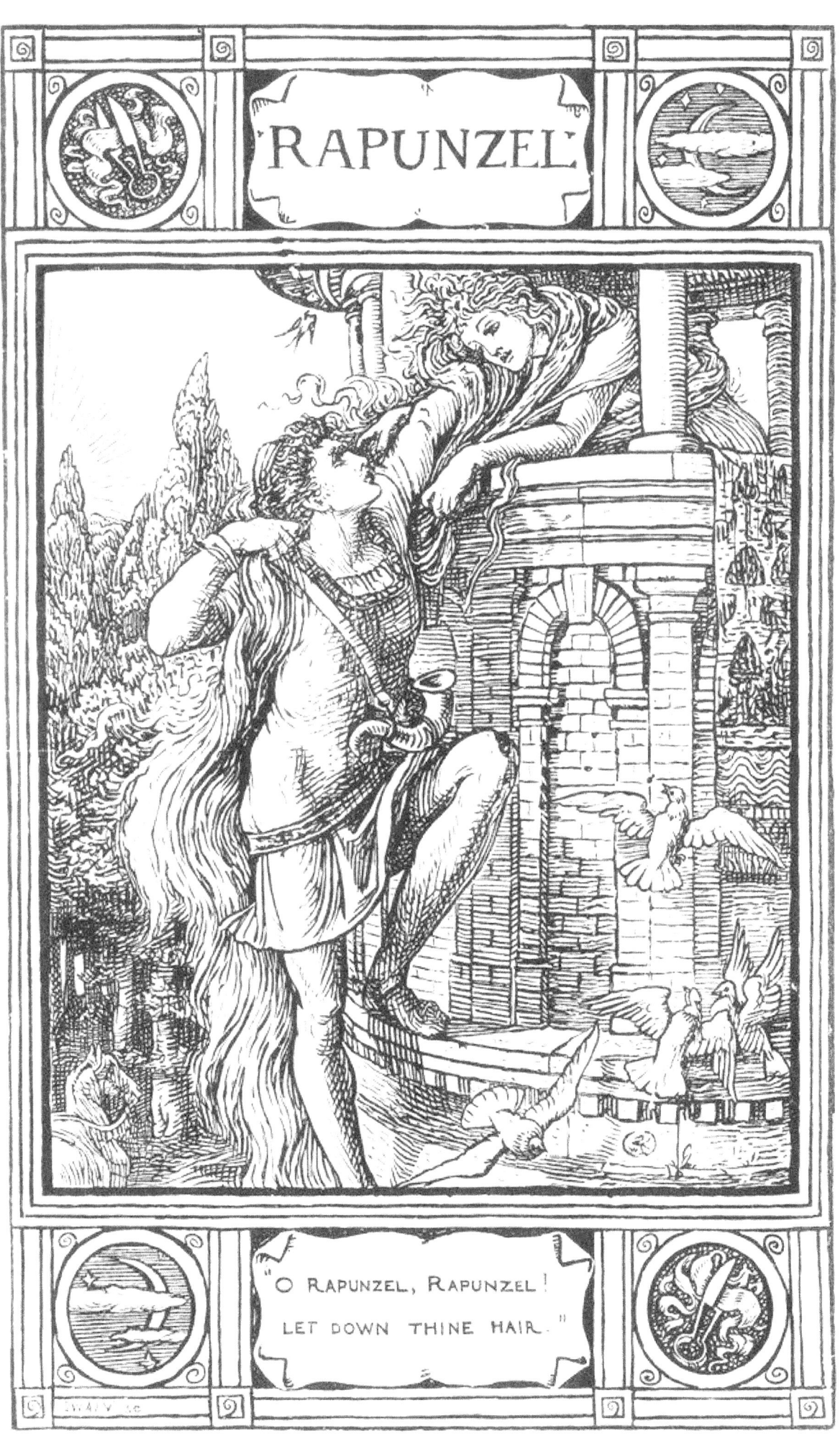

RAPUNZEL

"O RAPUNZEL, RAPUNZEL!
LET DOWN THINE HAIR."

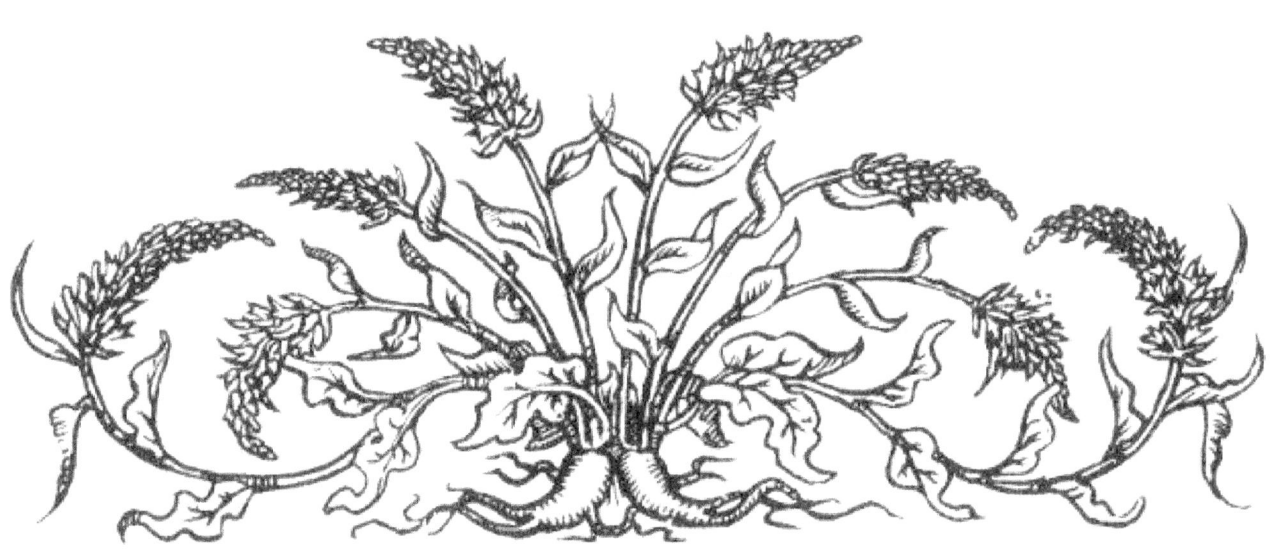

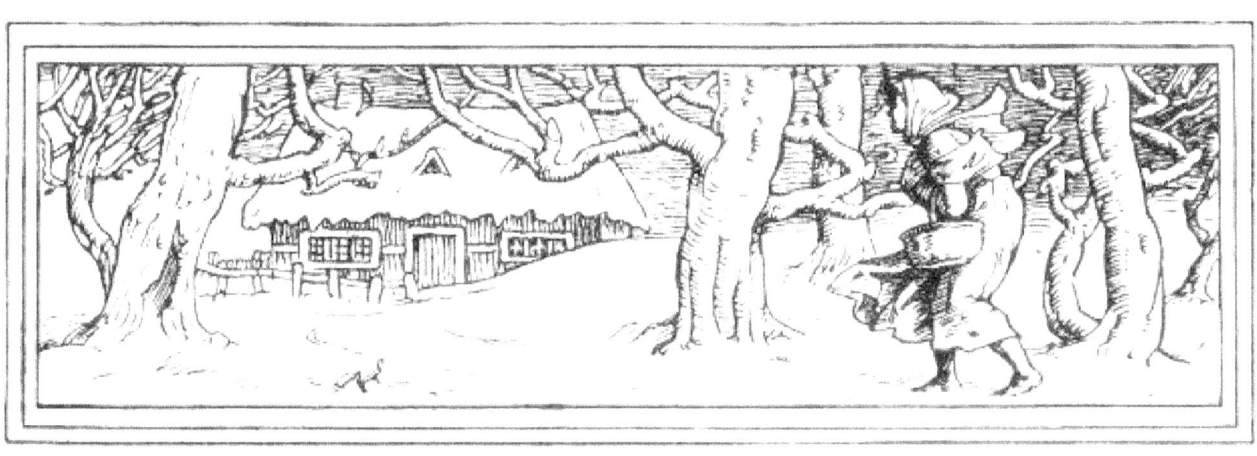

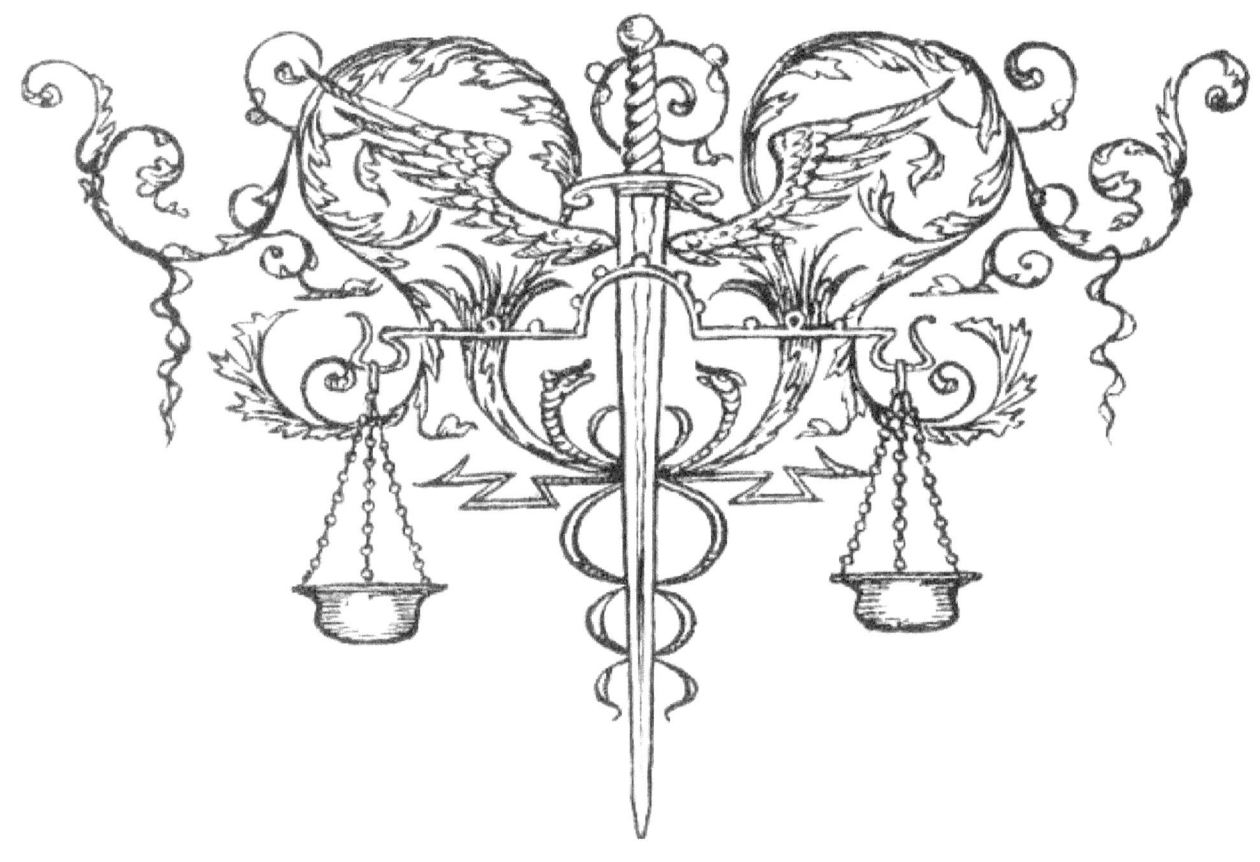

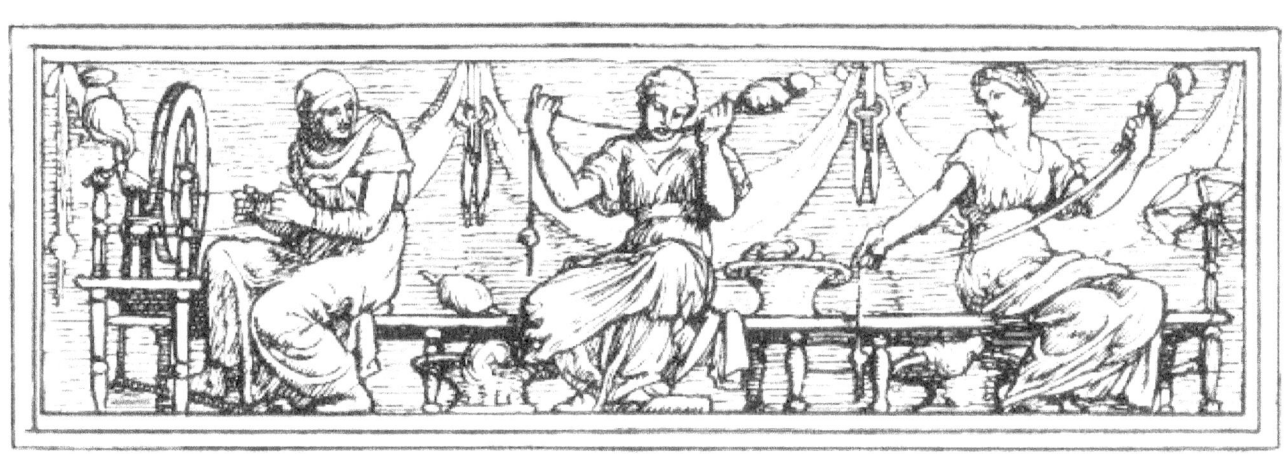

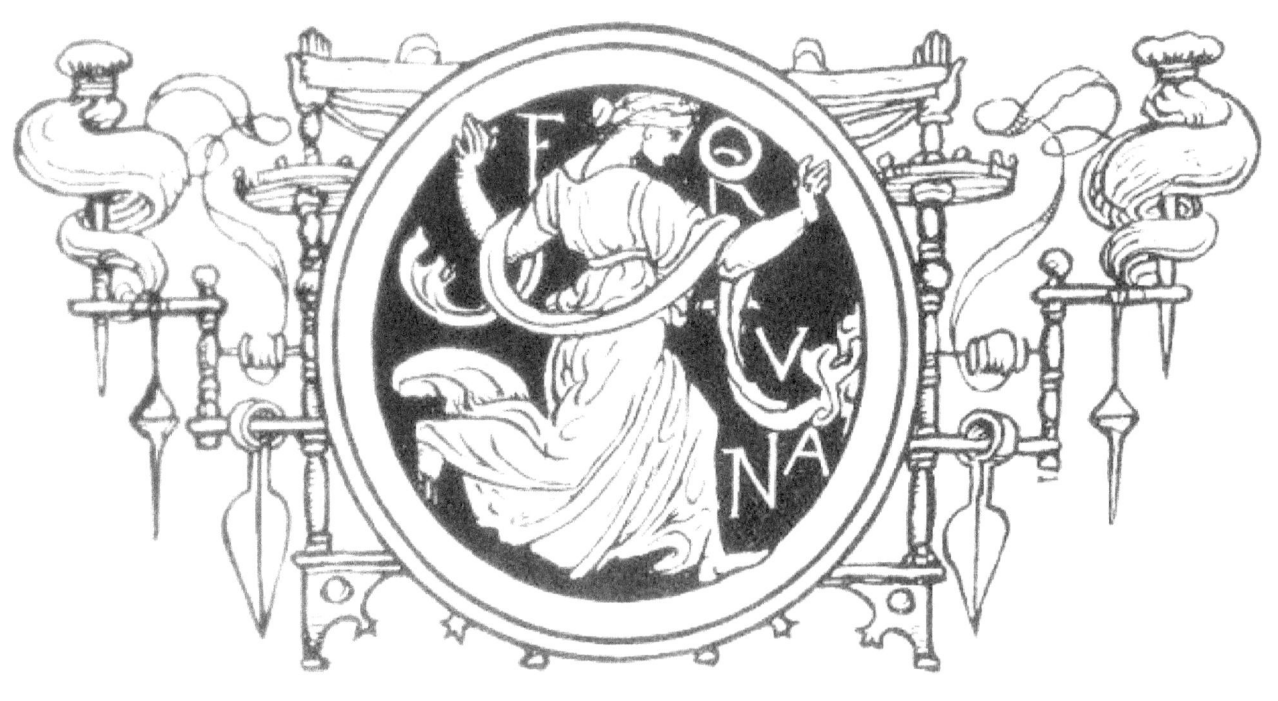

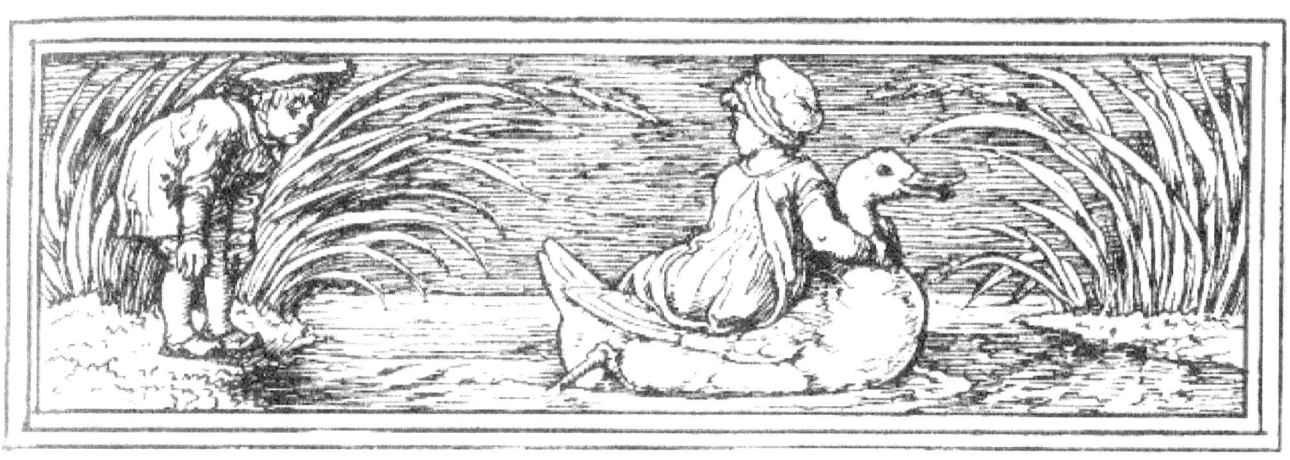

Sing every one,
My story is done,
And look! round the house
There runs a little mouse,
He that can catch her before she scampers in,
May make himself a very very large fur-cap
out of her skin.

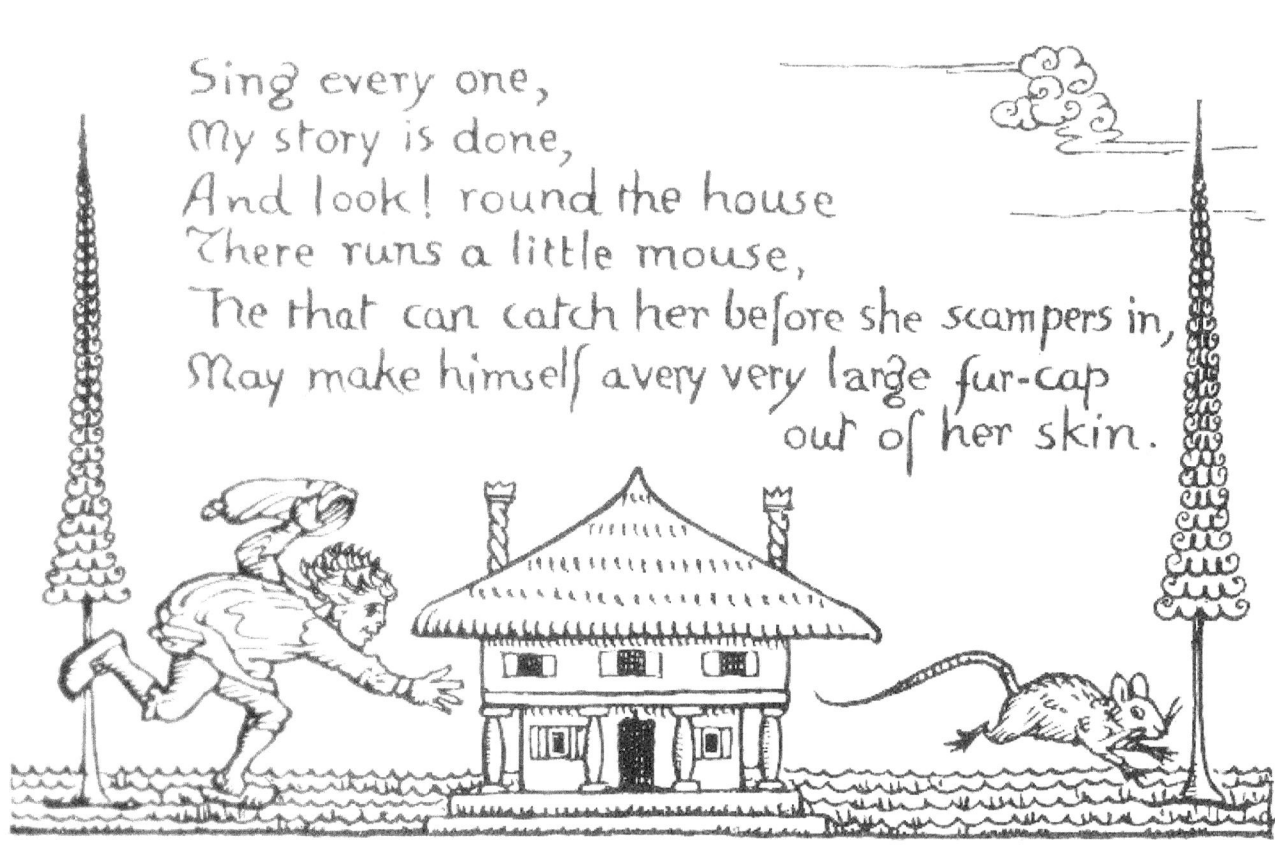

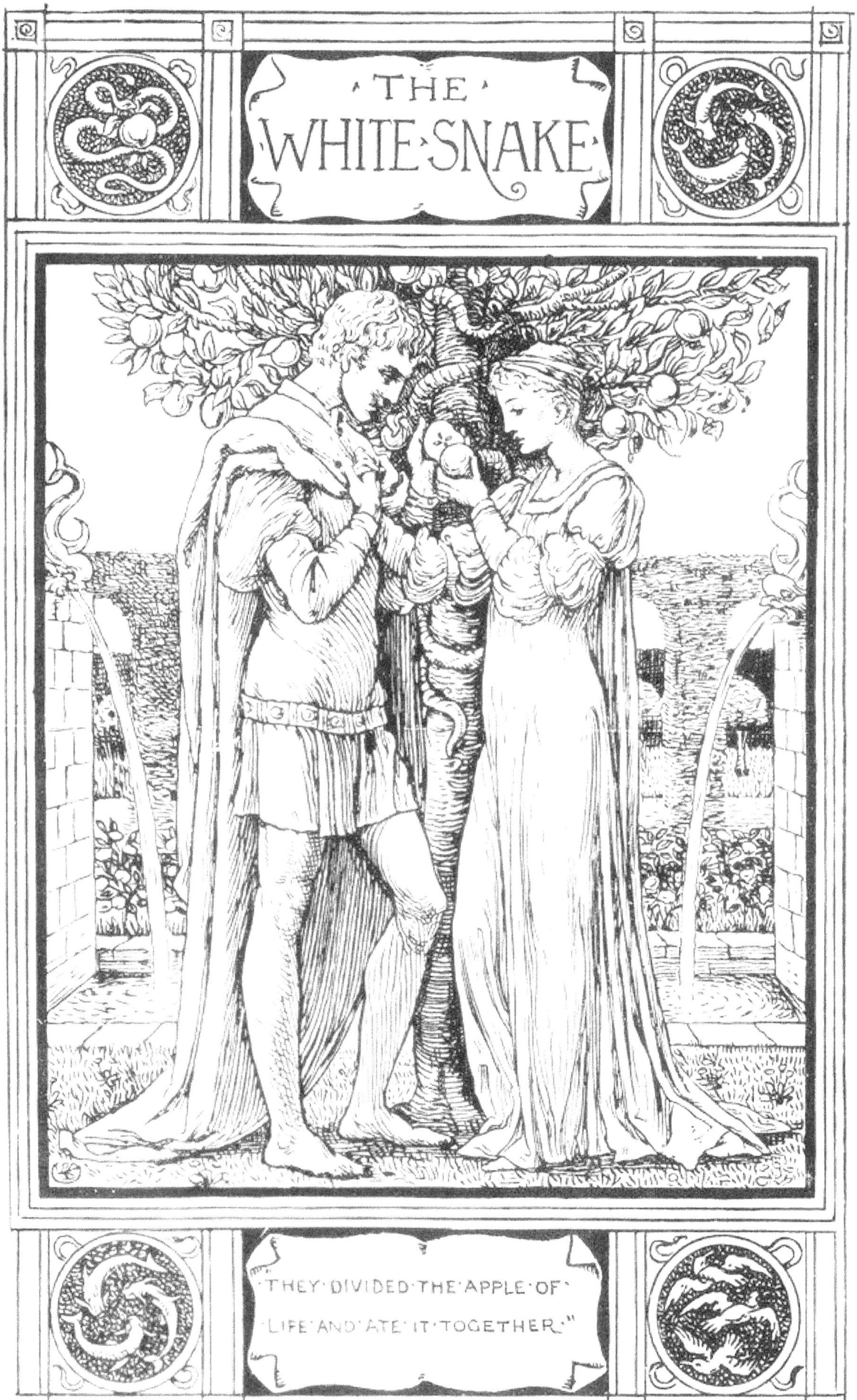

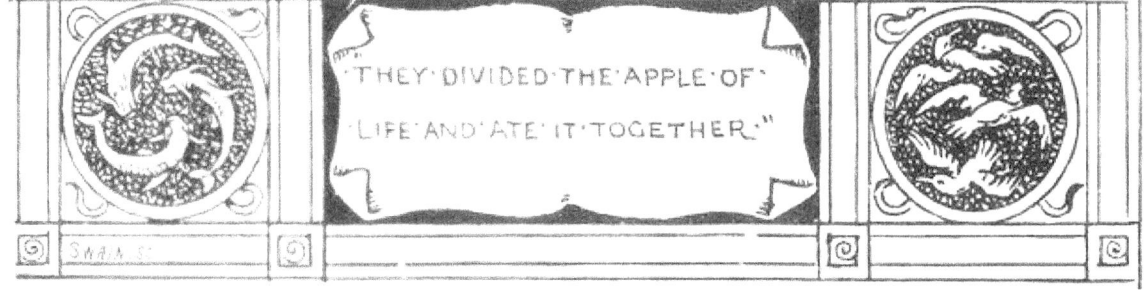

THE WHITE·SNAKE

"THEY·DIVIDED·THE·APPLE·OF·
LIFE·AND·ATE·IT·TOGETHER."

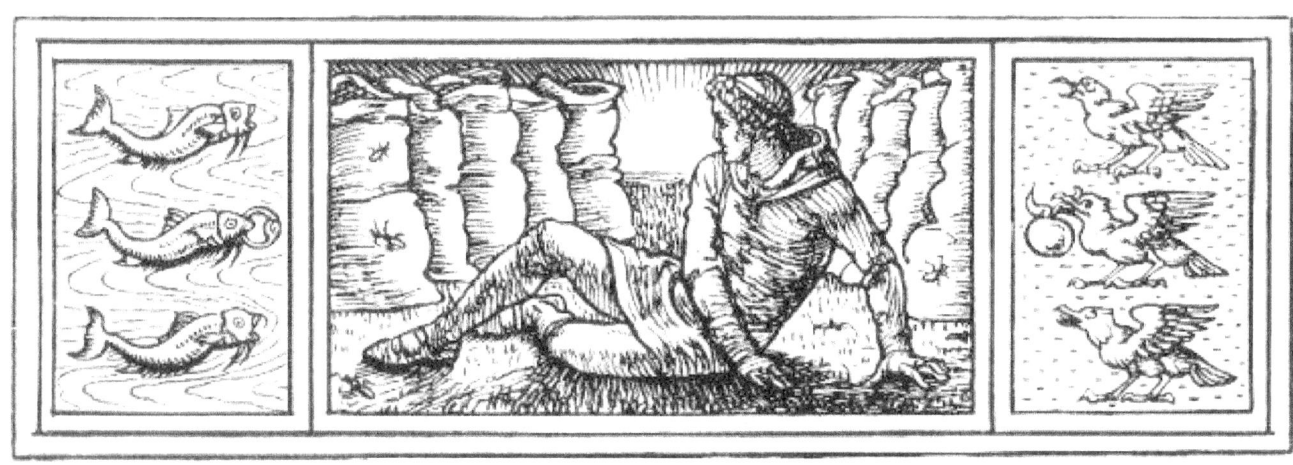

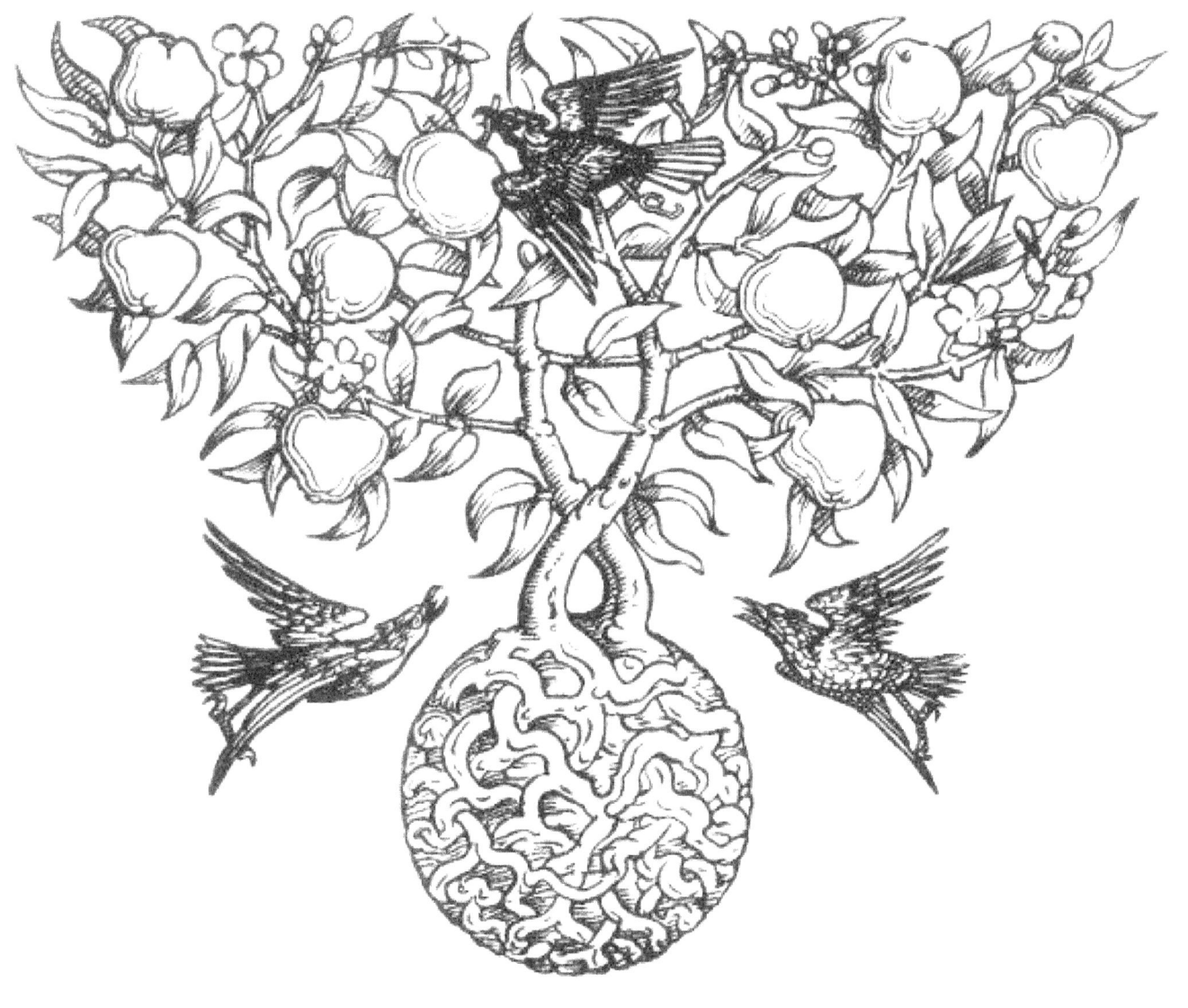

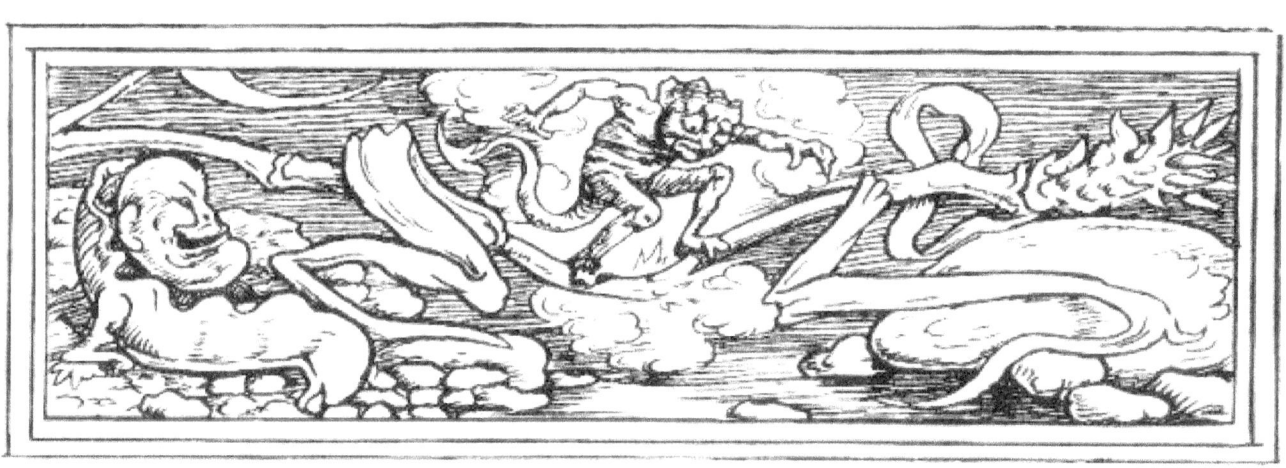

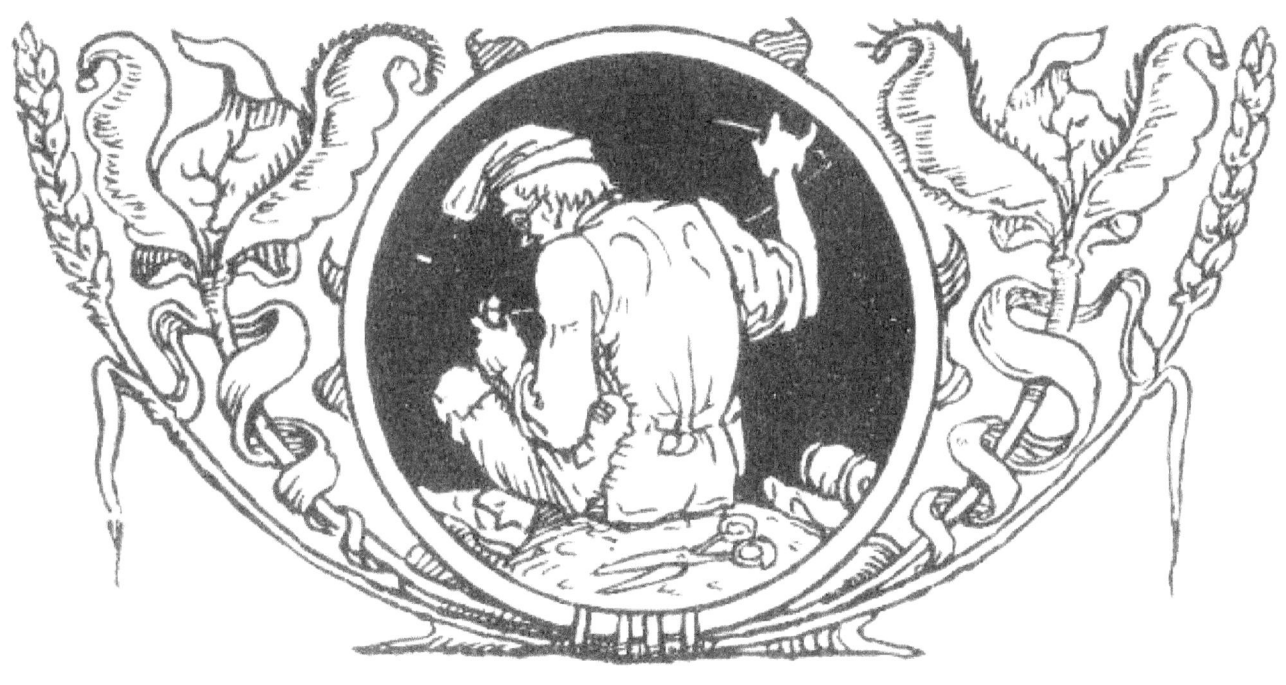

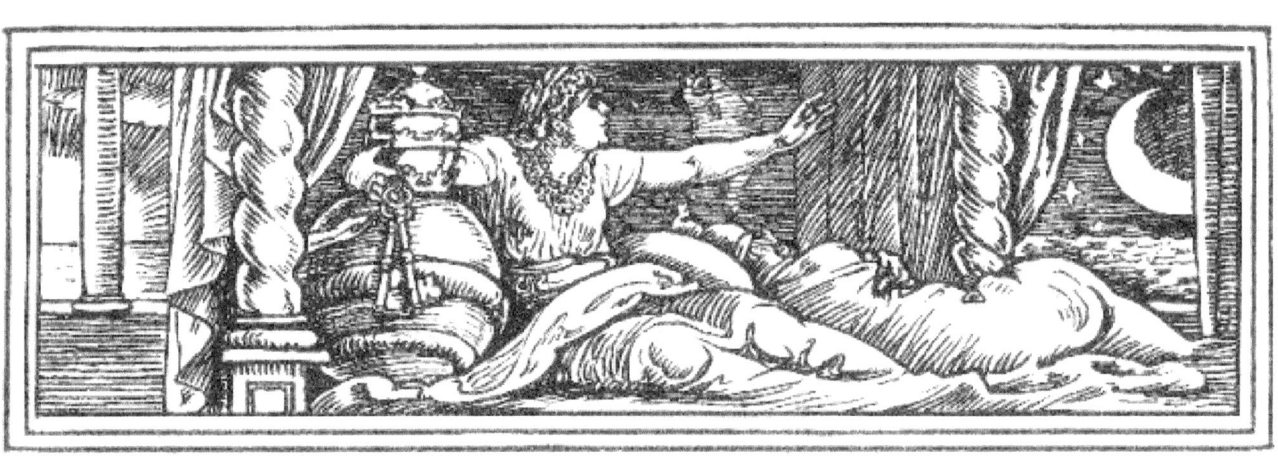

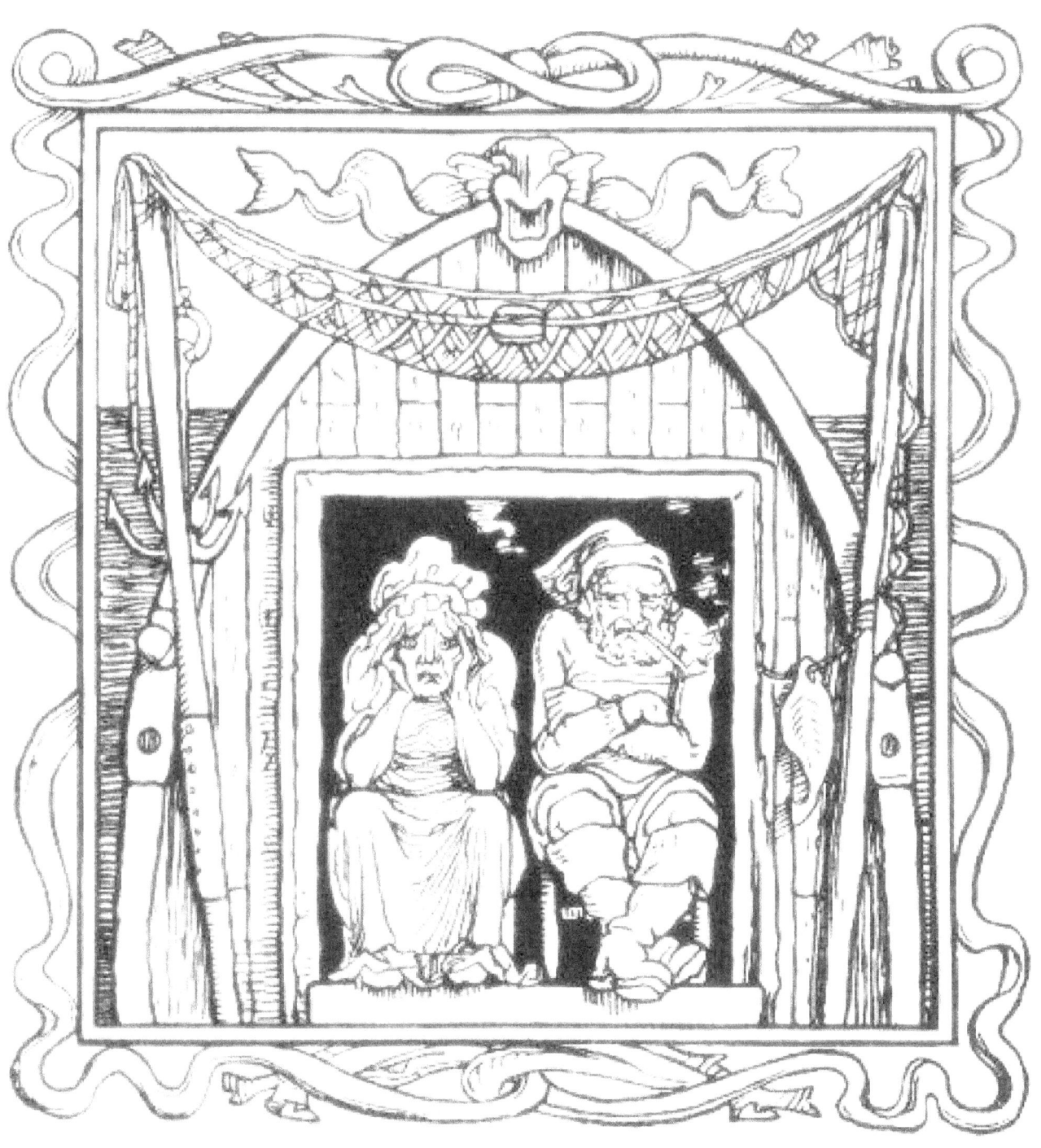

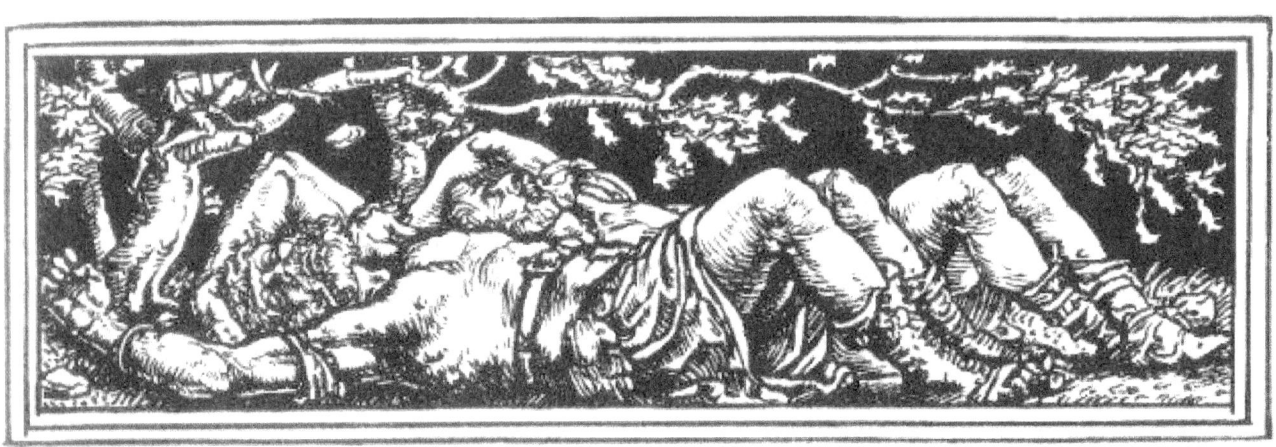

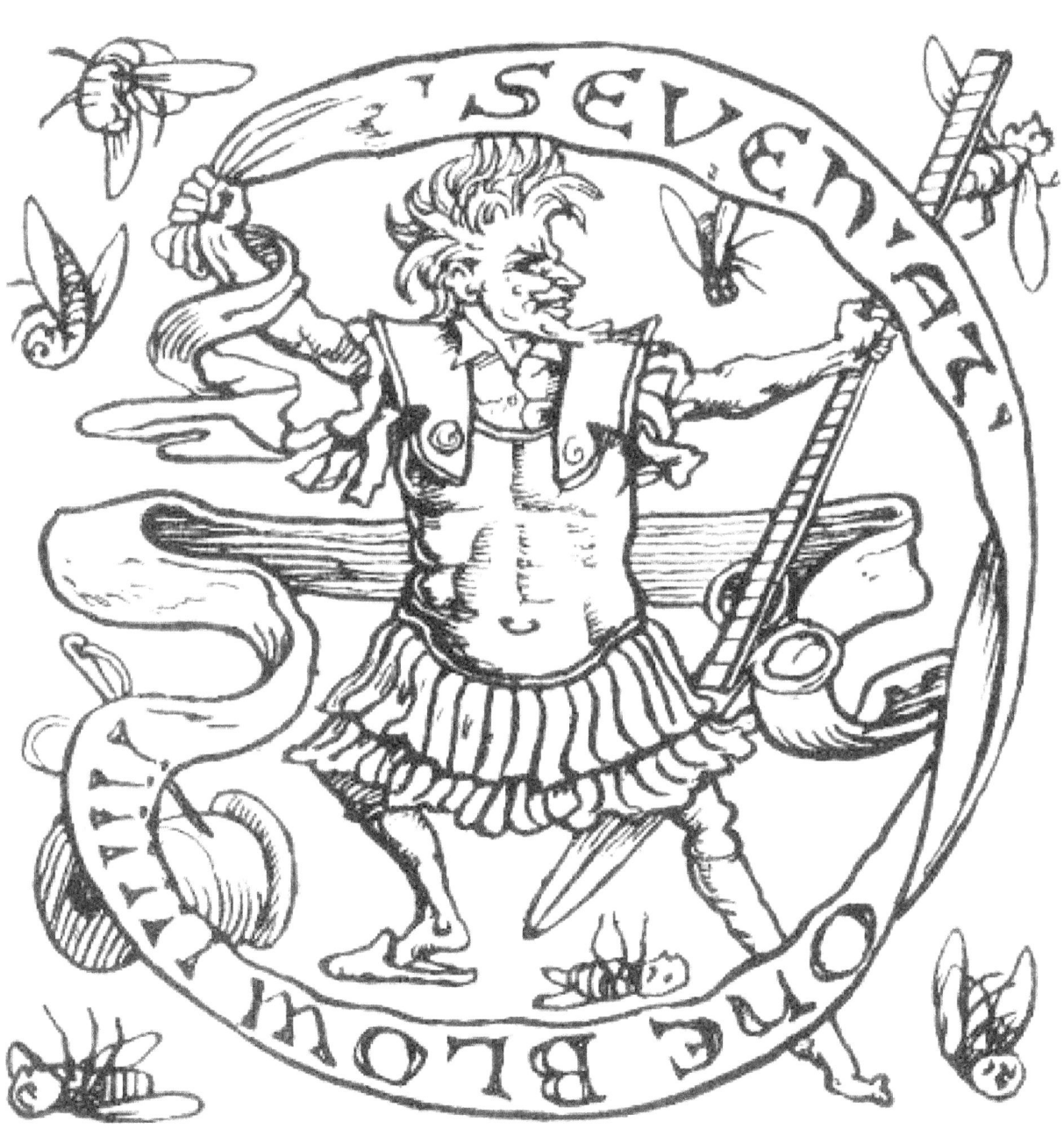

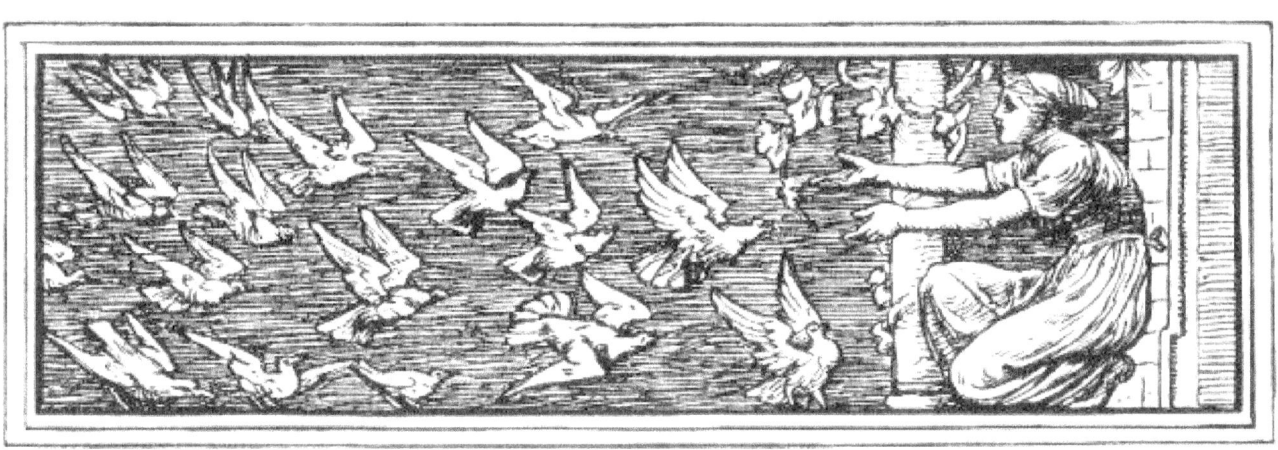

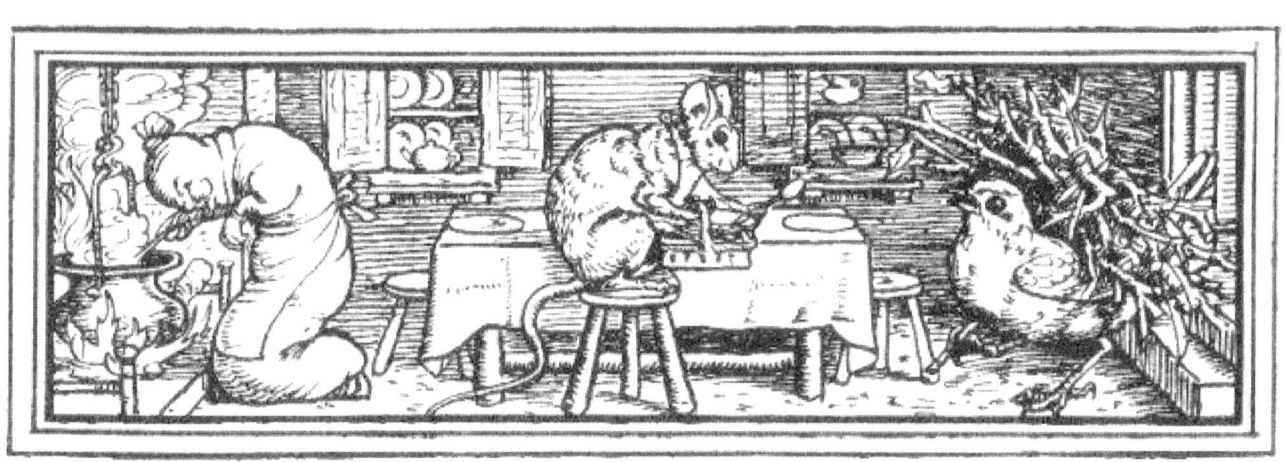

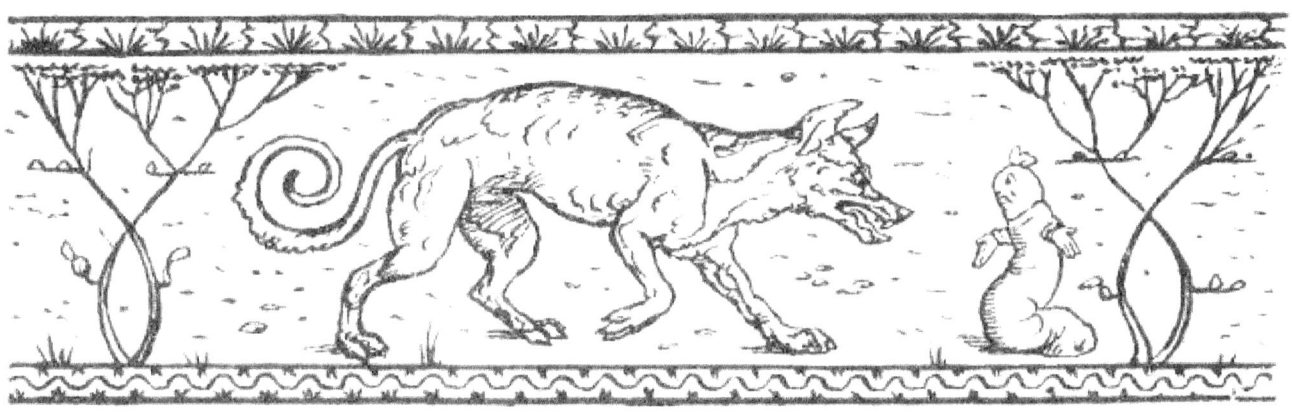

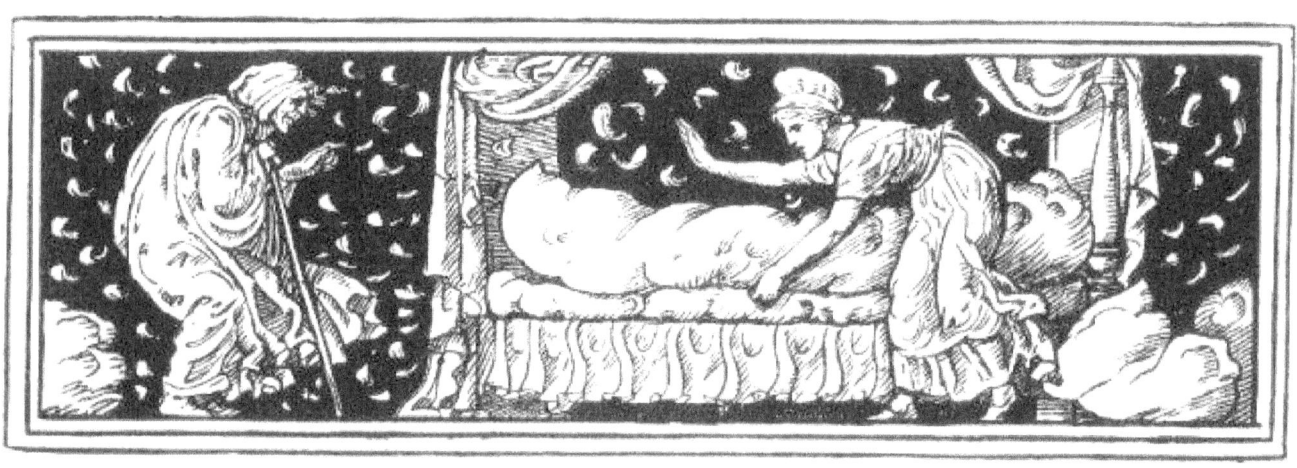

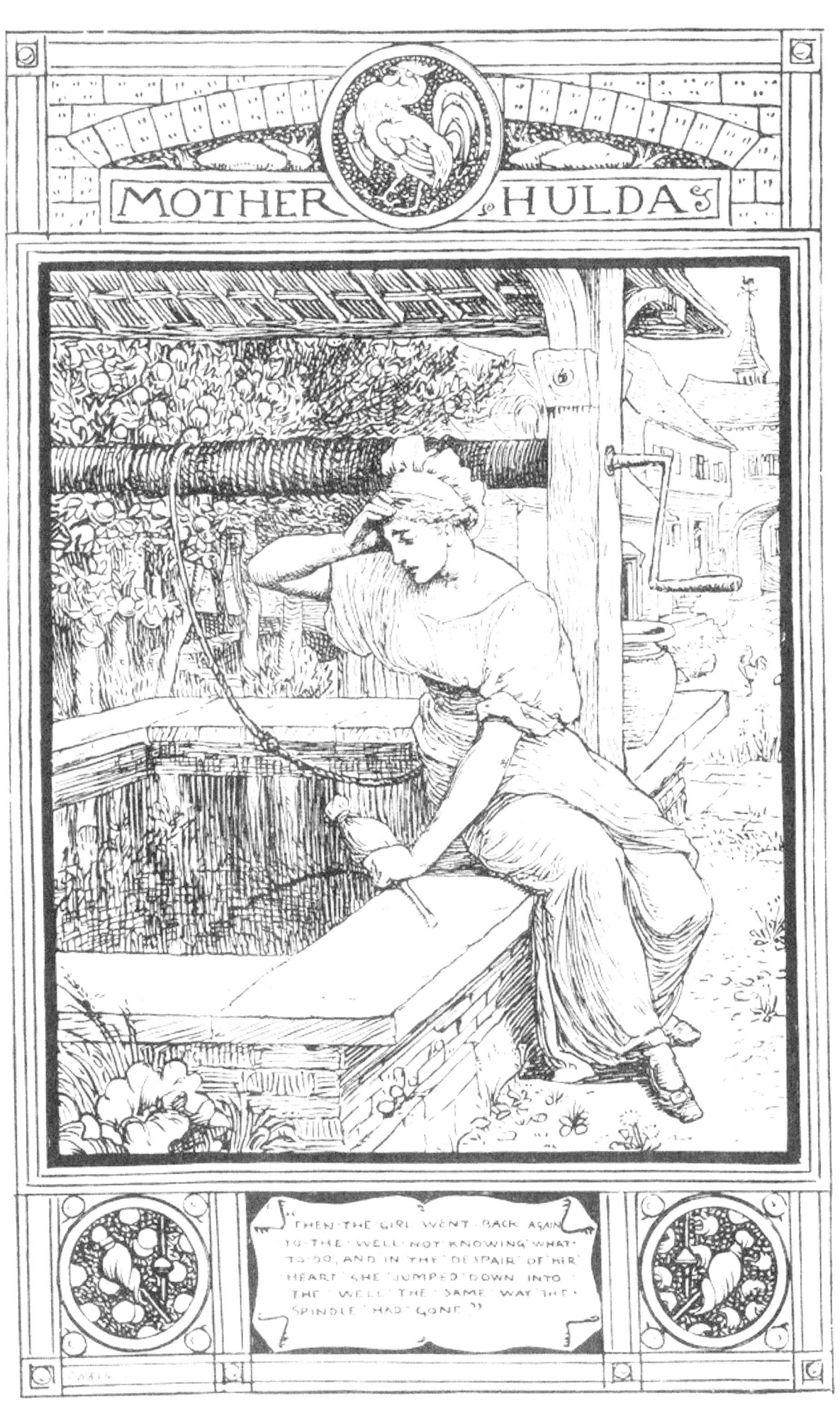

MOTHER HULDA

"THEN THE GIRL WENT BACK AGAIN TO THE WELL NOT KNOWING WHAT TO DO, AND IN THE DESPAIR OF HER HEART SHE JUMPED DOWN INTO THE WELL THE SAME WAY THE SPINDLE HAD GONE"

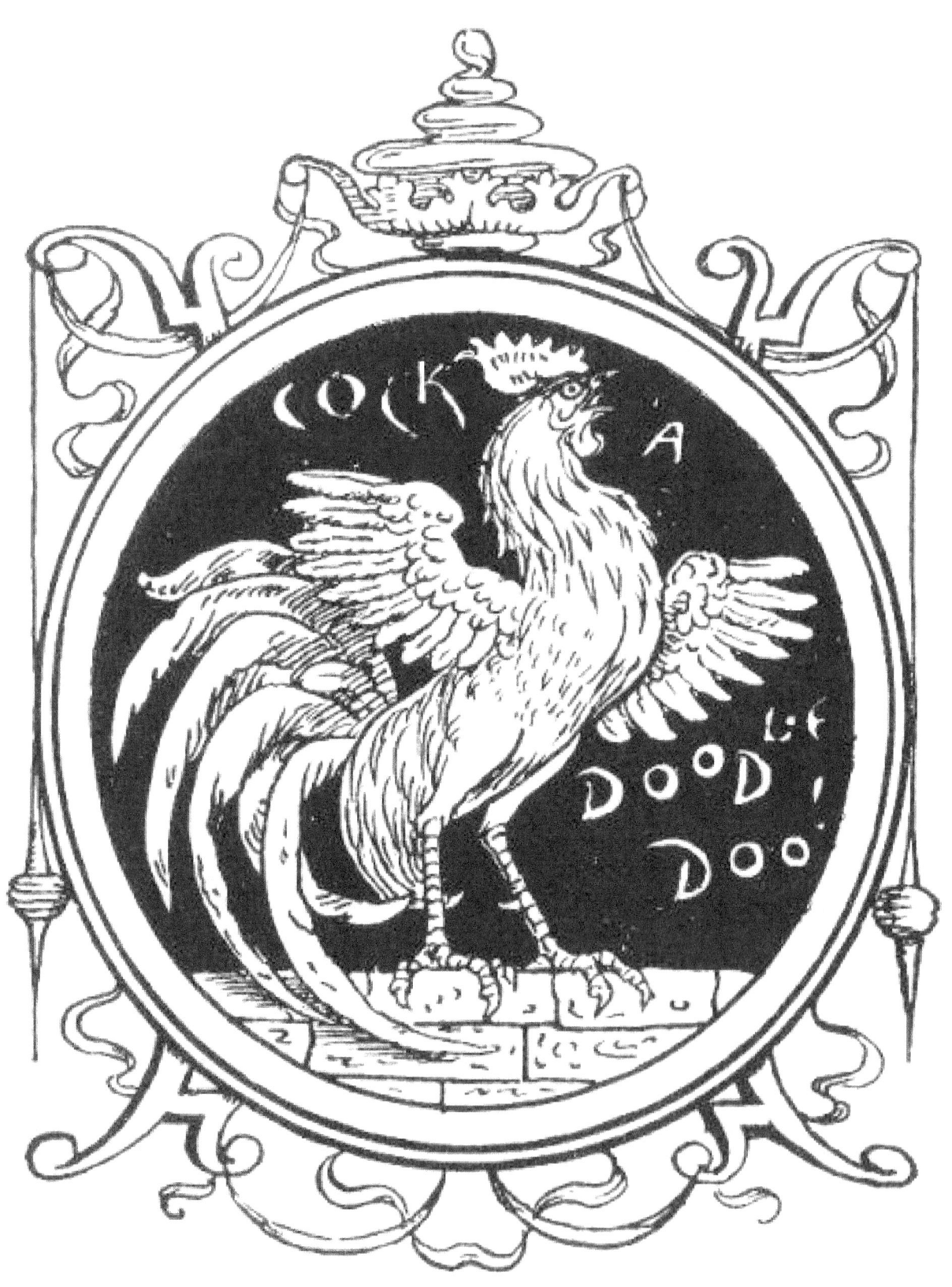

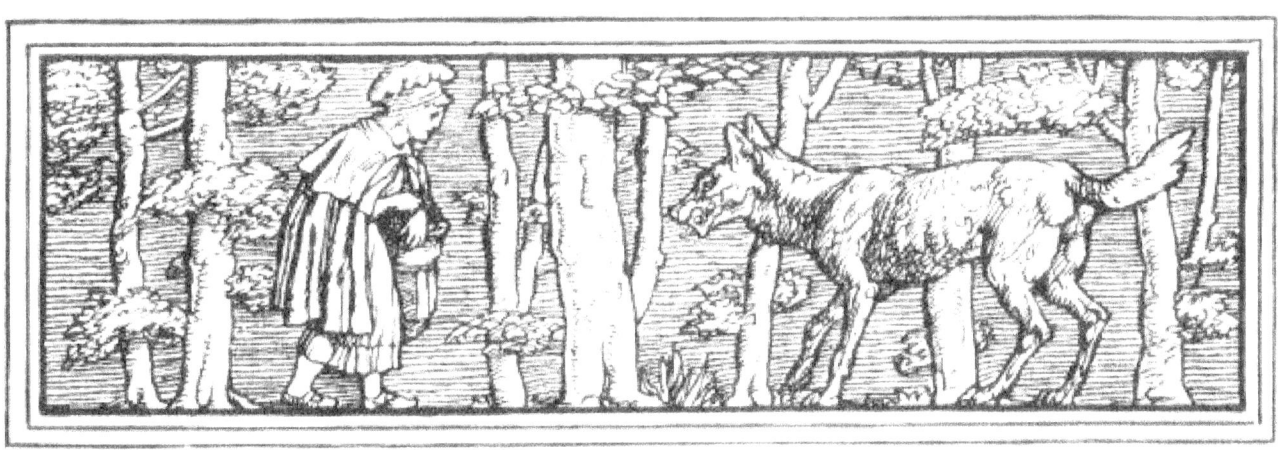

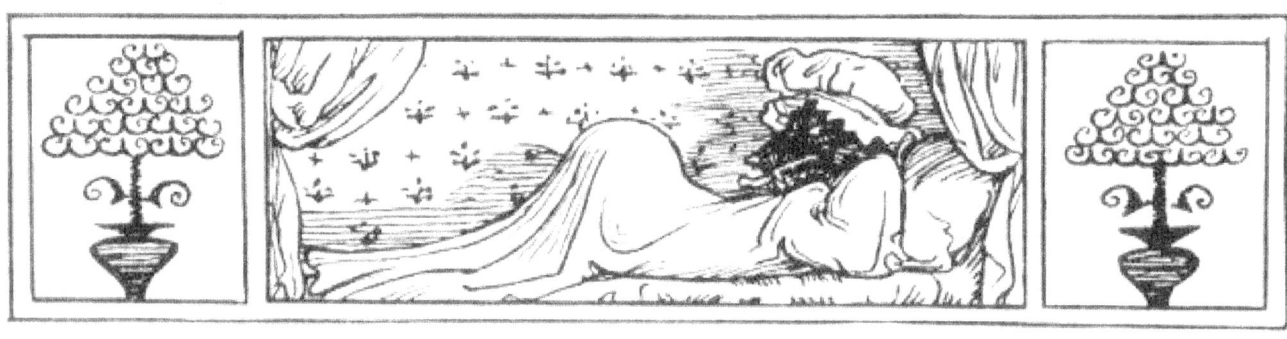

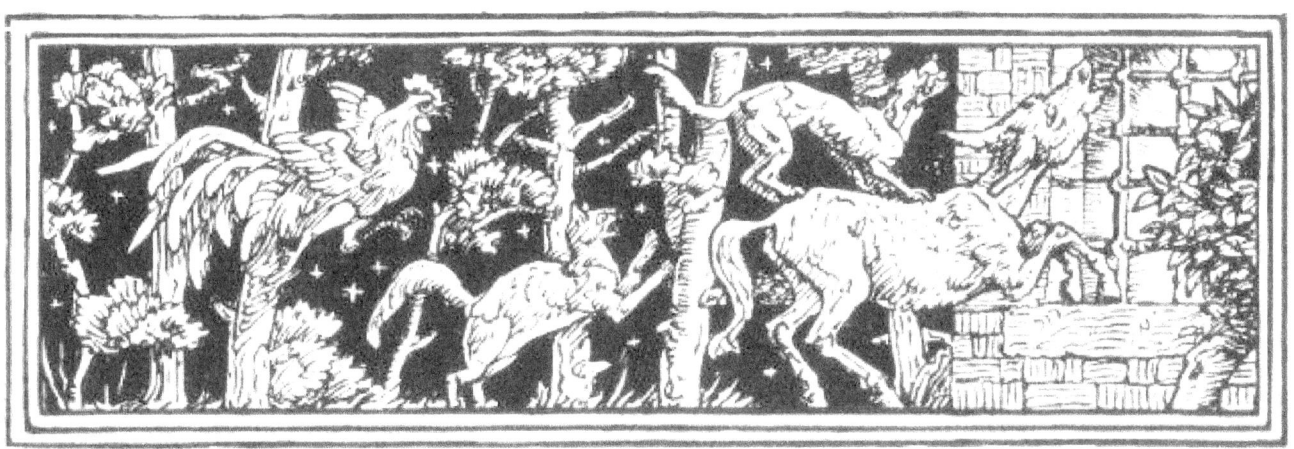

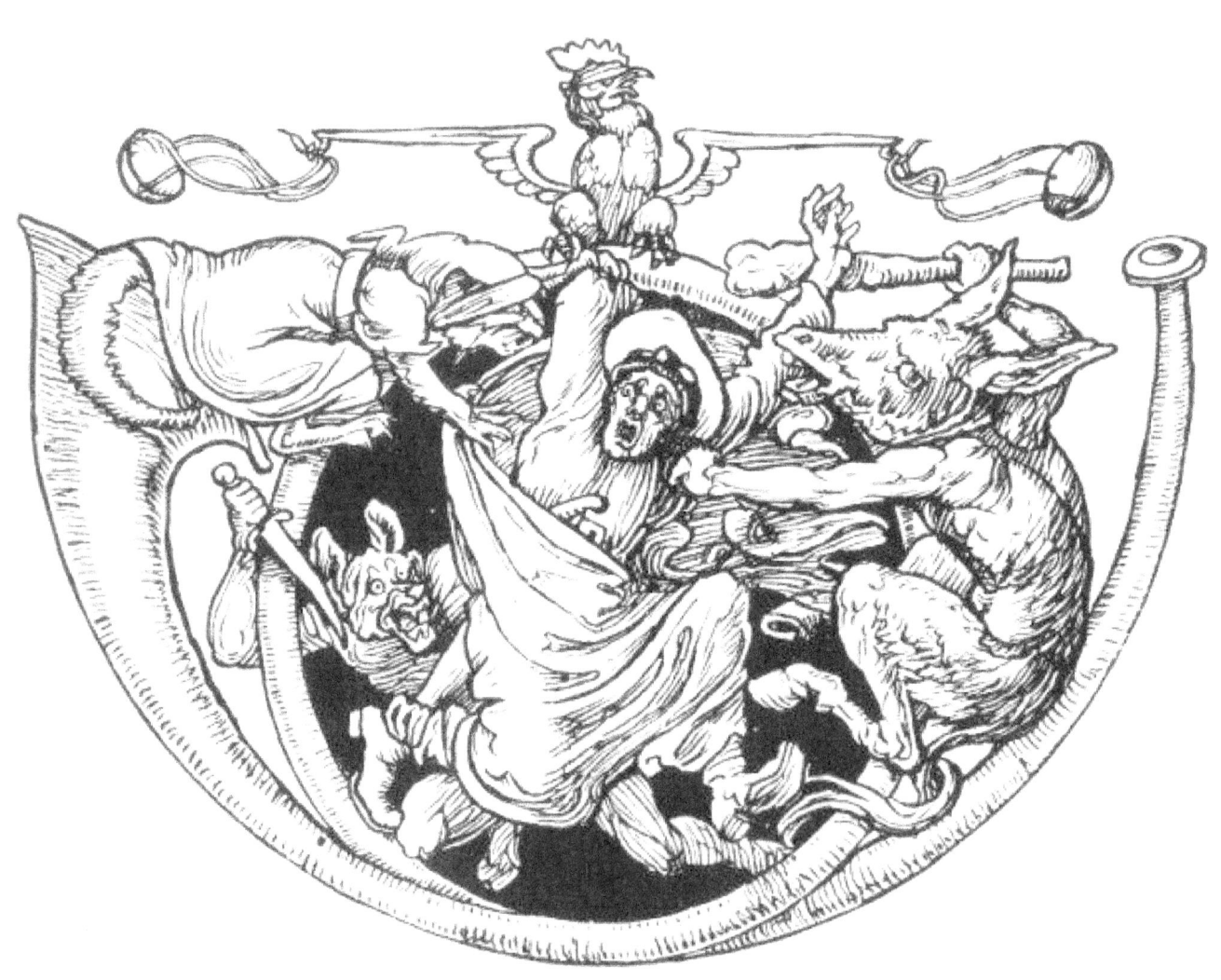

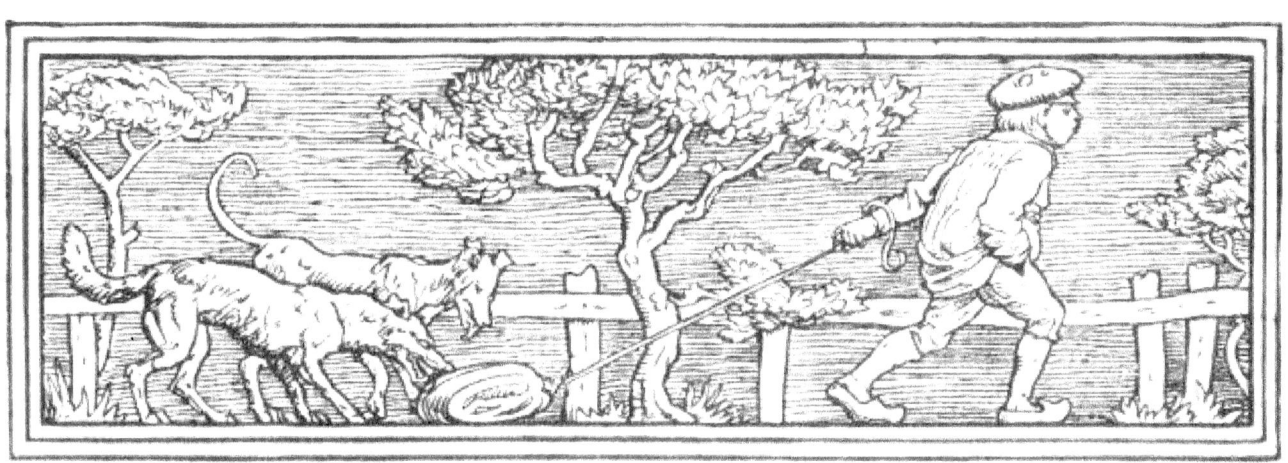

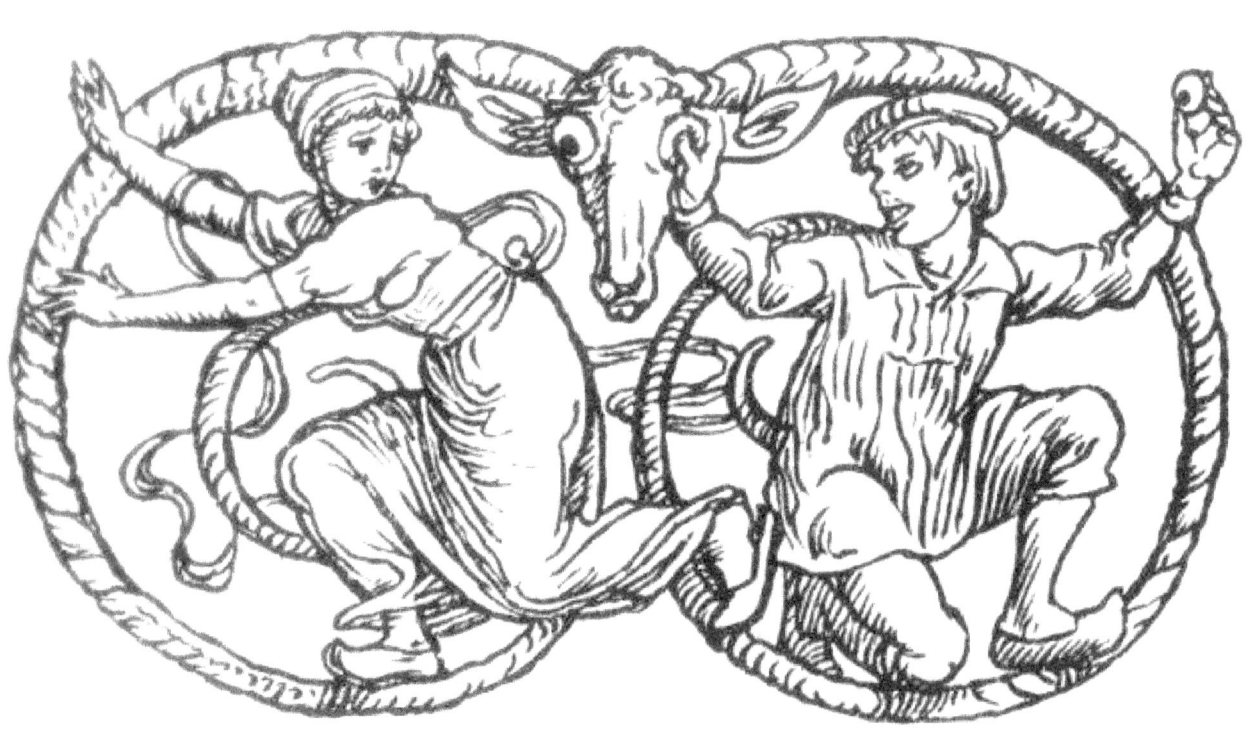

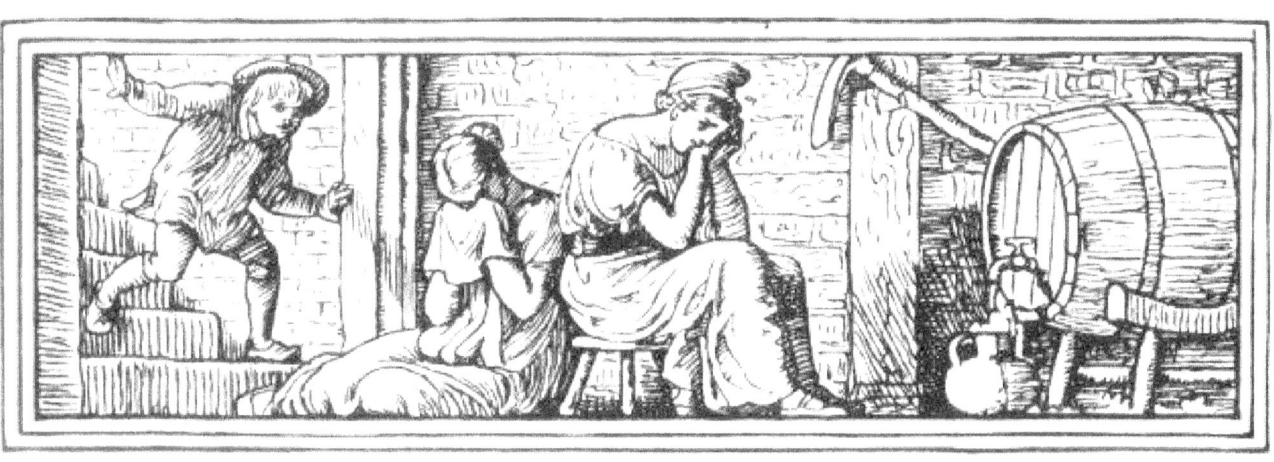

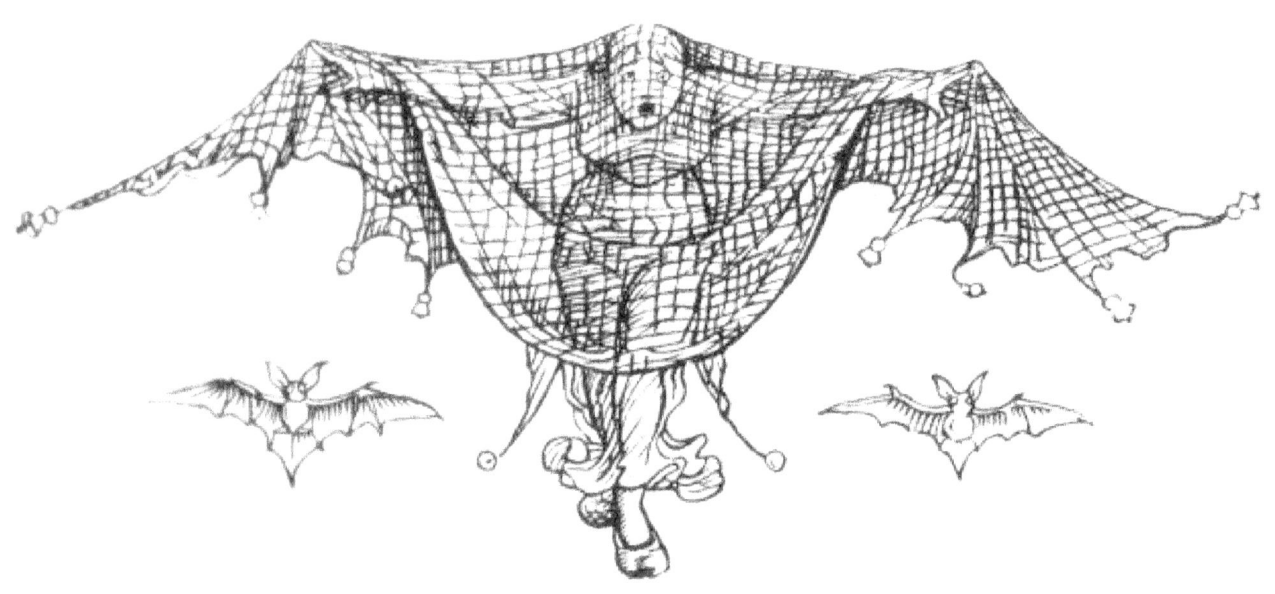

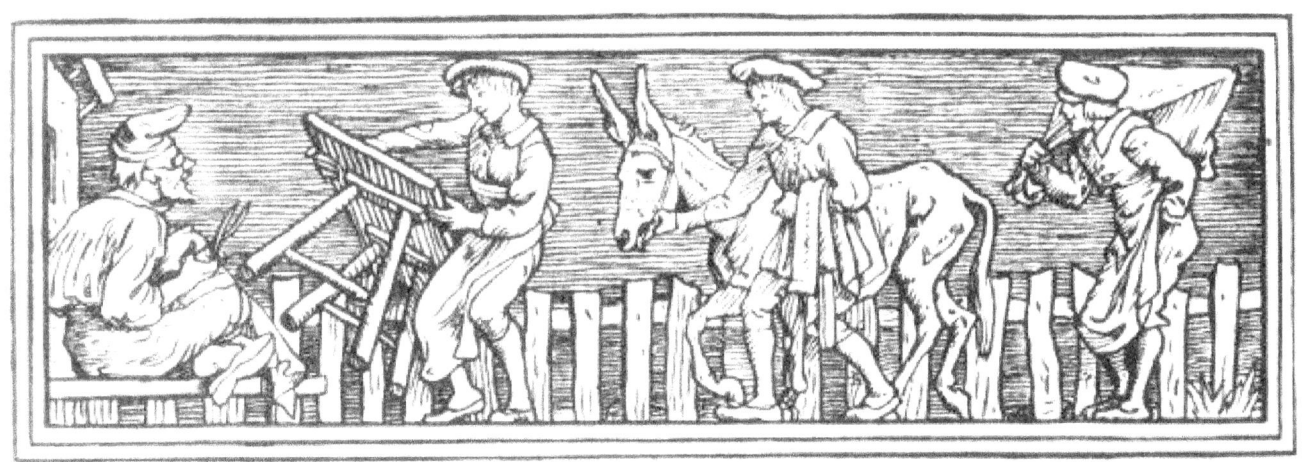

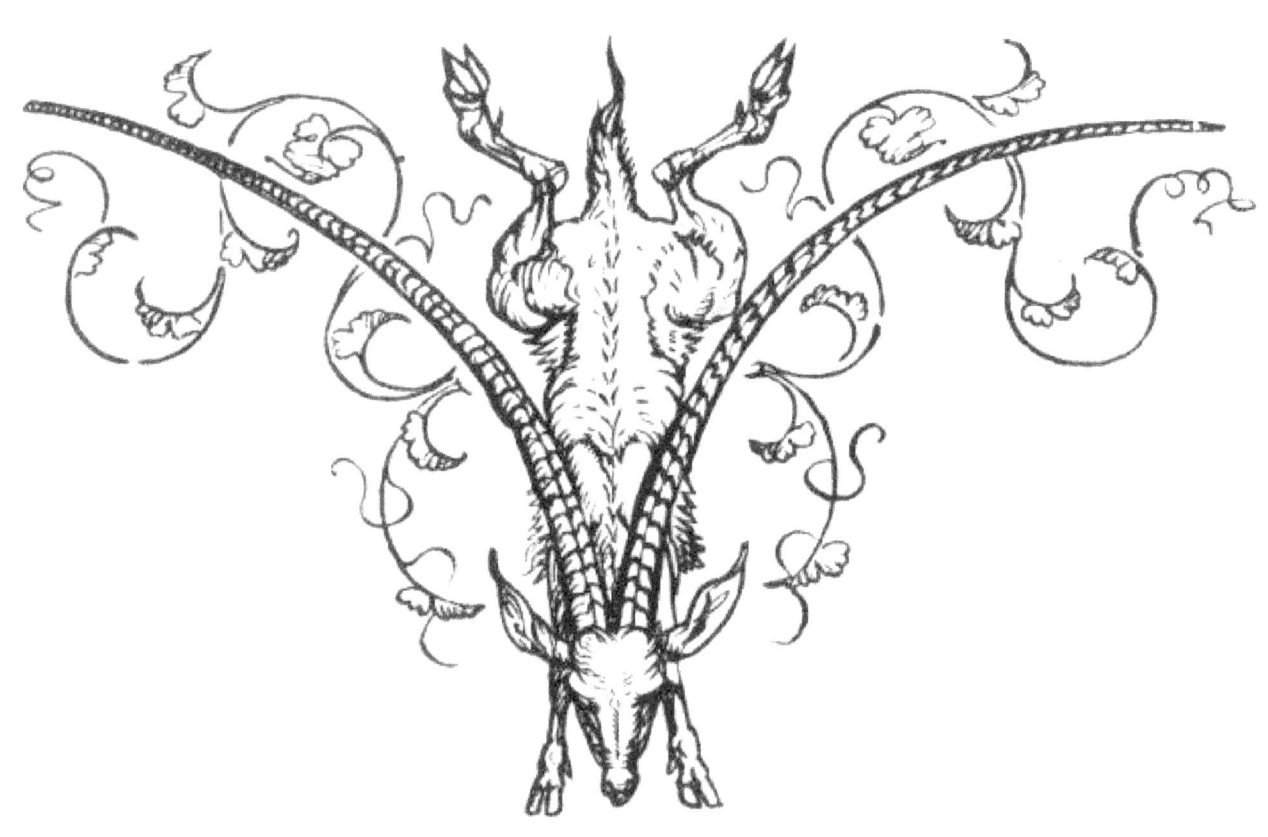

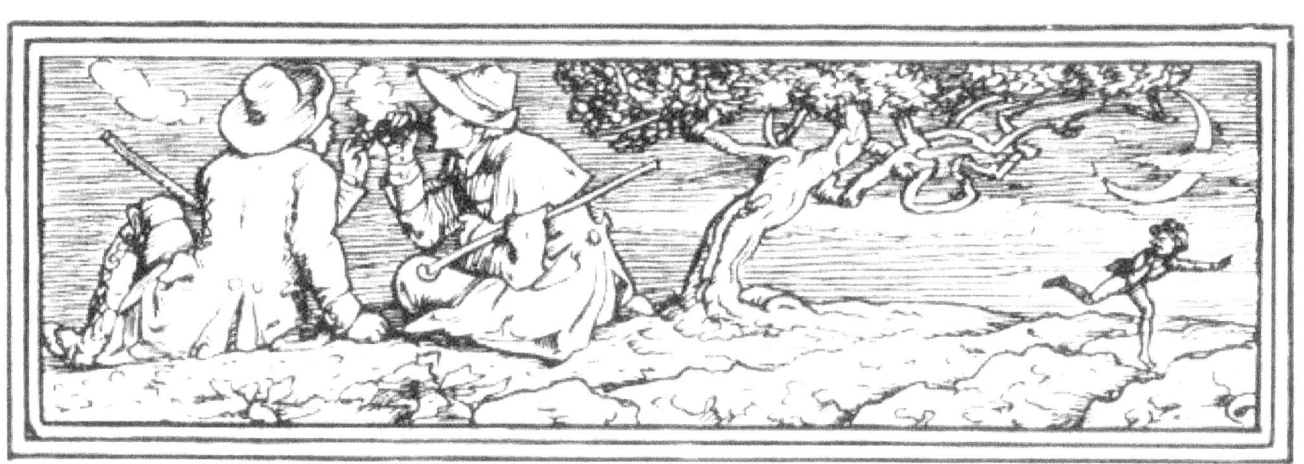

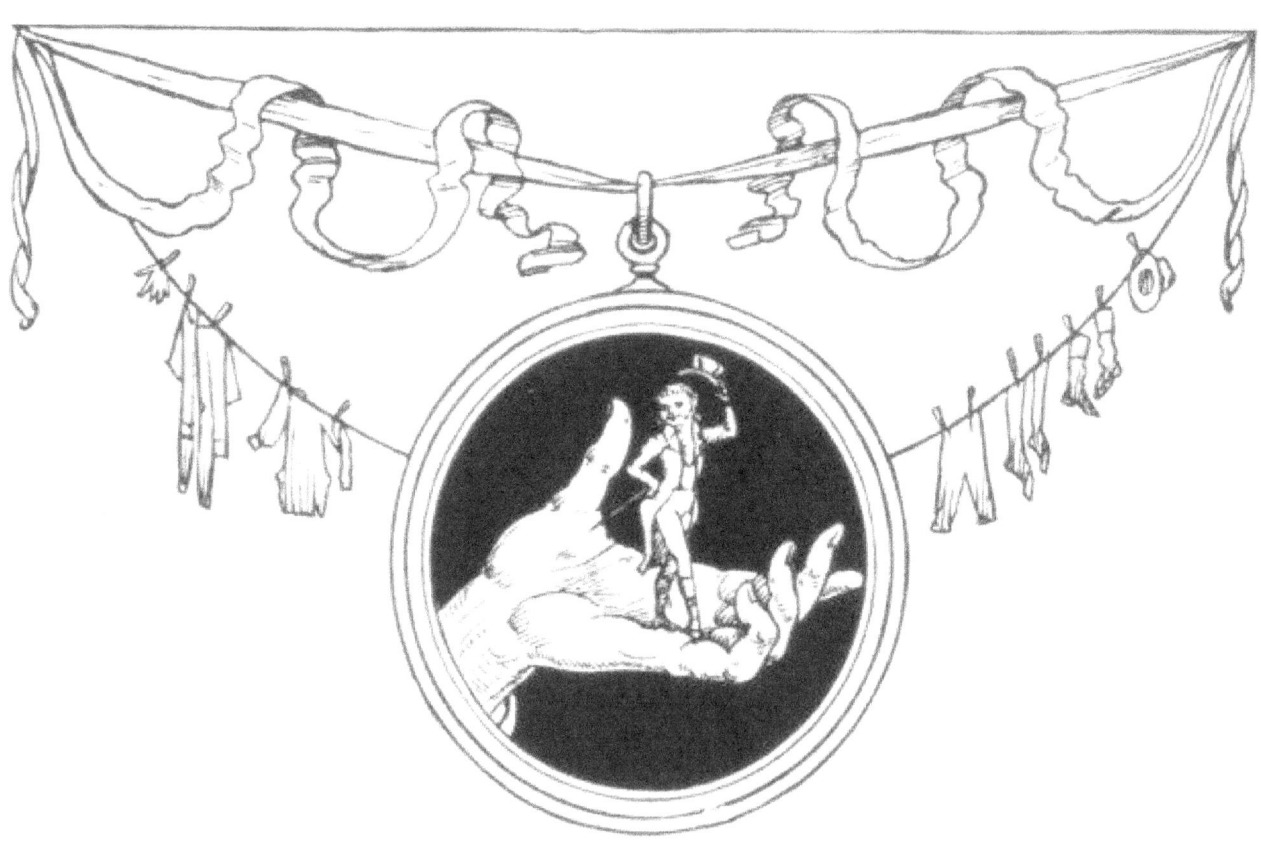

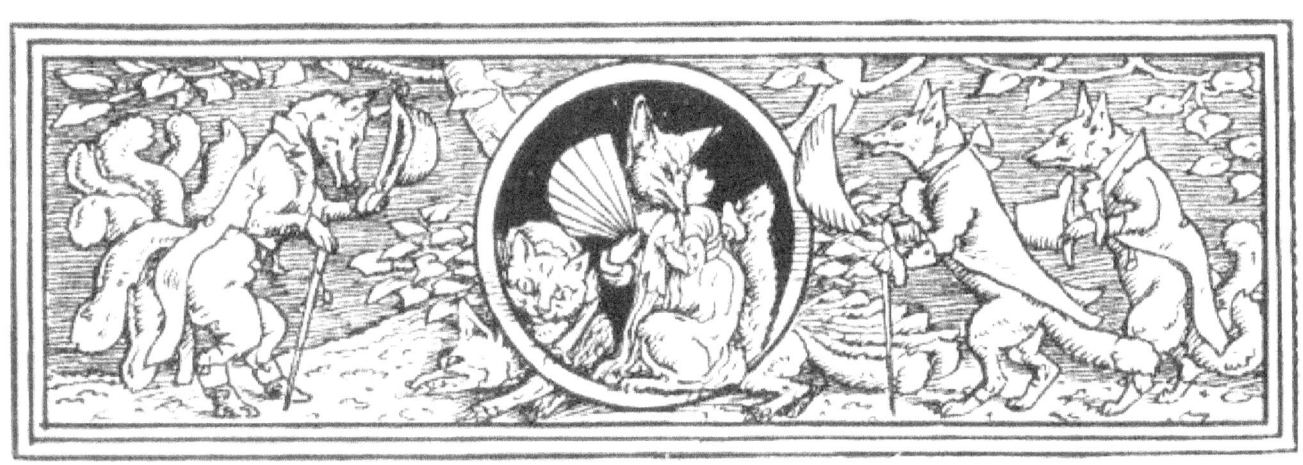

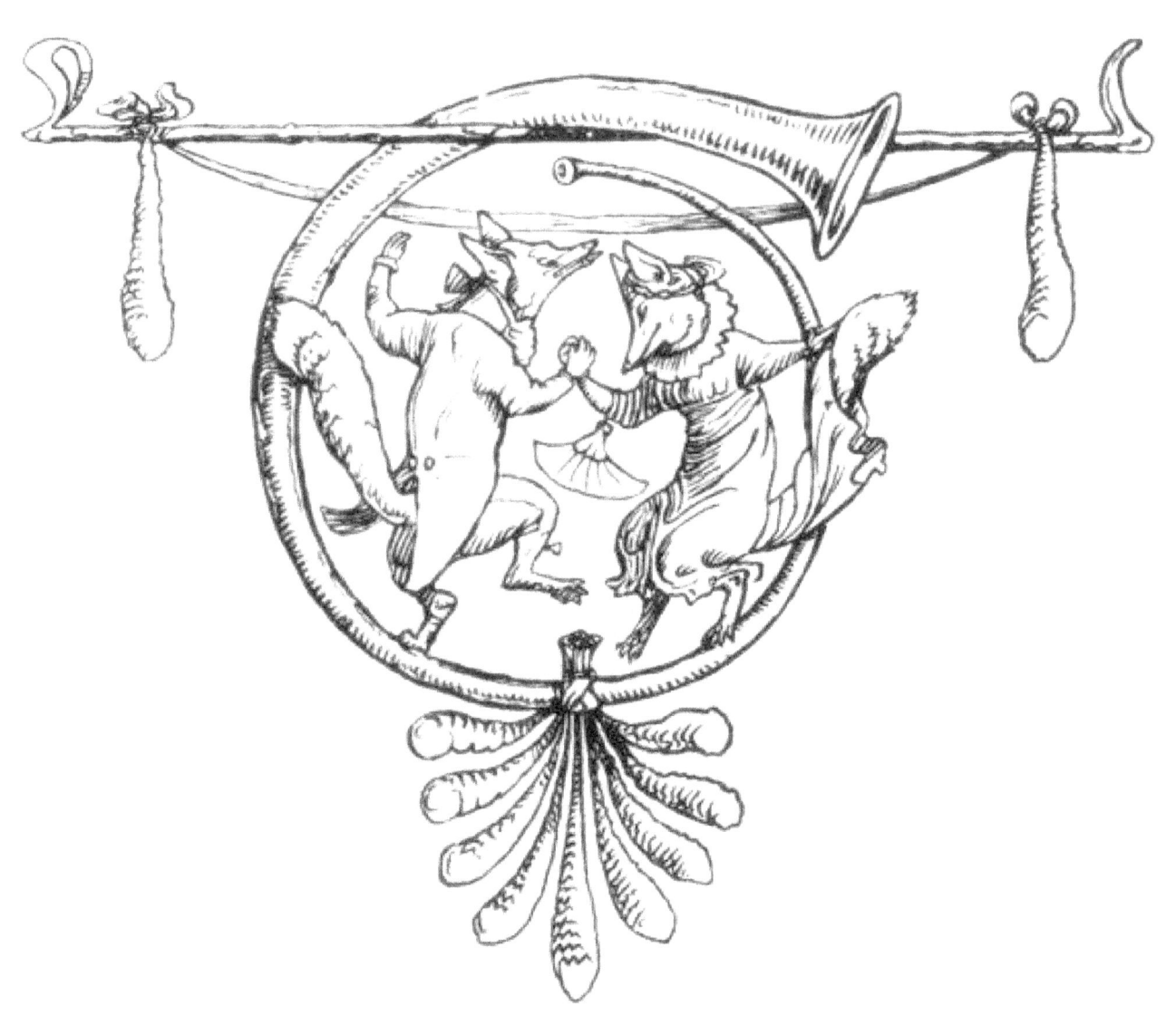

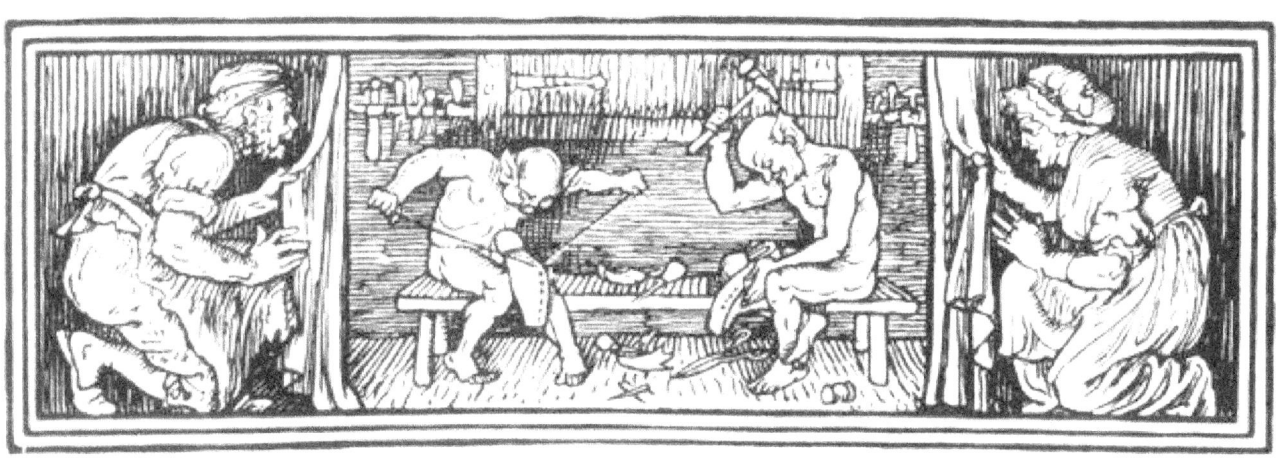

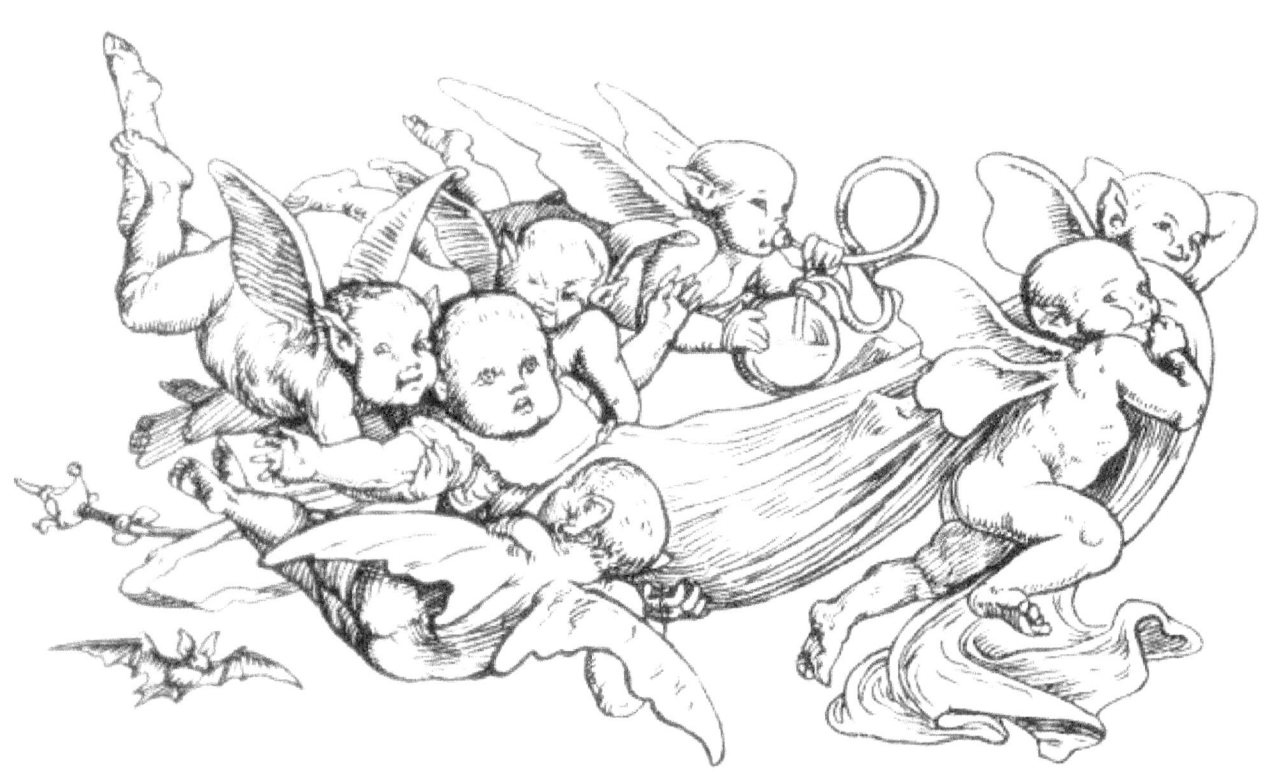

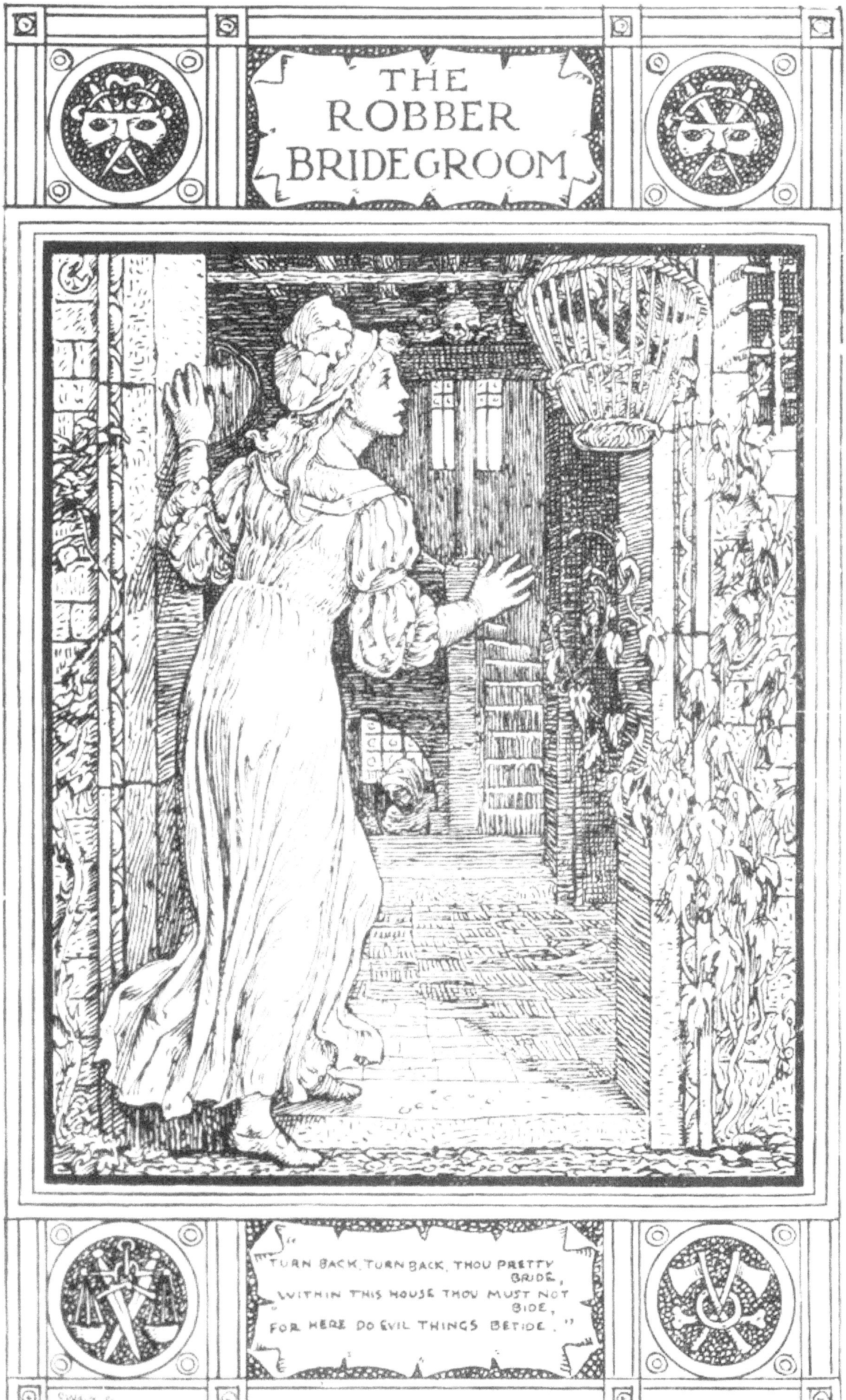

THE ROBBER BRIDEGROOM

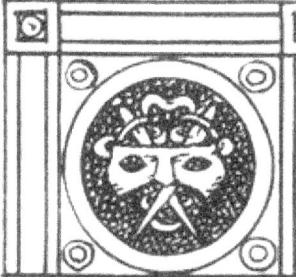
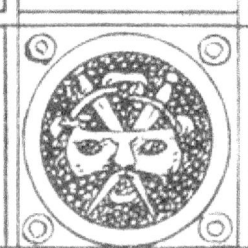

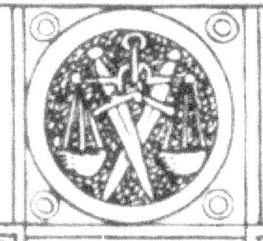
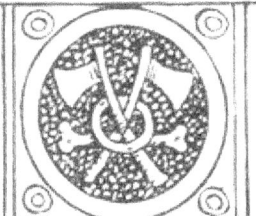

"TURN BACK, TURN BACK, THOU PRETTY BRIDE,
WITHIN THIS HOUSE THOU MUST NOT BIDE,
FOR HERE DO EVIL THINGS BETIDE."

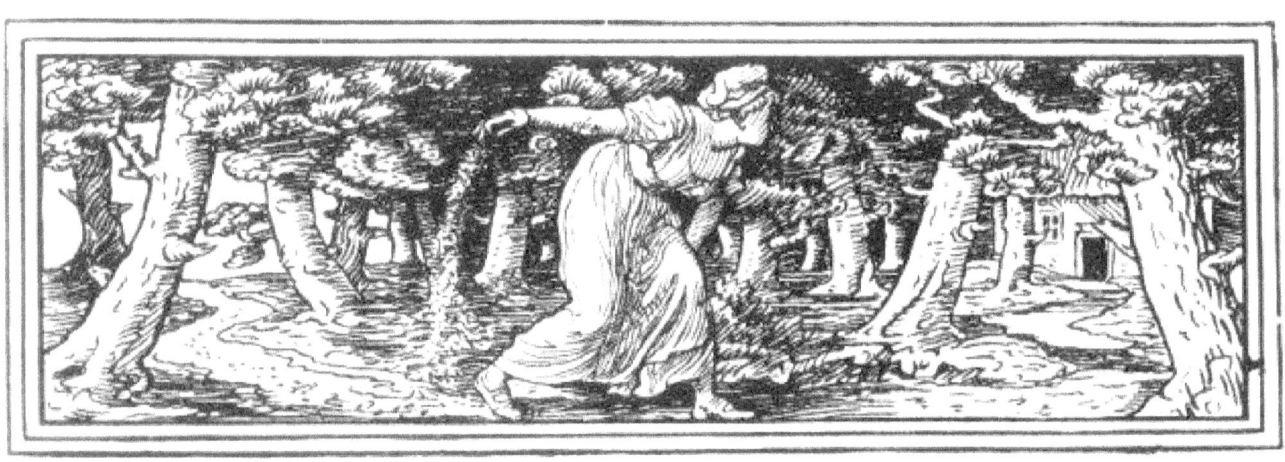

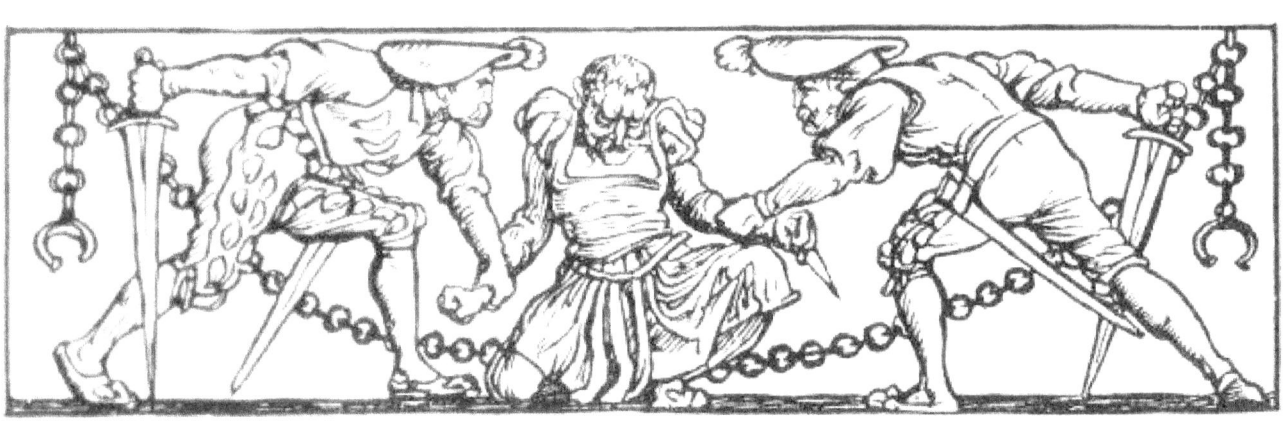

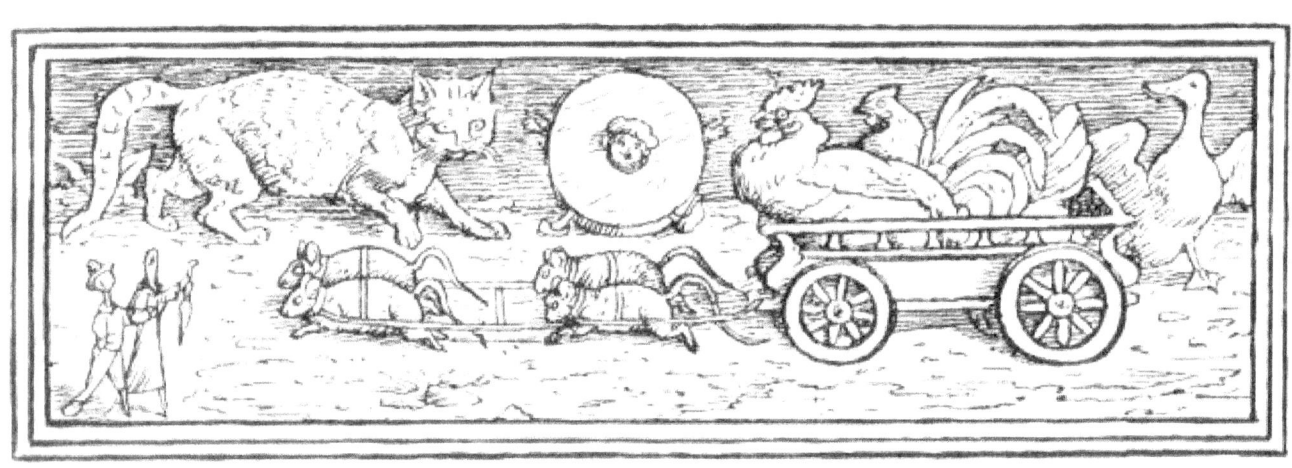

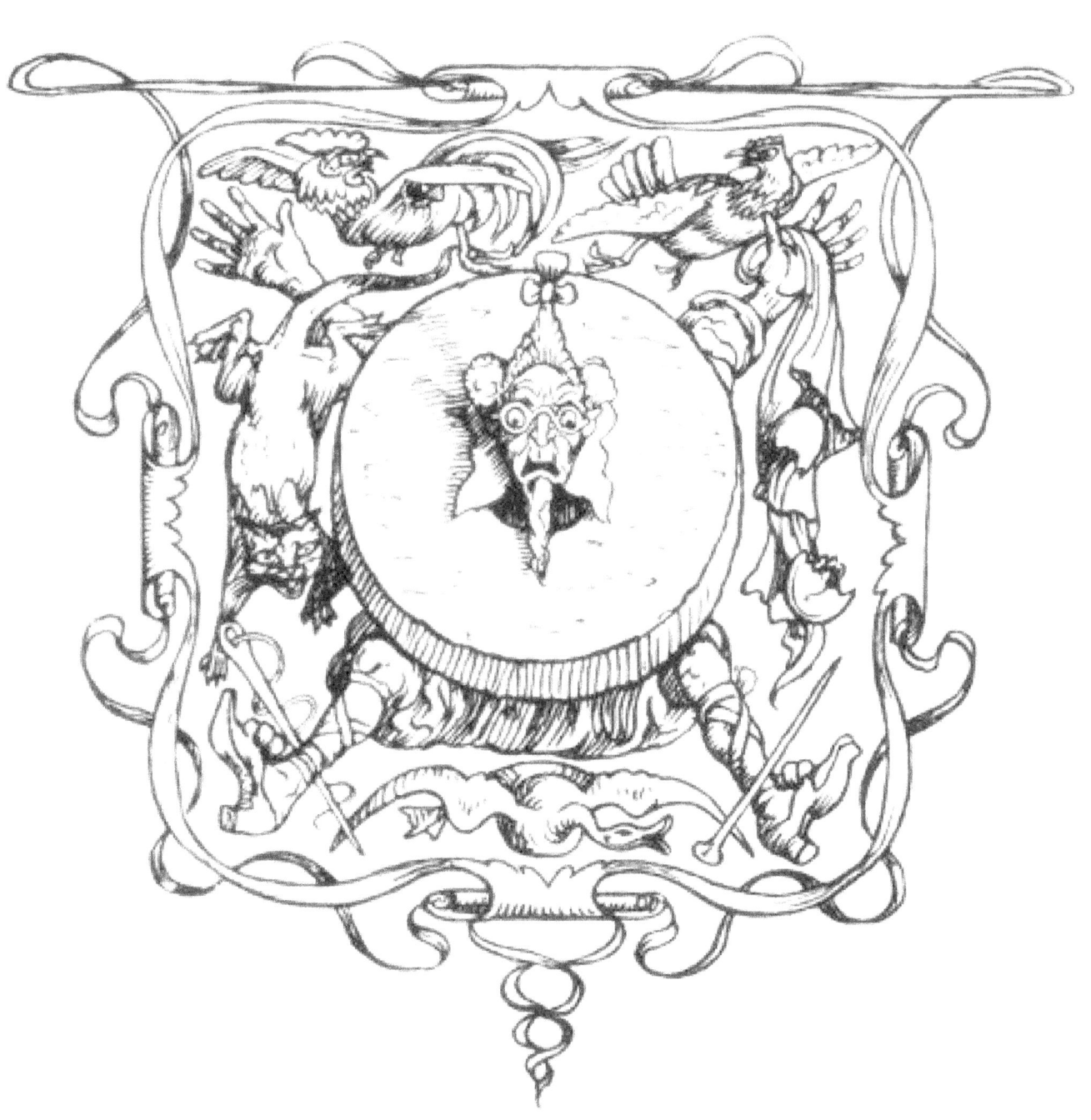

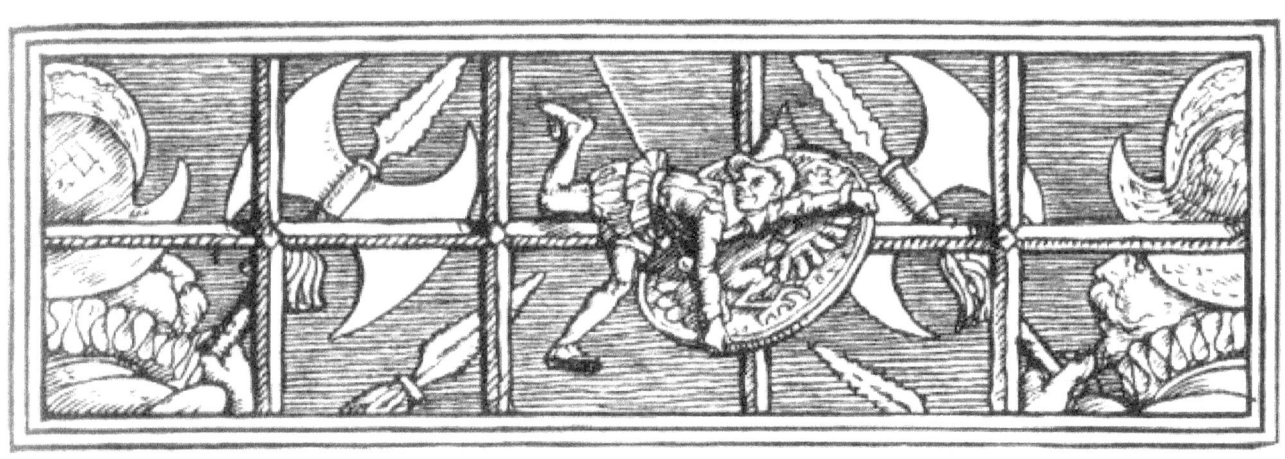

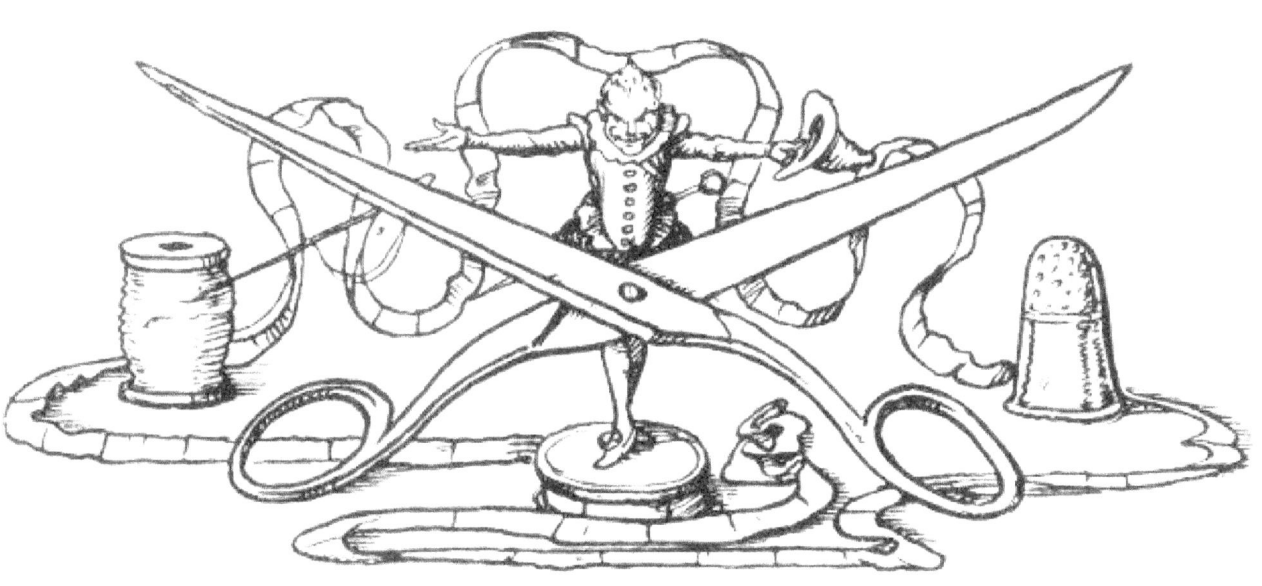

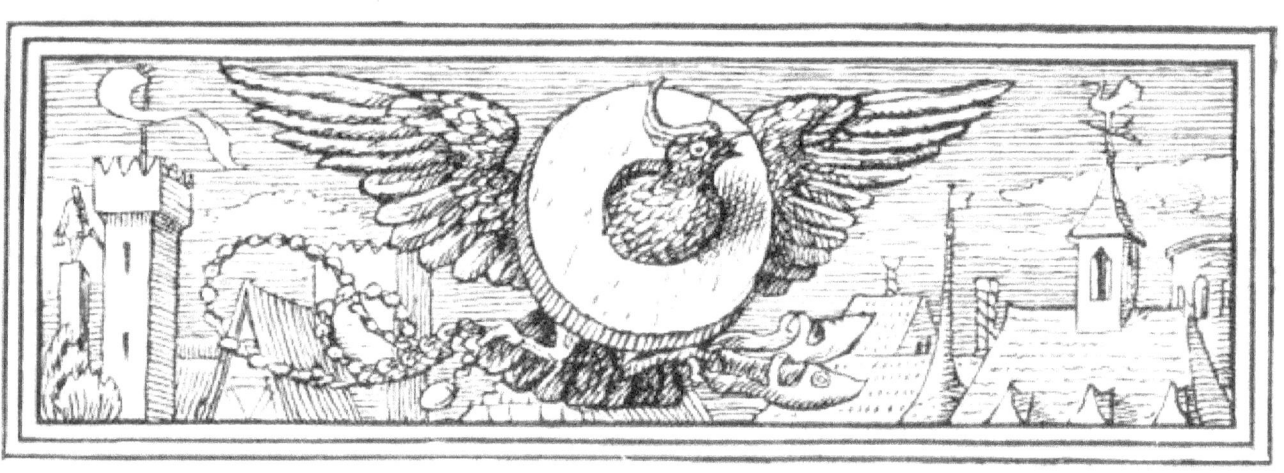

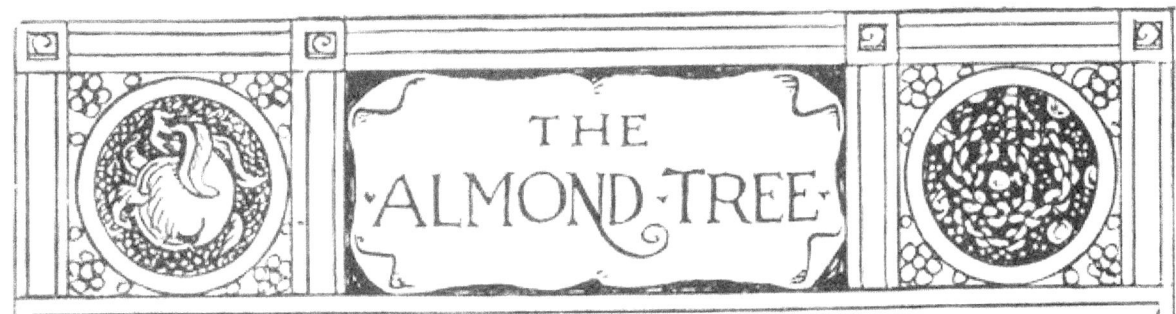

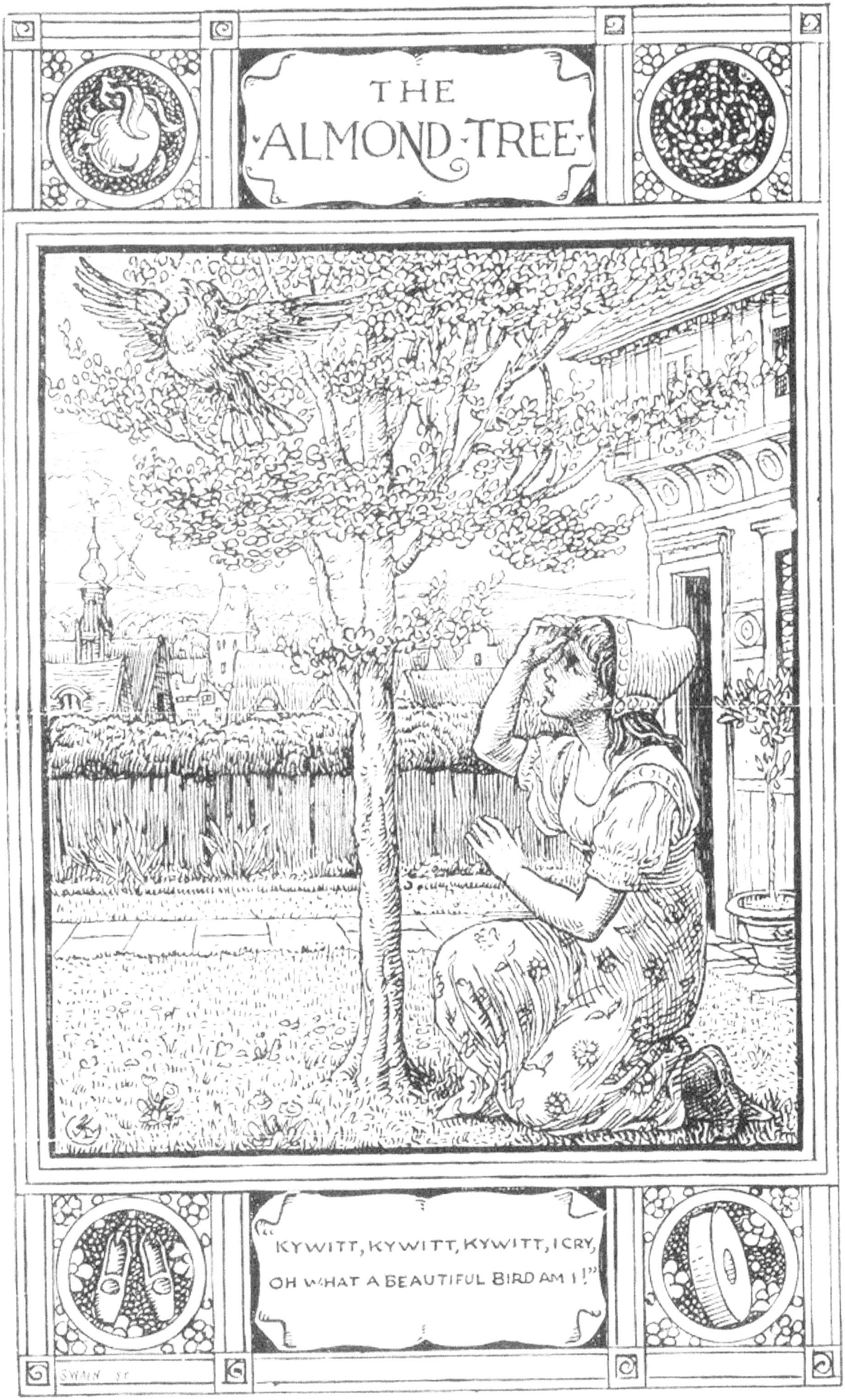

THE ALMOND·TREE·

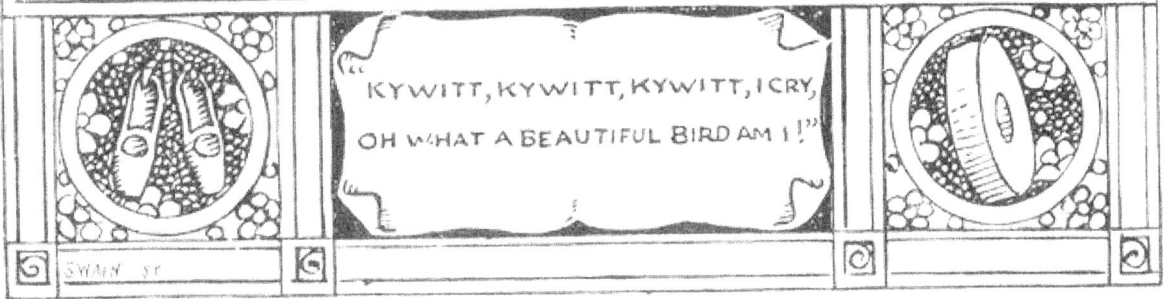

"KYWITT, KYWITT, KYWITT, I CRY,
OH WHAT A BEAUTIFUL BIRD AM I!"

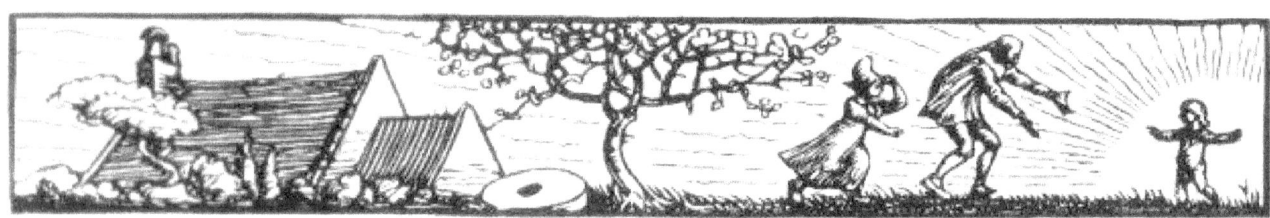

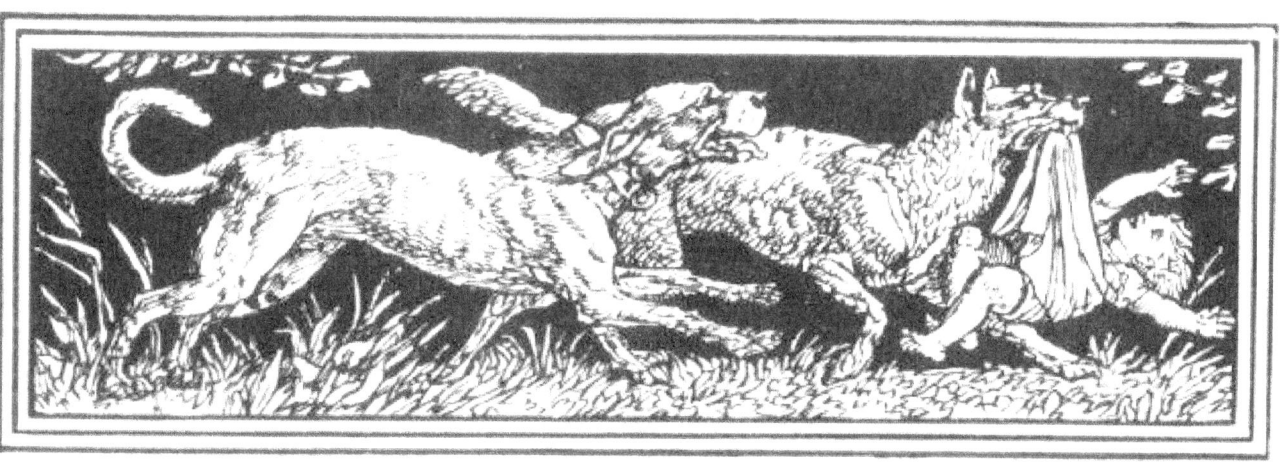

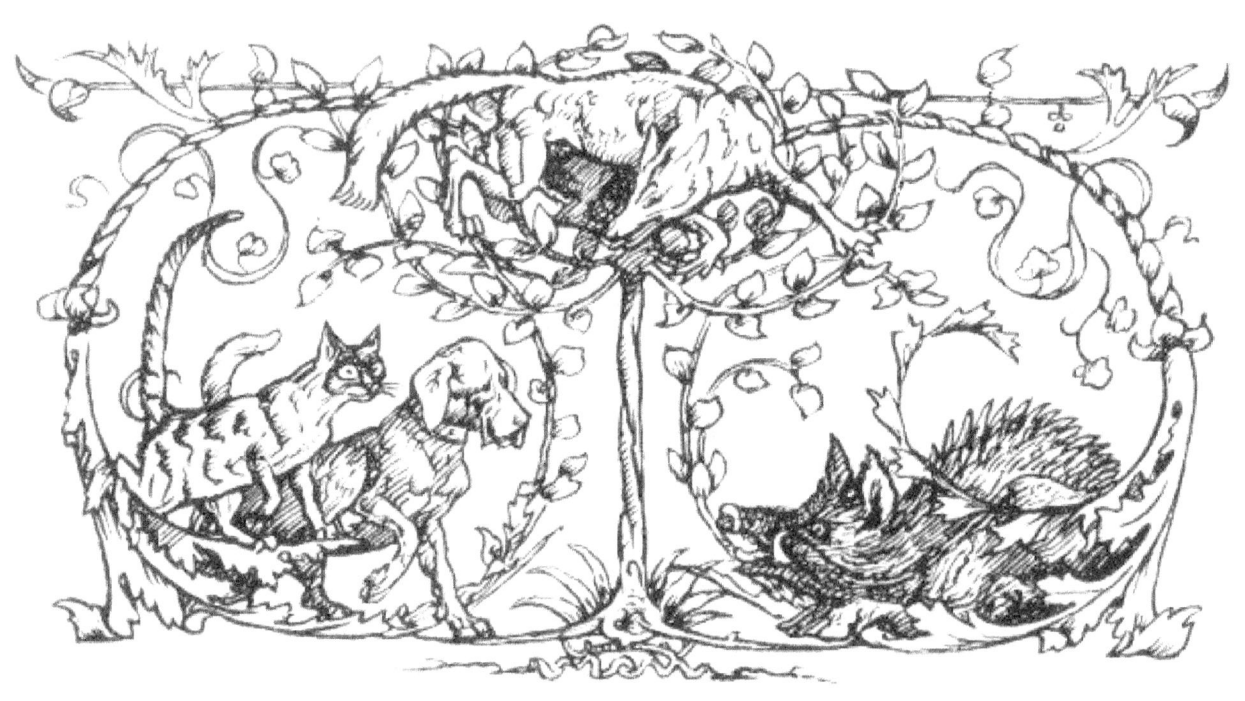

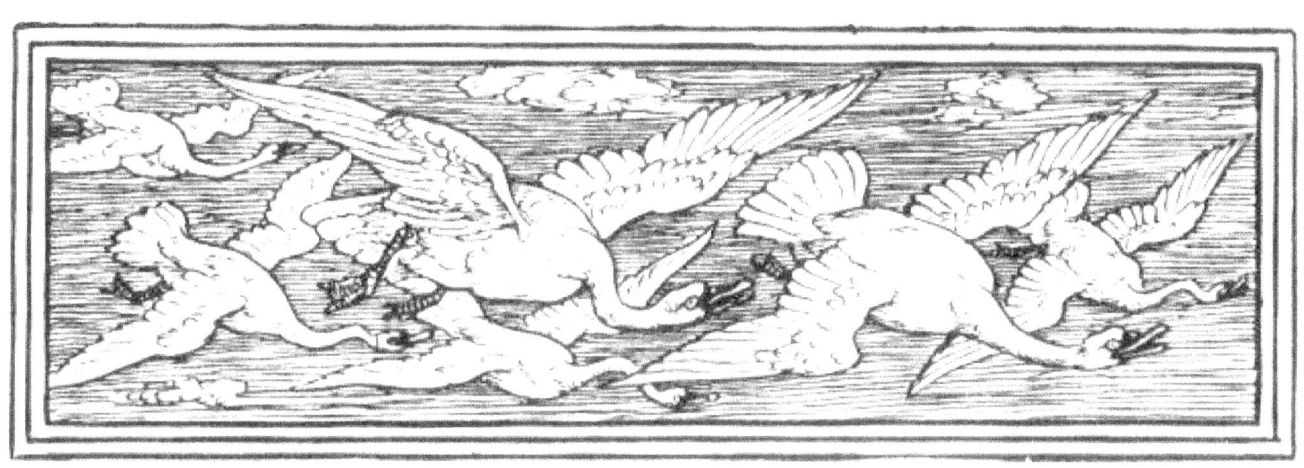

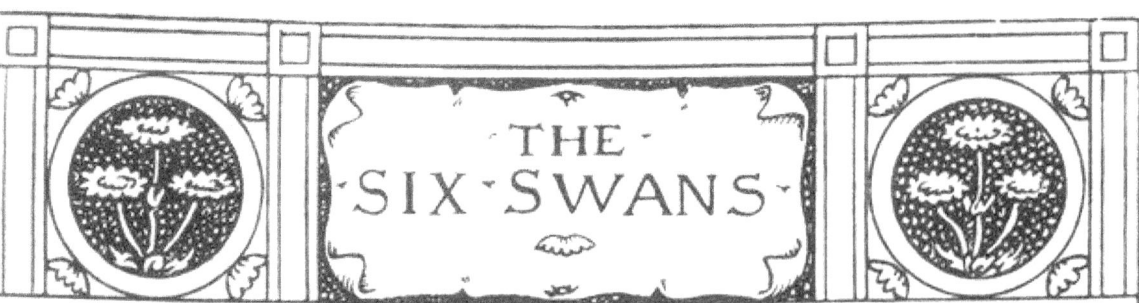

THE · SIX · SWANS

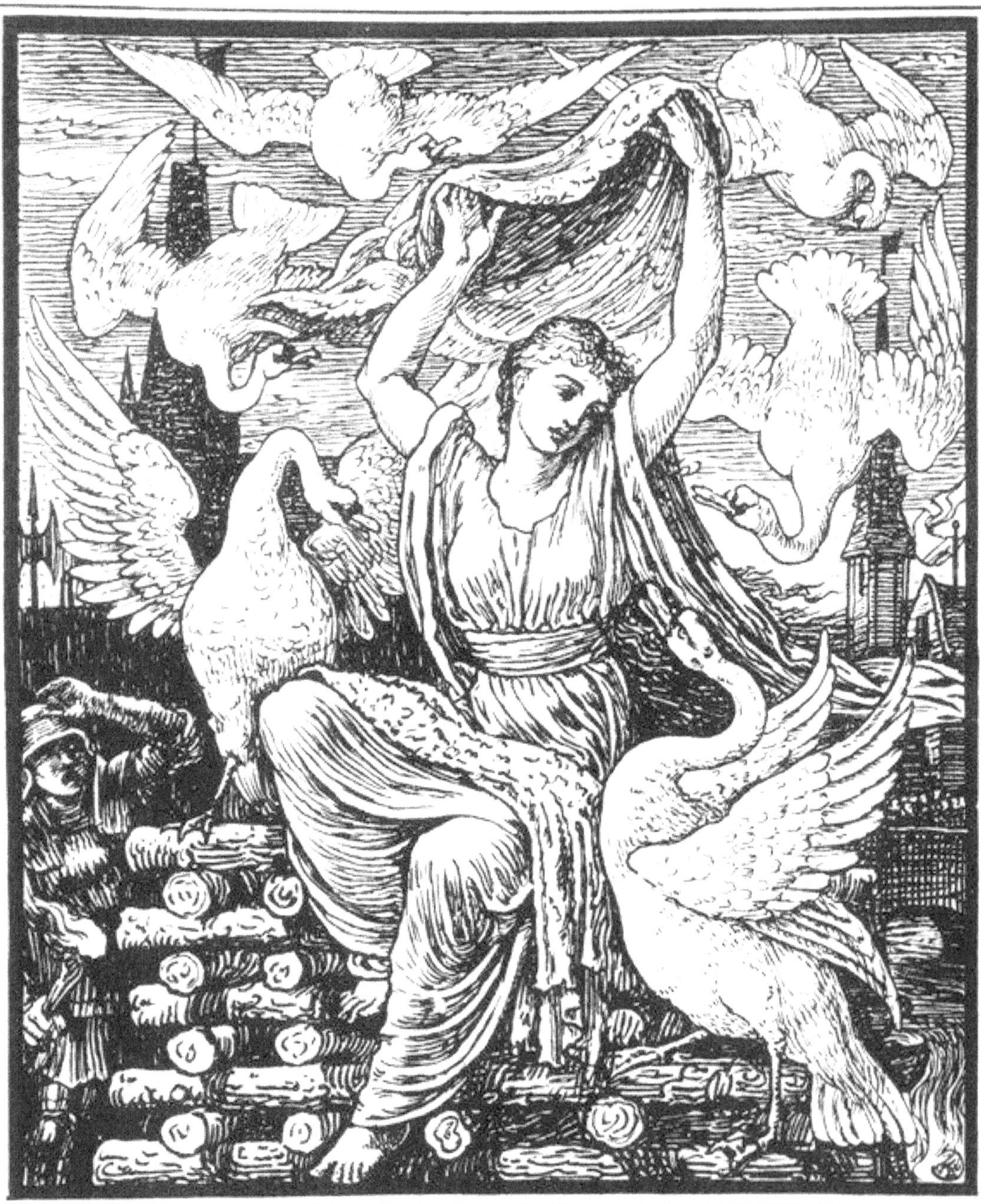

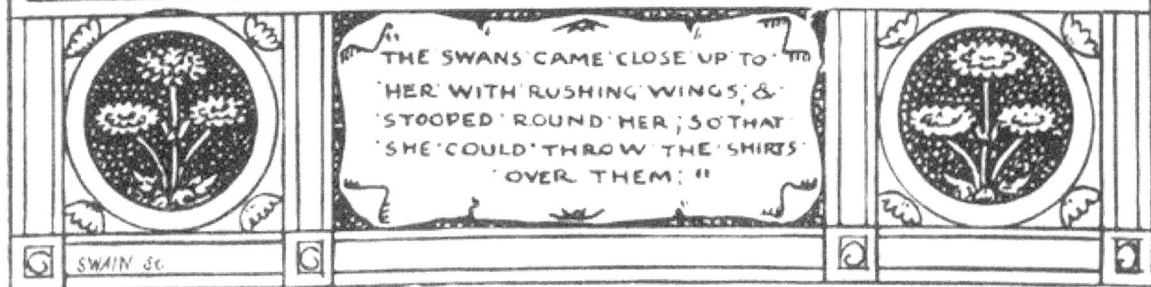

THE·SWANS·CAME·CLOSE·UP·TO·
HER·WITH·RUSHING·WINGS, &·
STOOPED·ROUND·HER; SO·THAT·
SHE·COULD·THROW·THE·SHIRTS·
OVER·THEM: "

SWAIN sc.

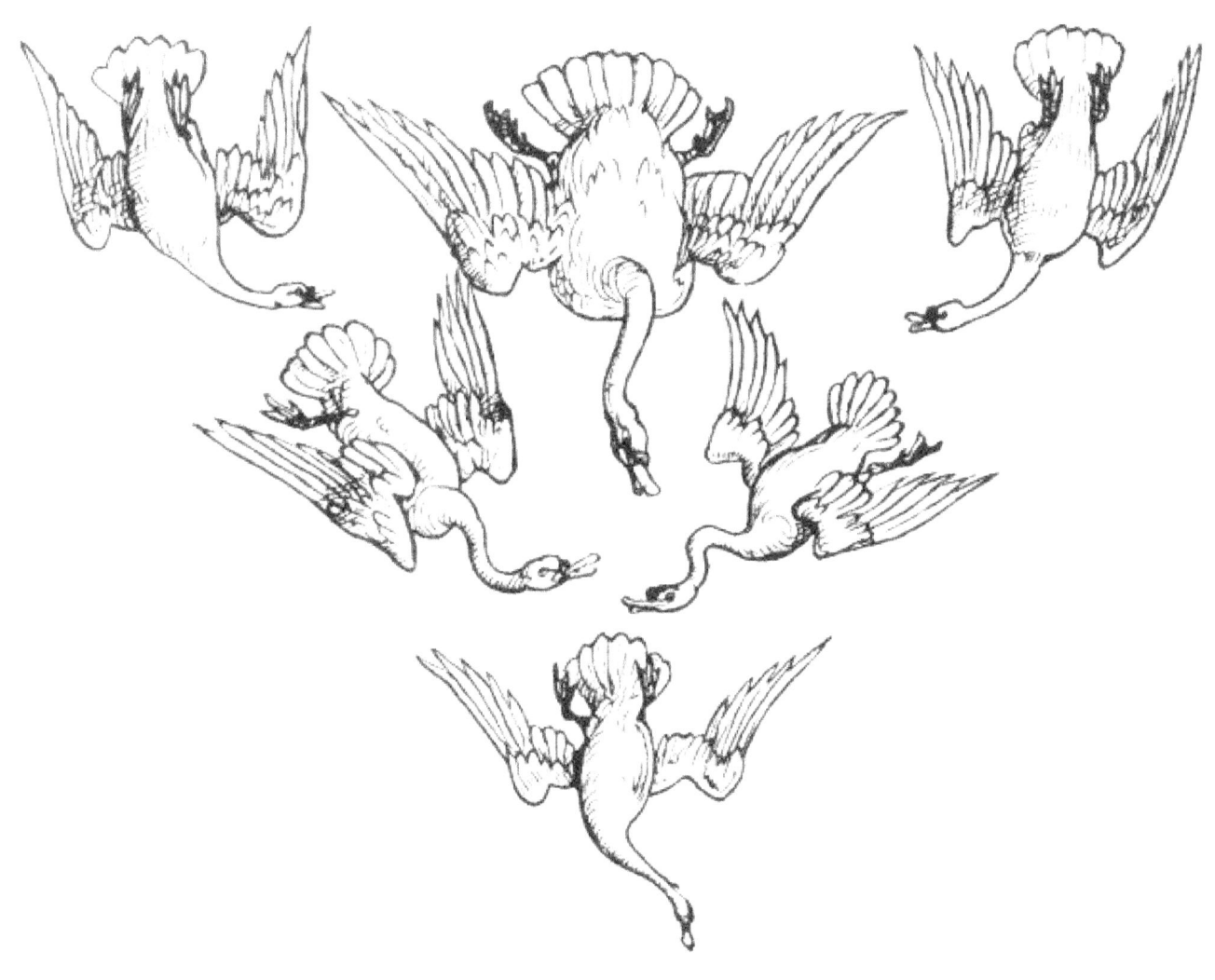

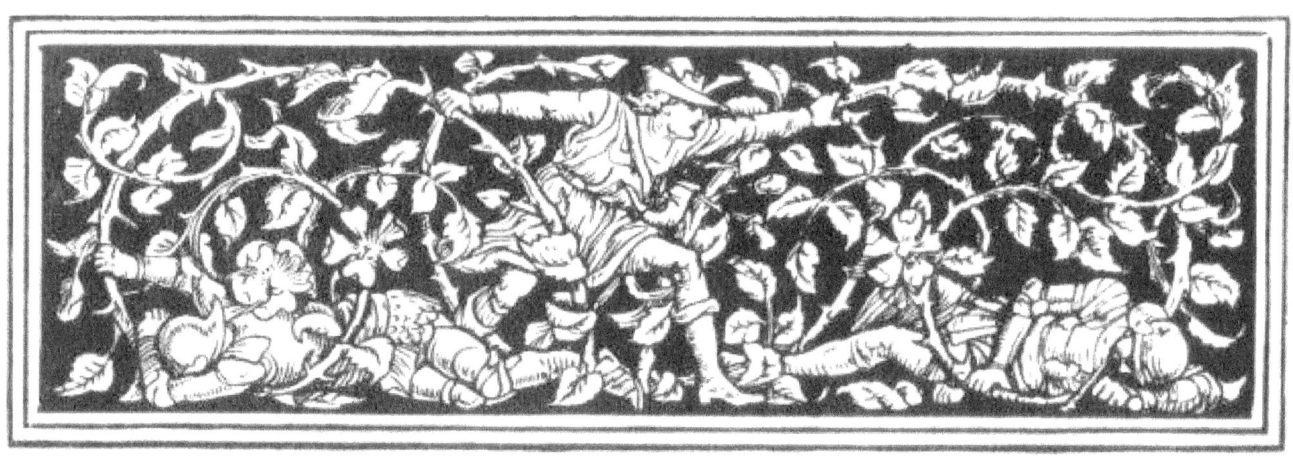

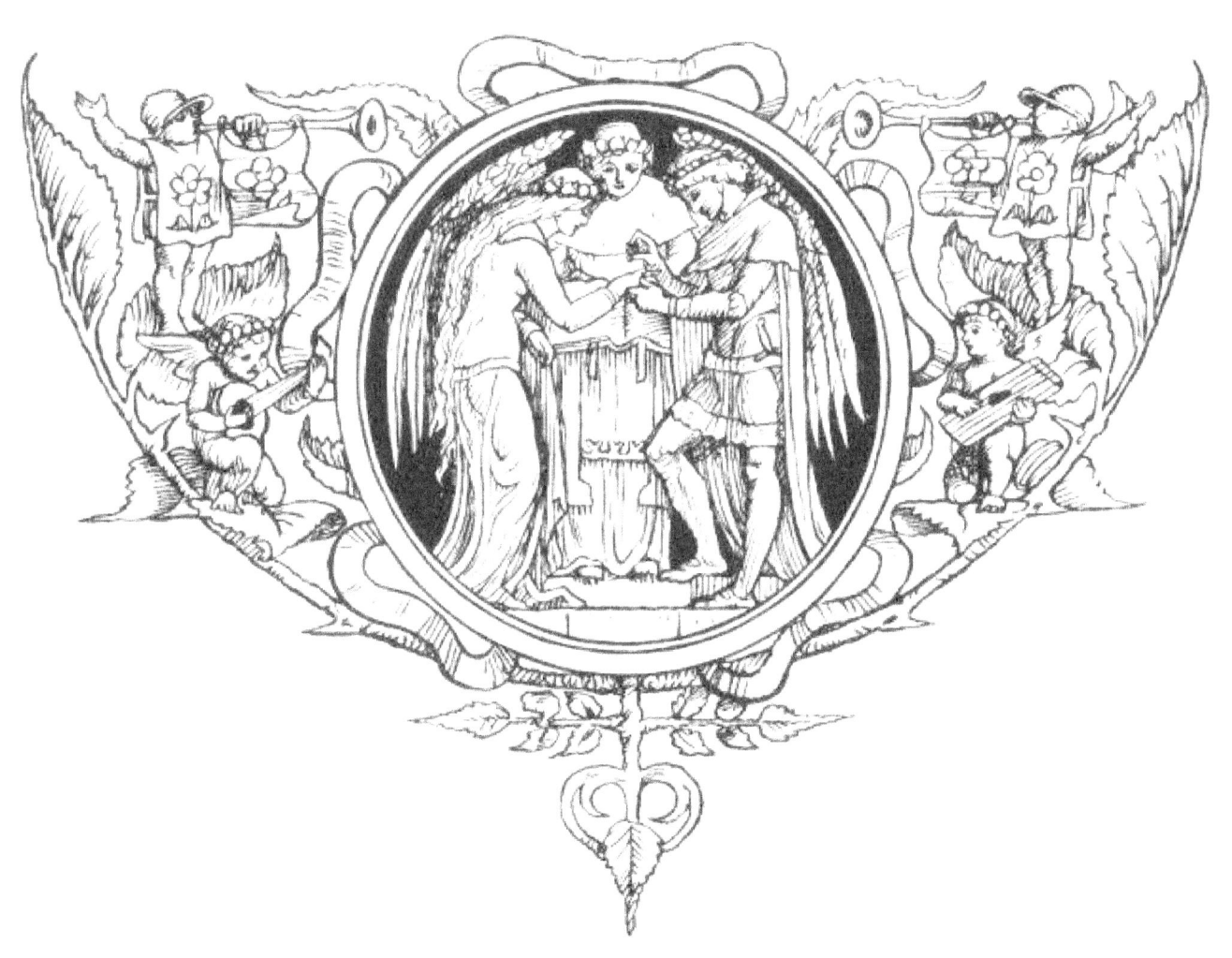

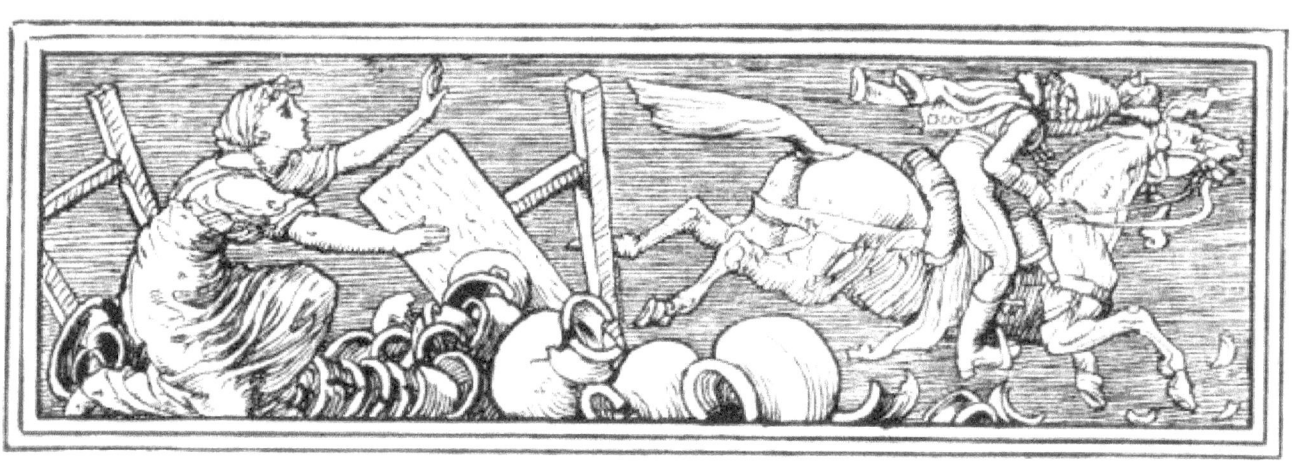

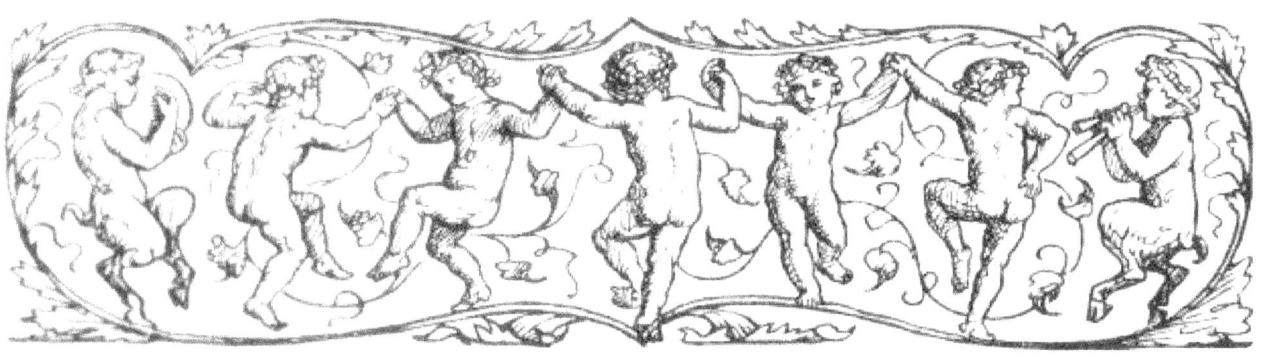

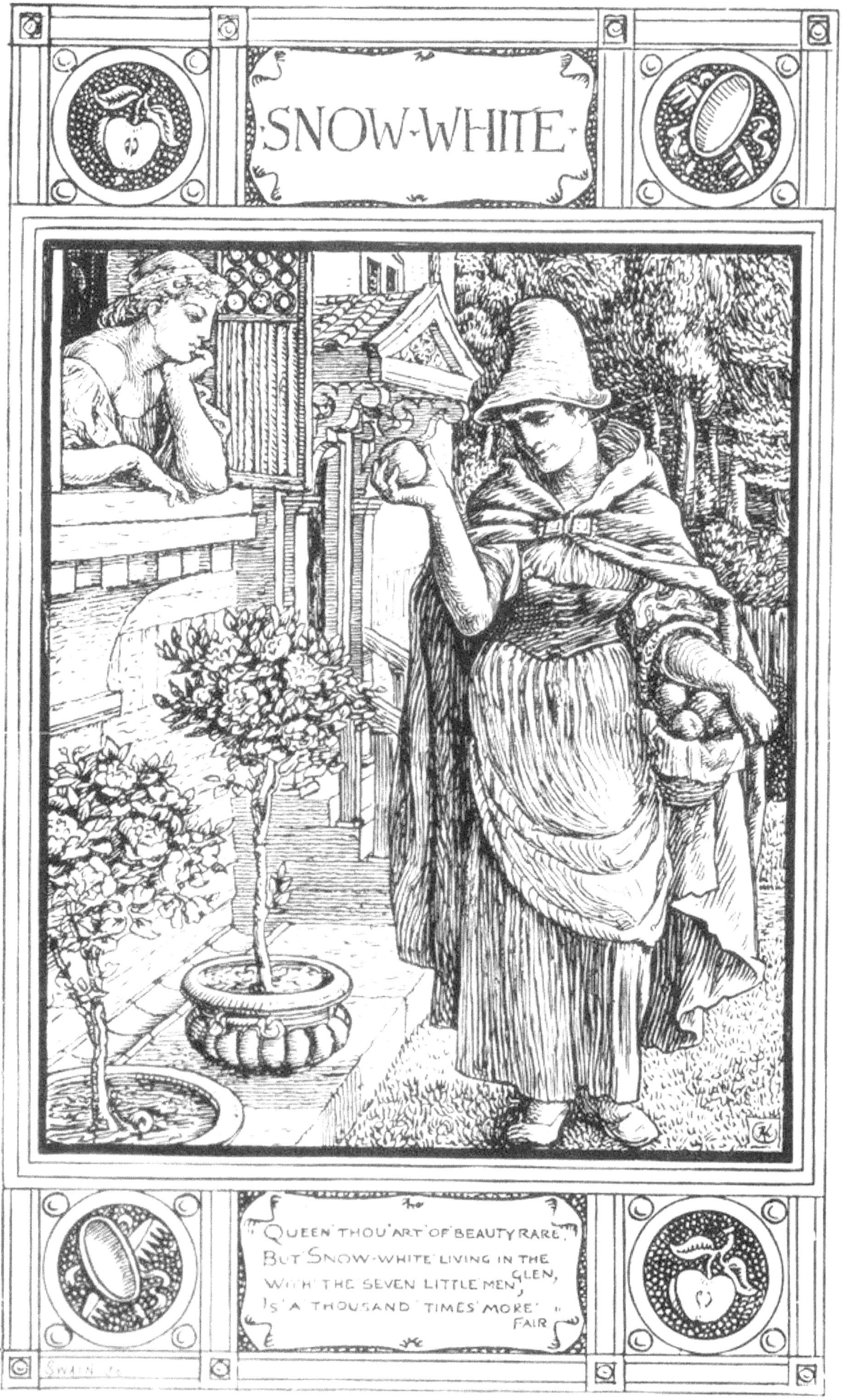

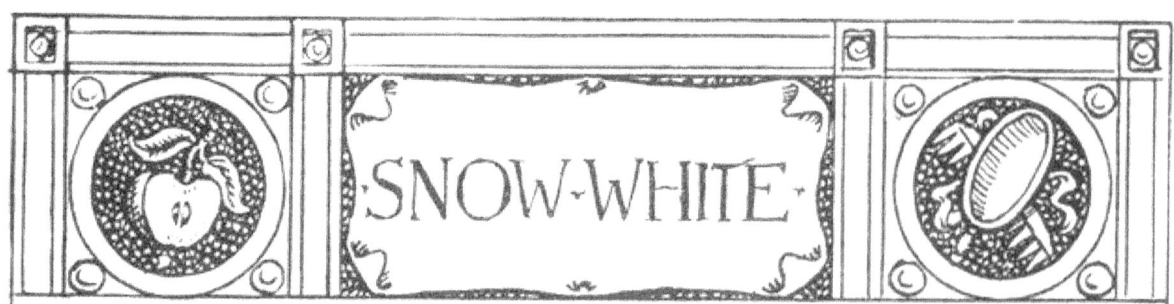

SNOW-WHITE

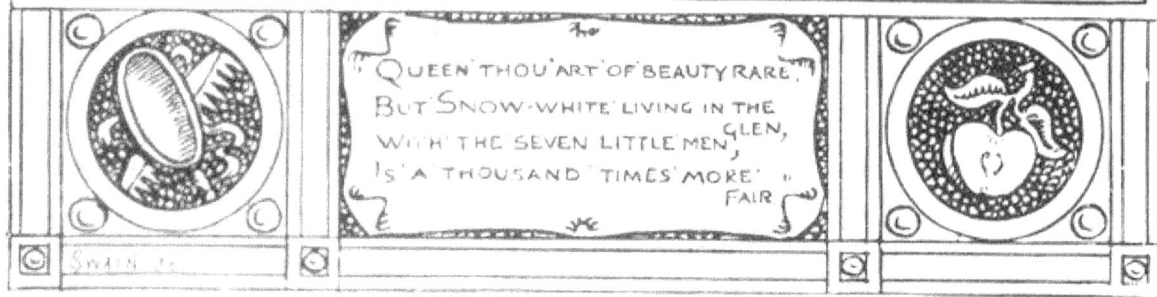

"QUEEN THOU ART OF BEAUTY RARE,
BUT SNOW-WHITE LIVING IN THE GLEN,
WITH THE SEVEN LITTLE MEN,
IS A THOUSAND TIMES MORE FAIR."

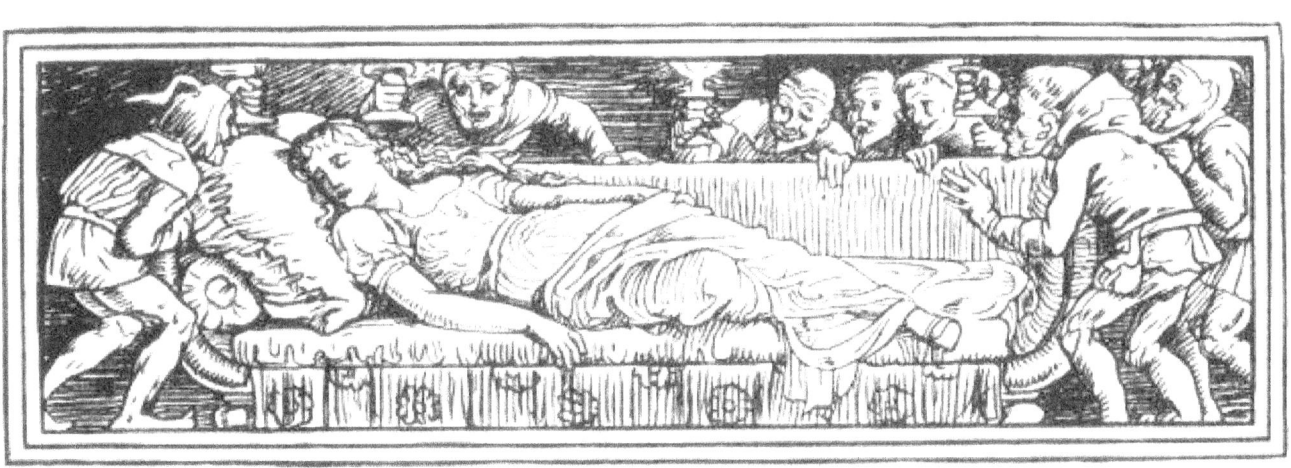

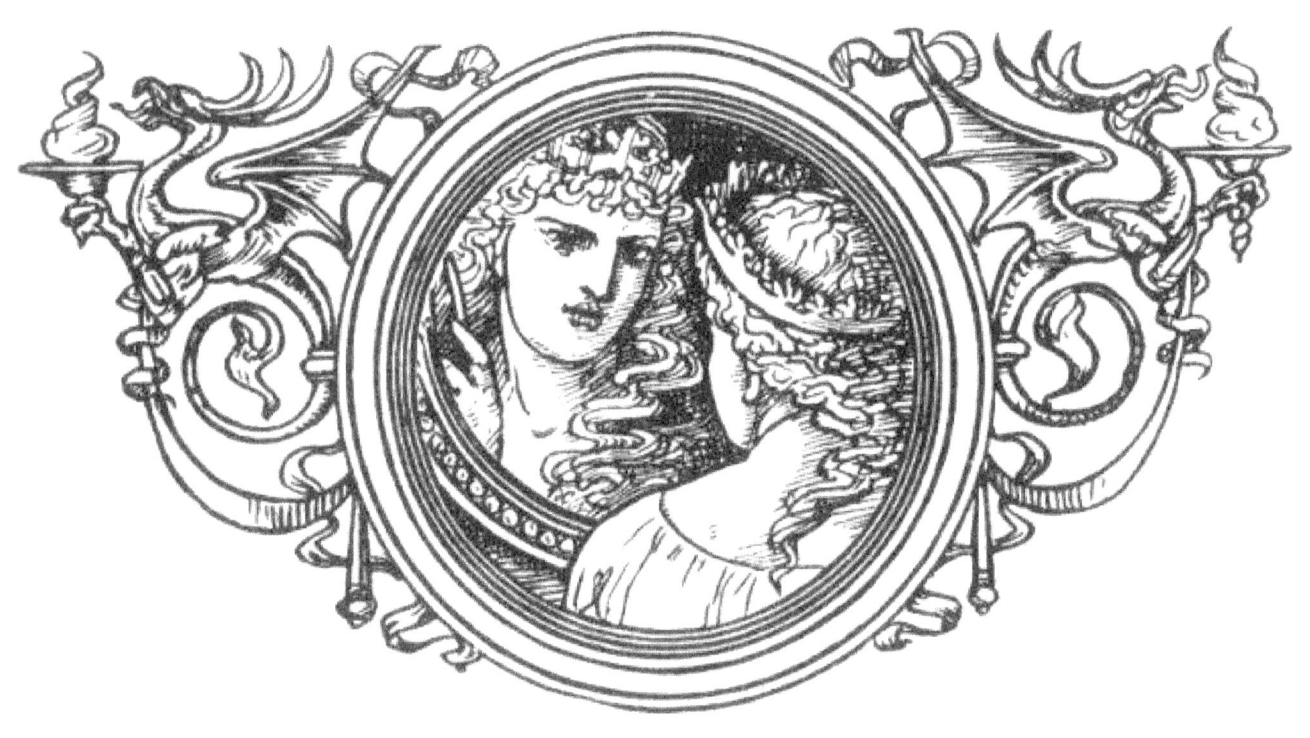

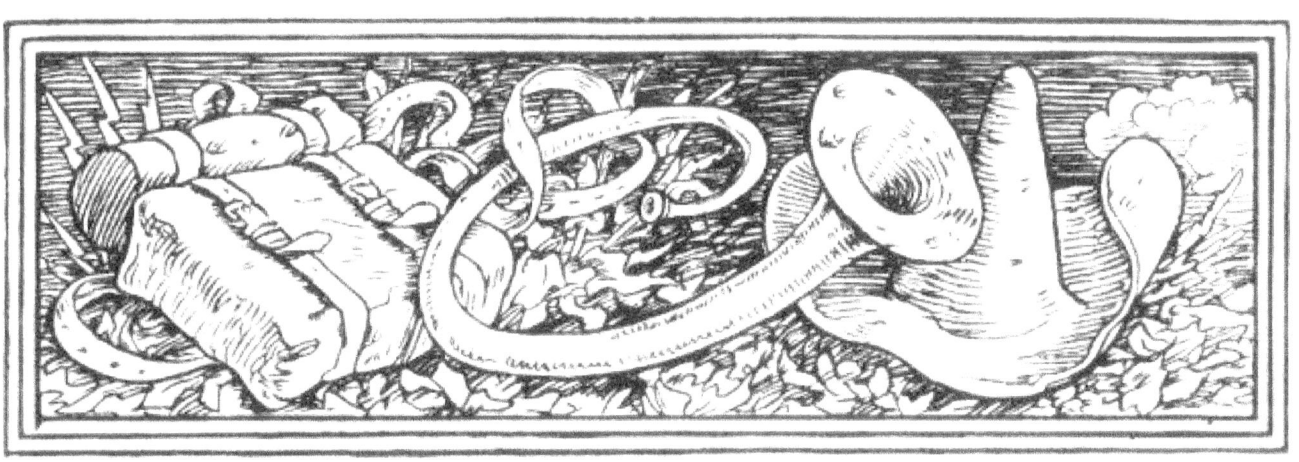

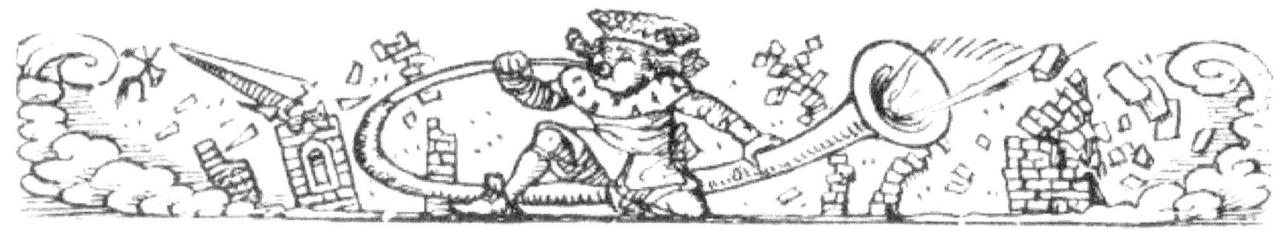

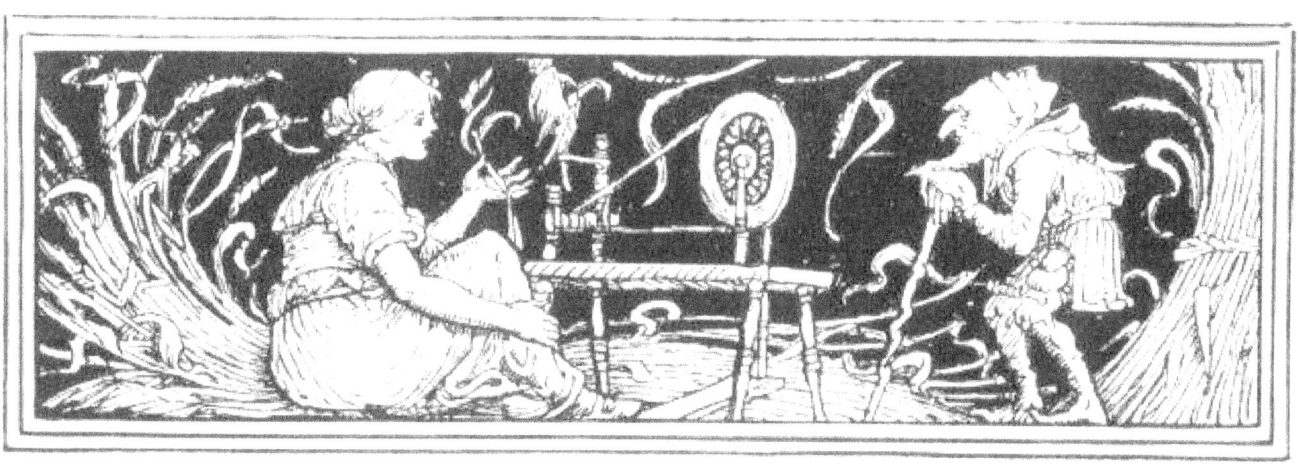

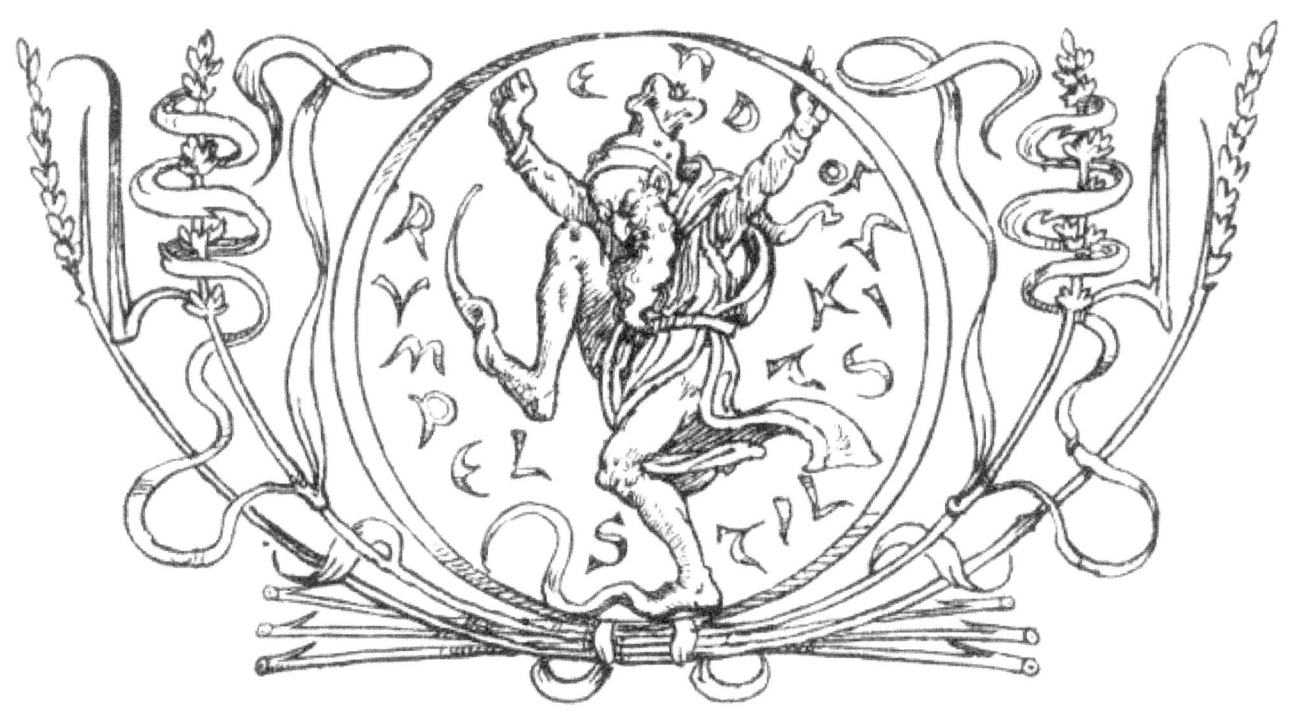

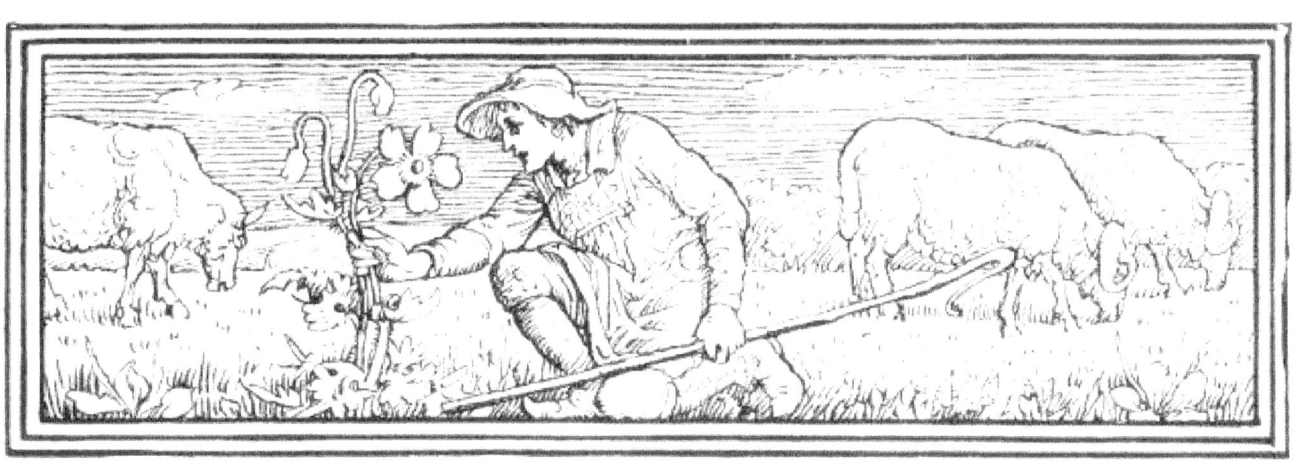

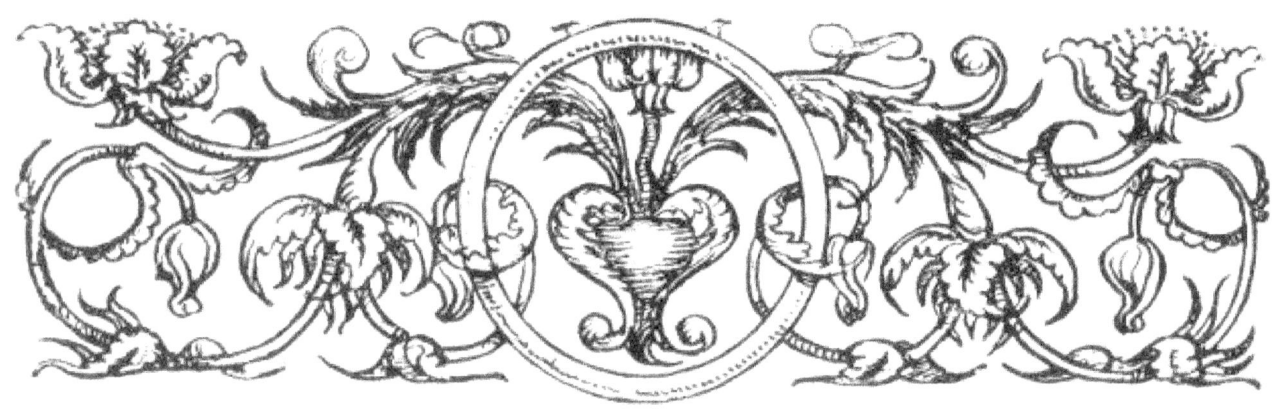

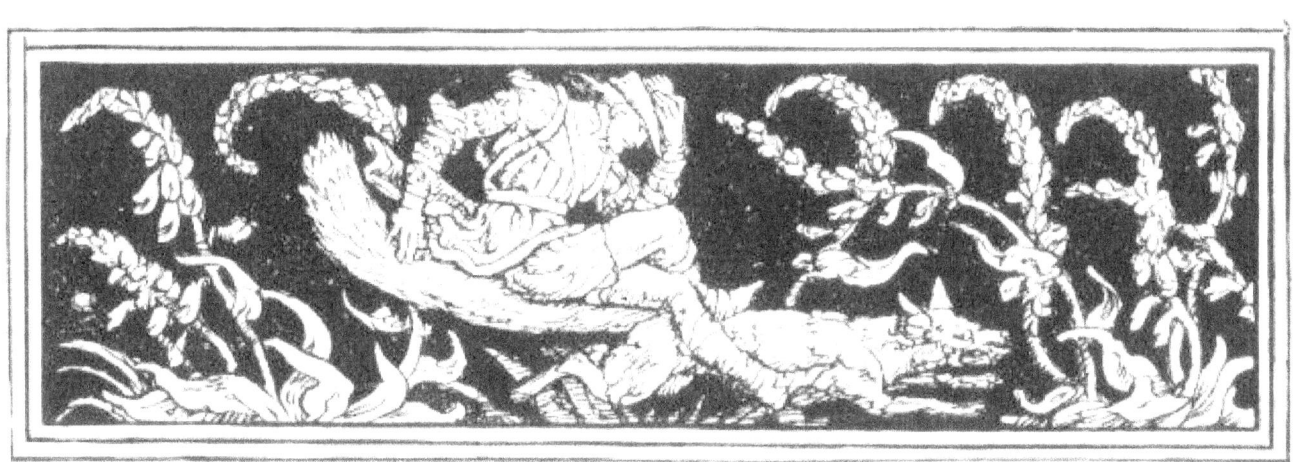

THE GOLDEN·BIRD

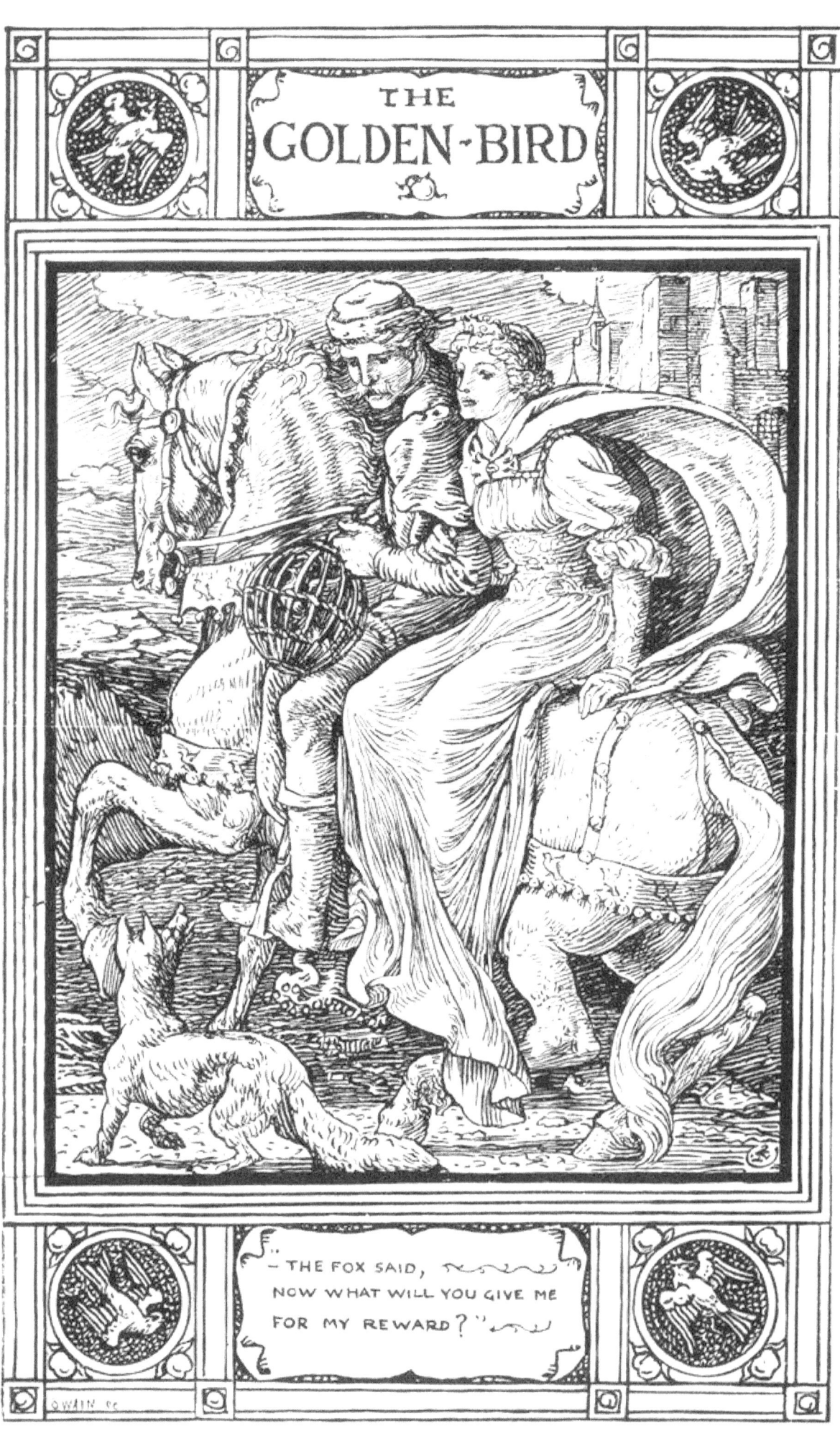

"— THE FOX SAID, NOW WHAT WILL YOU GIVE ME FOR MY REWARD?"

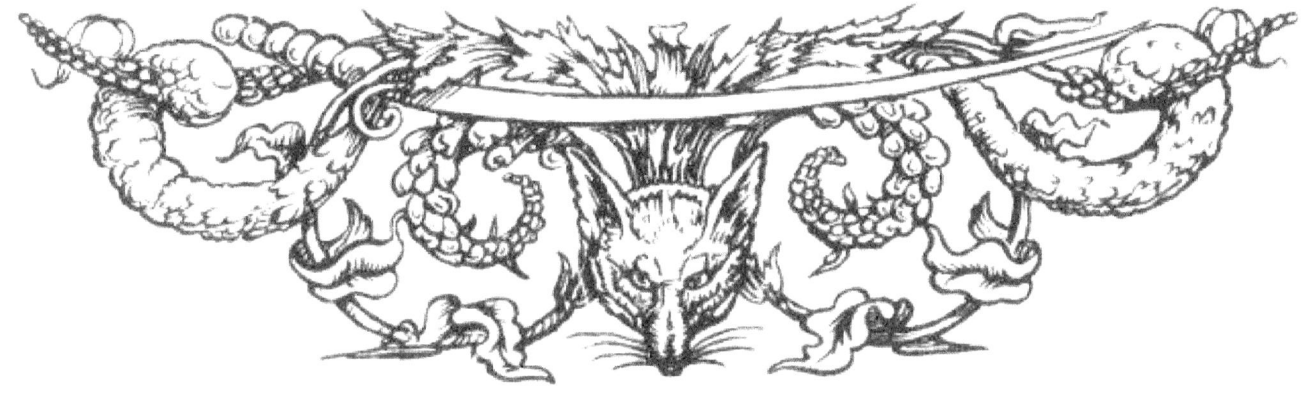

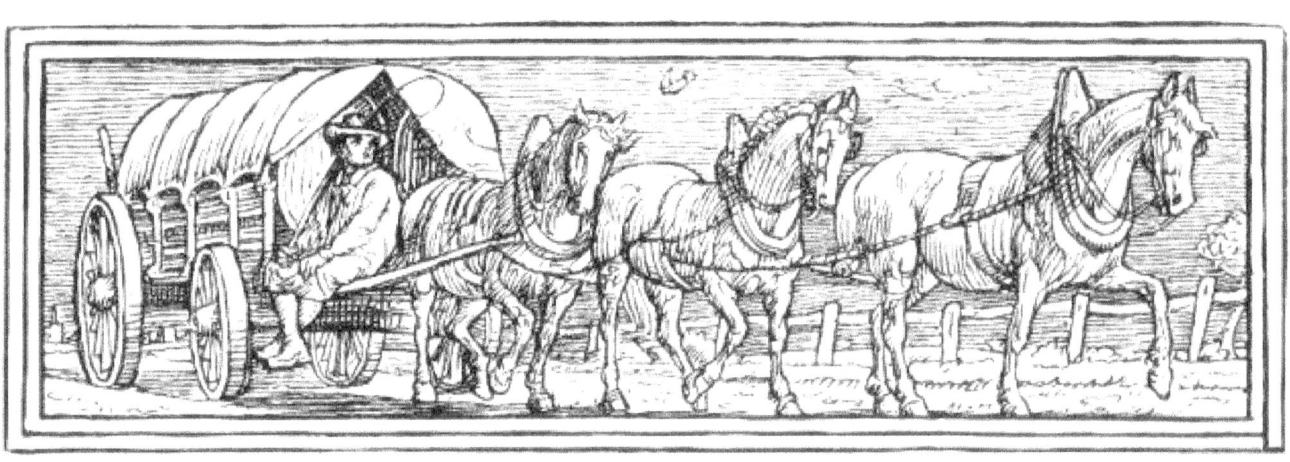

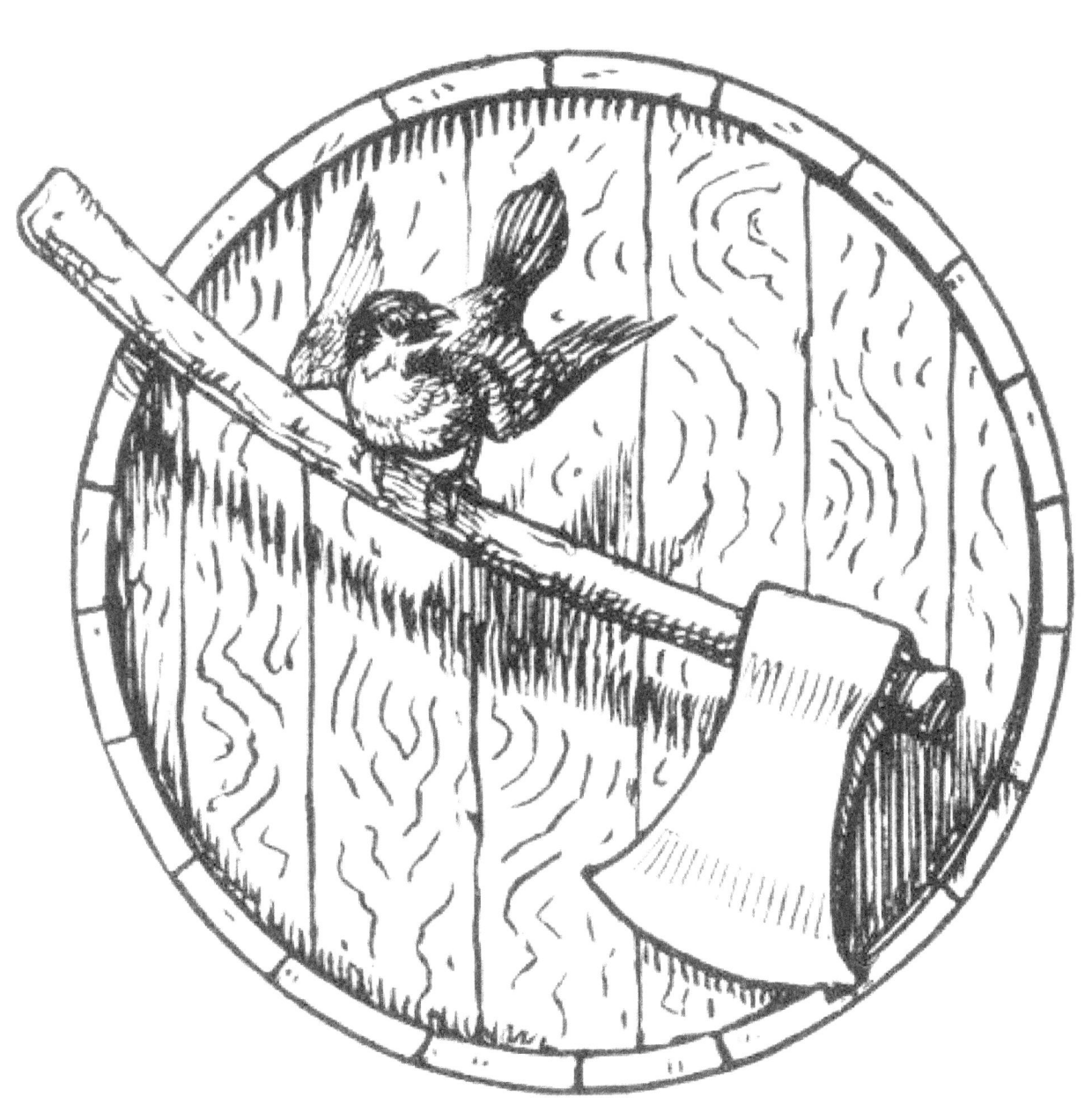

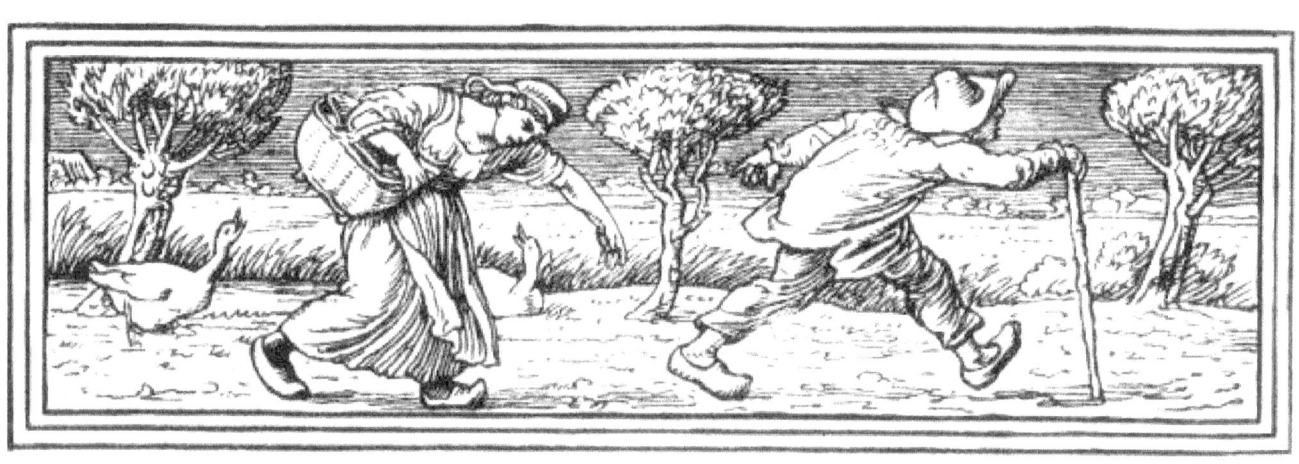

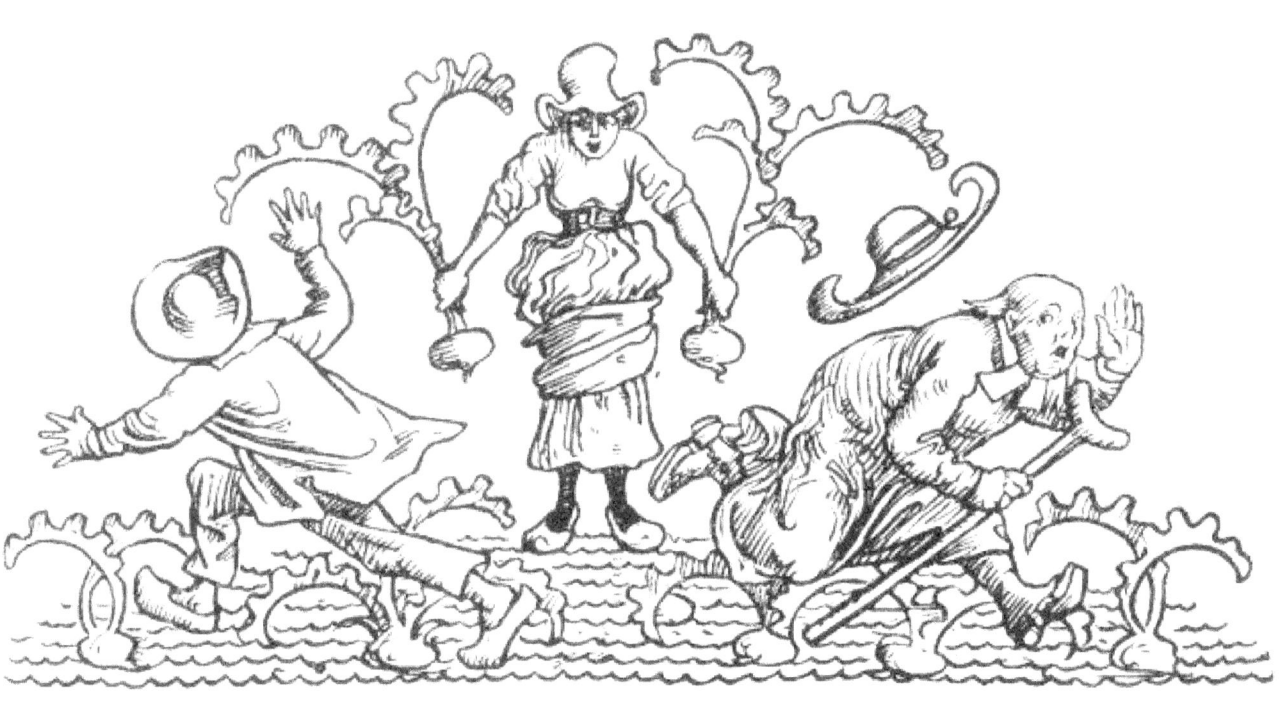

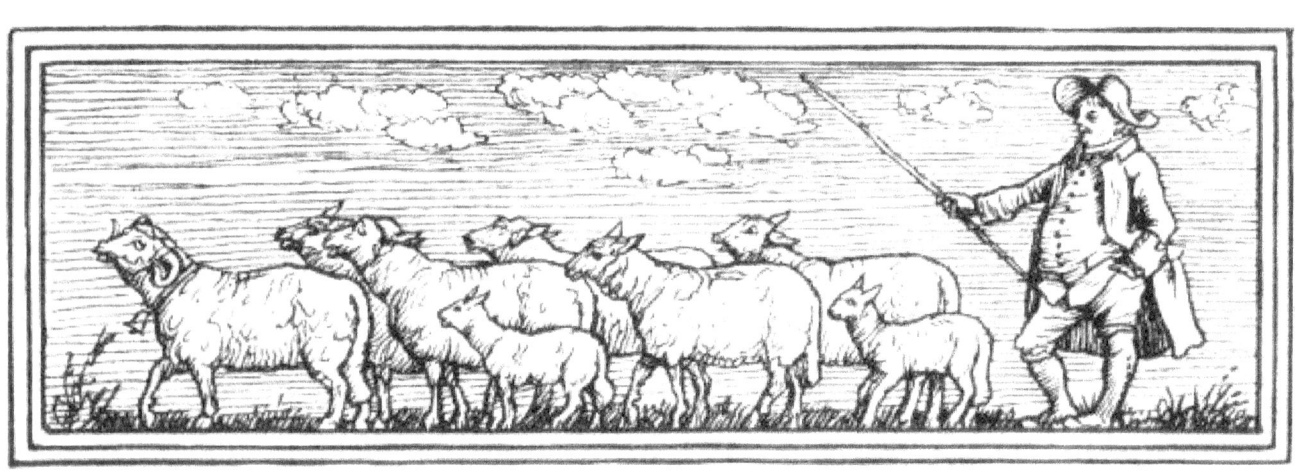

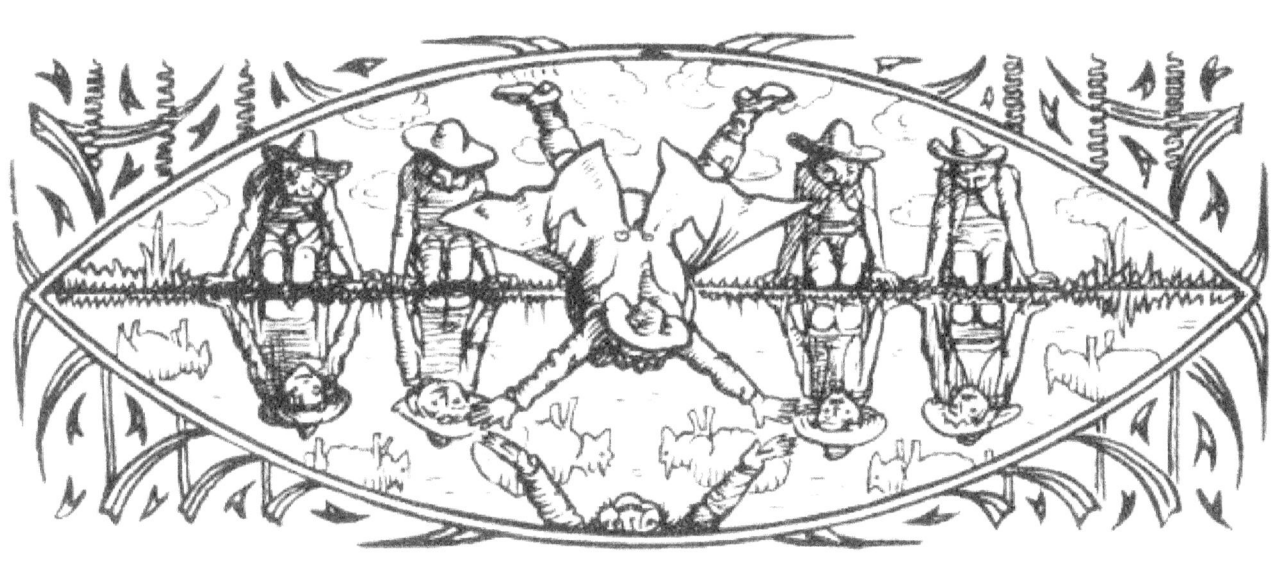

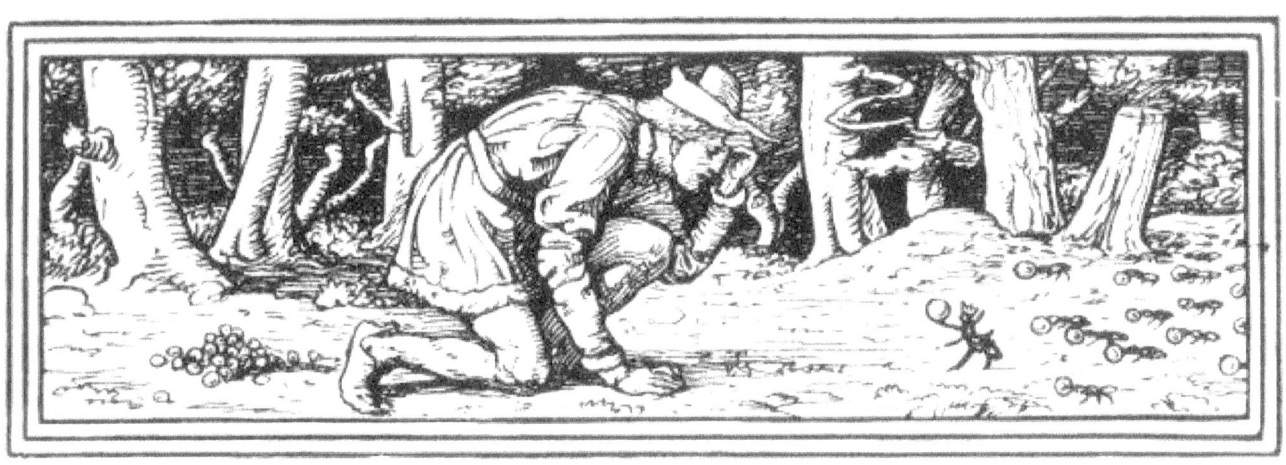

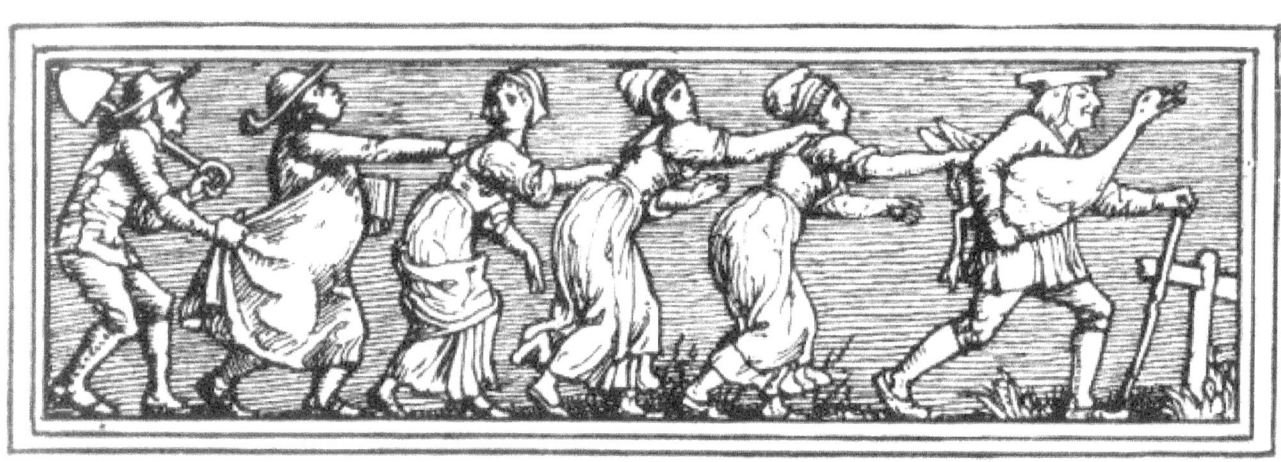

John B. Gruelle

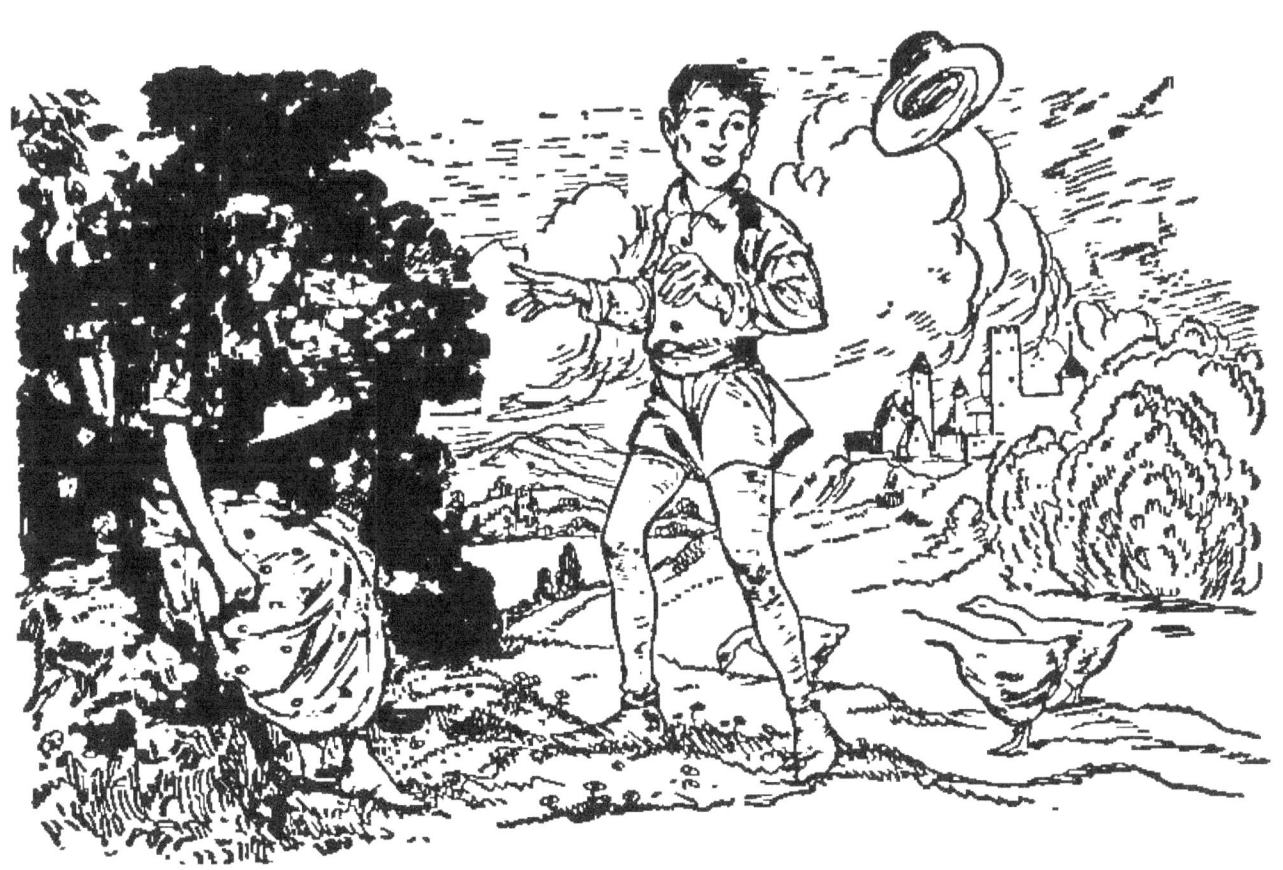

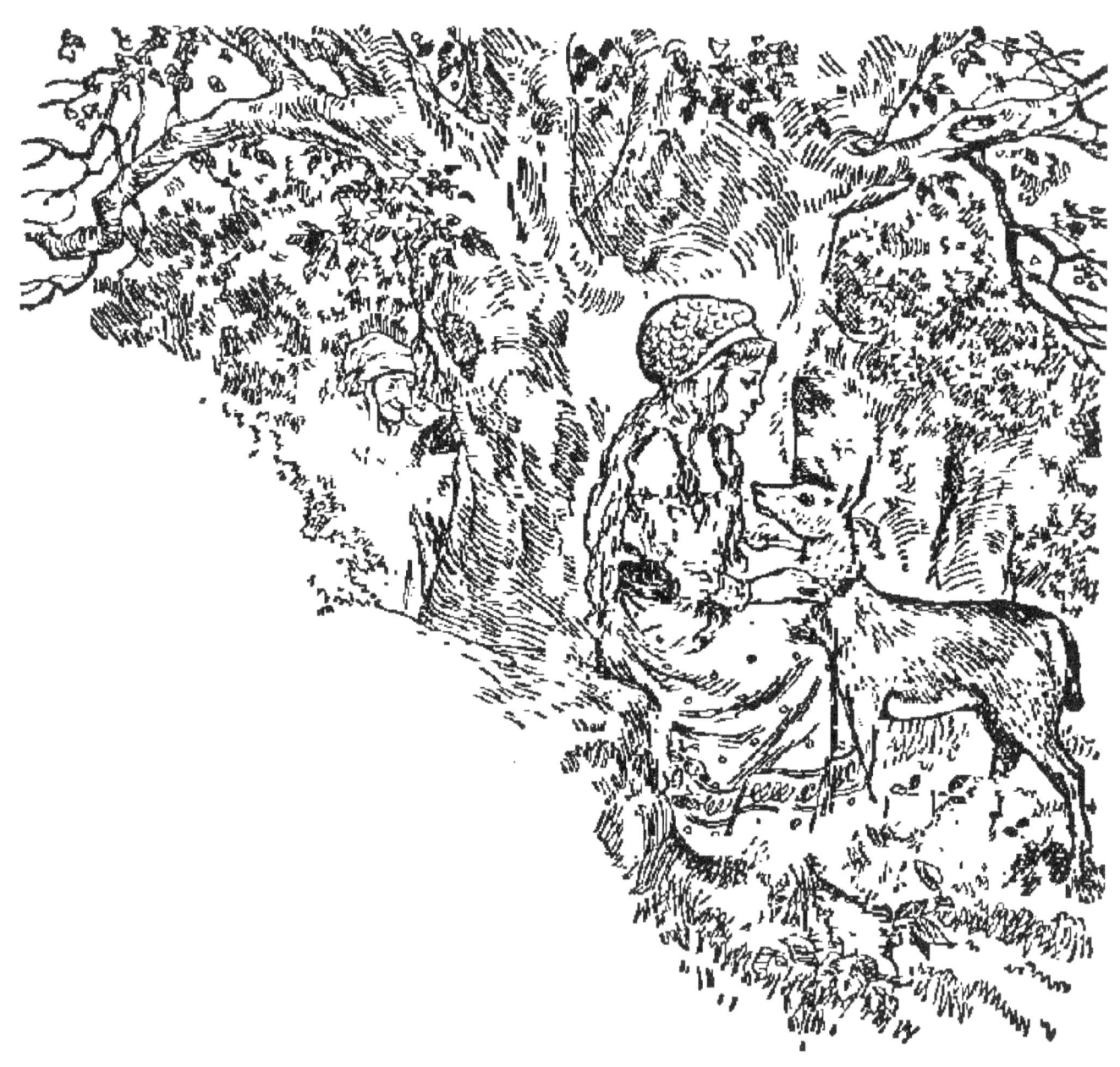

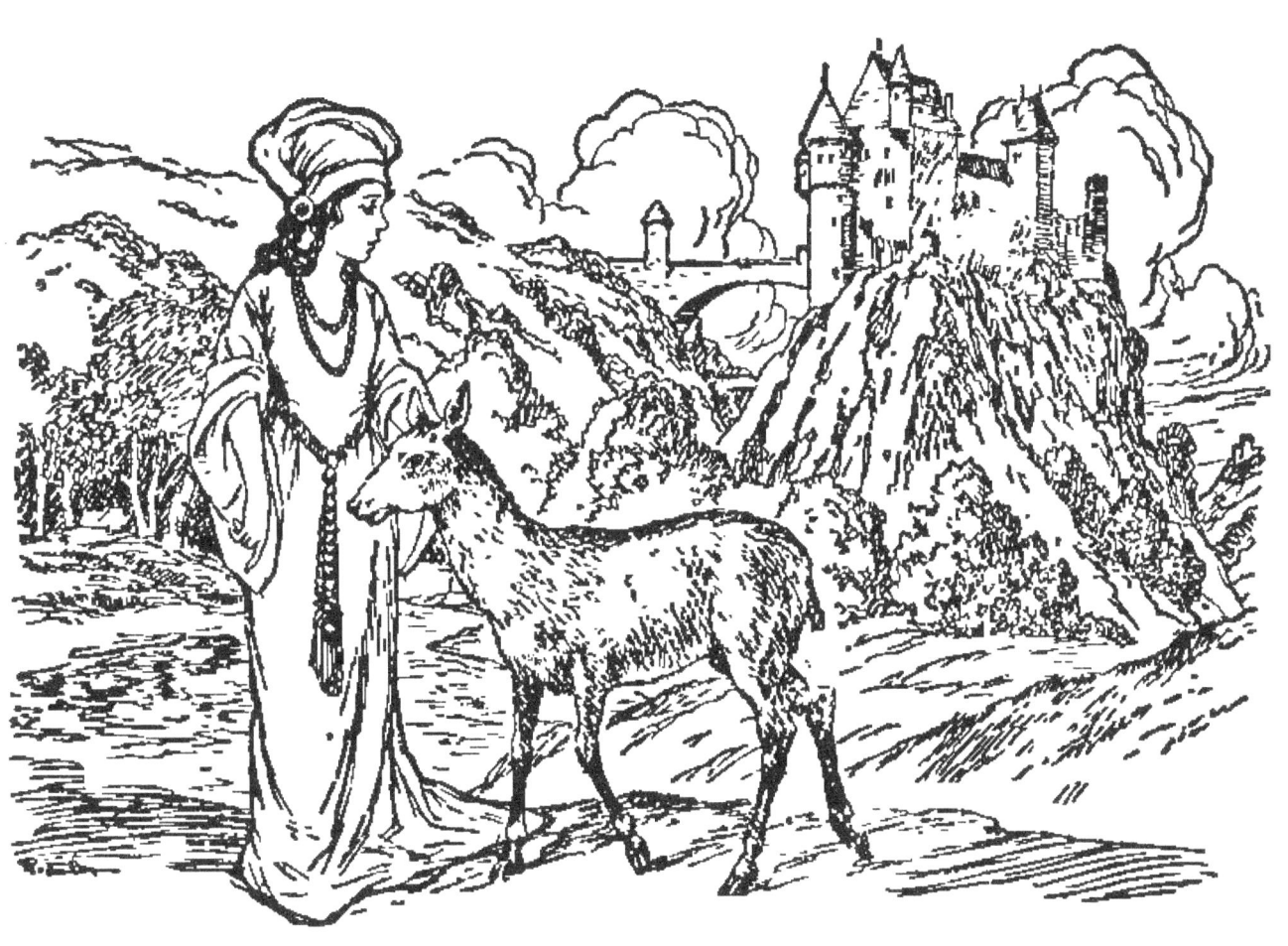

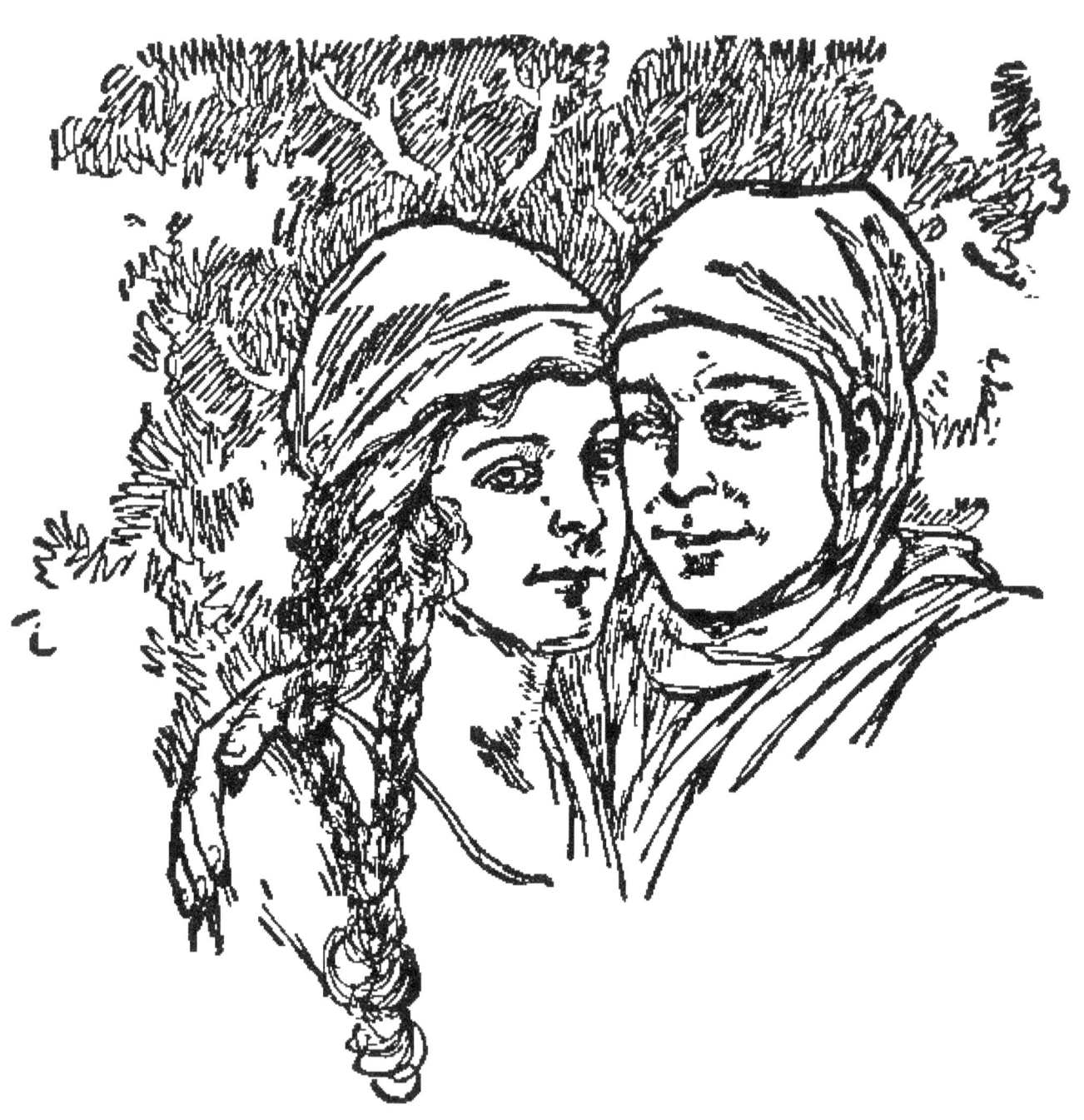

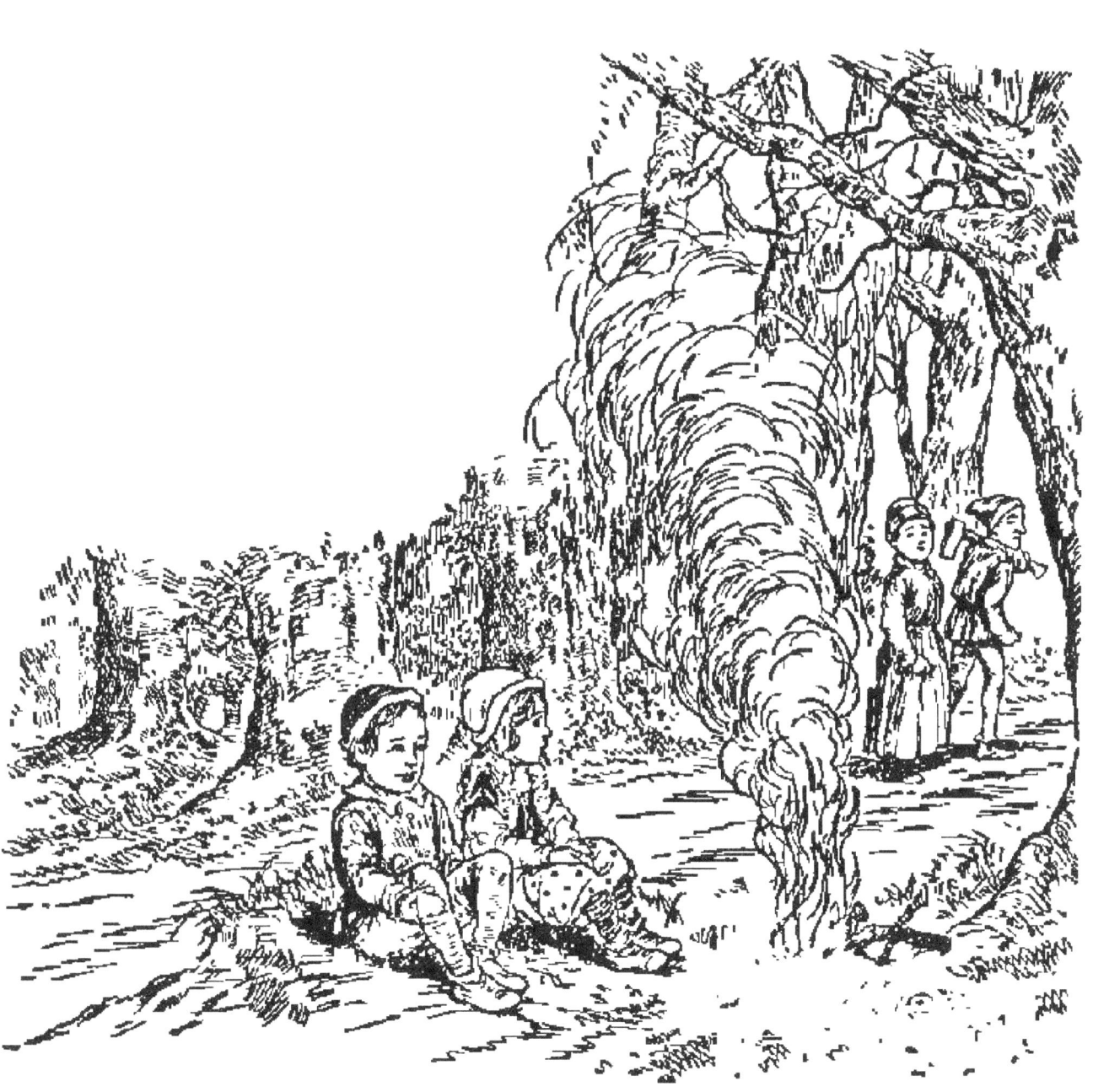

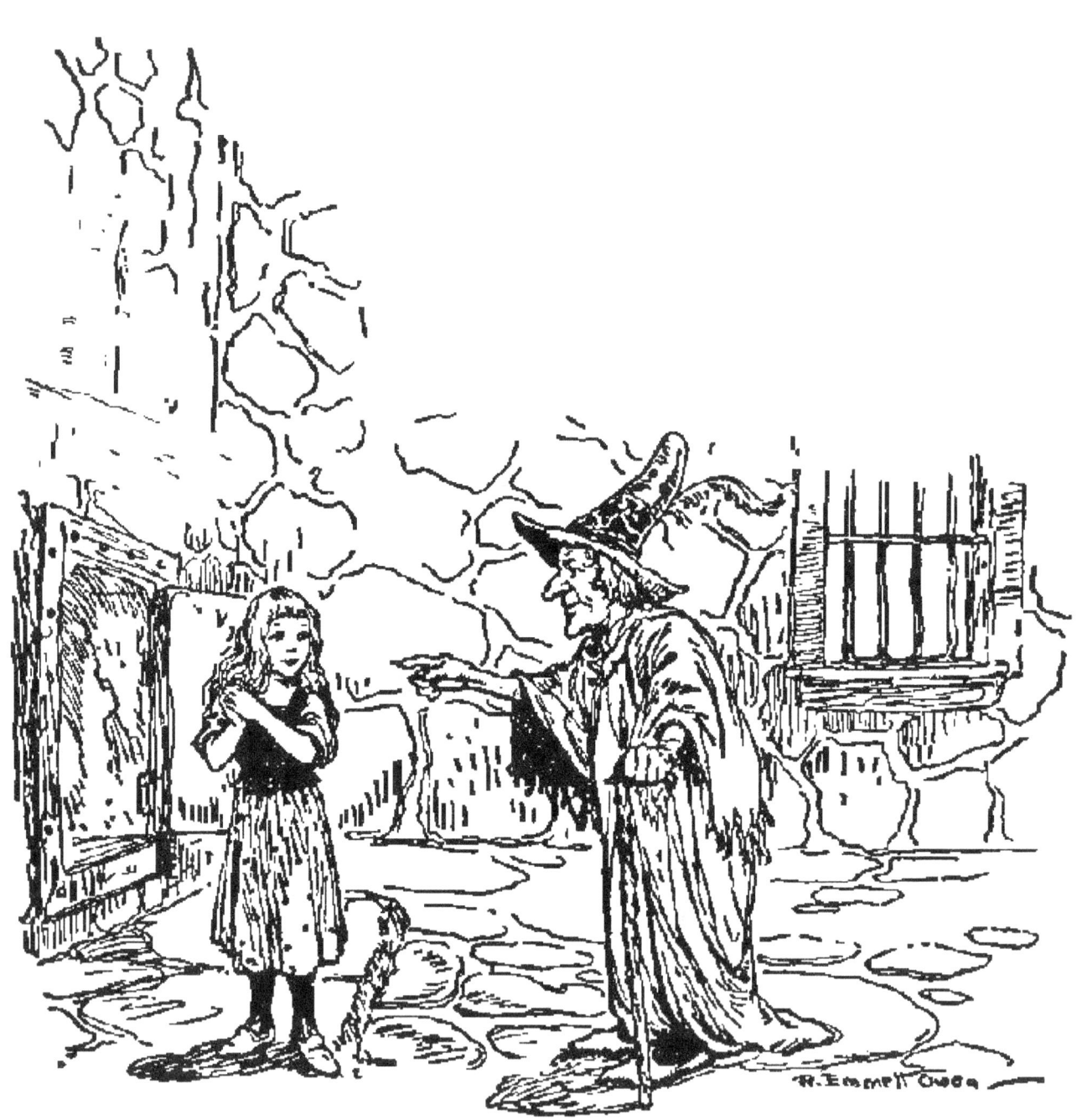

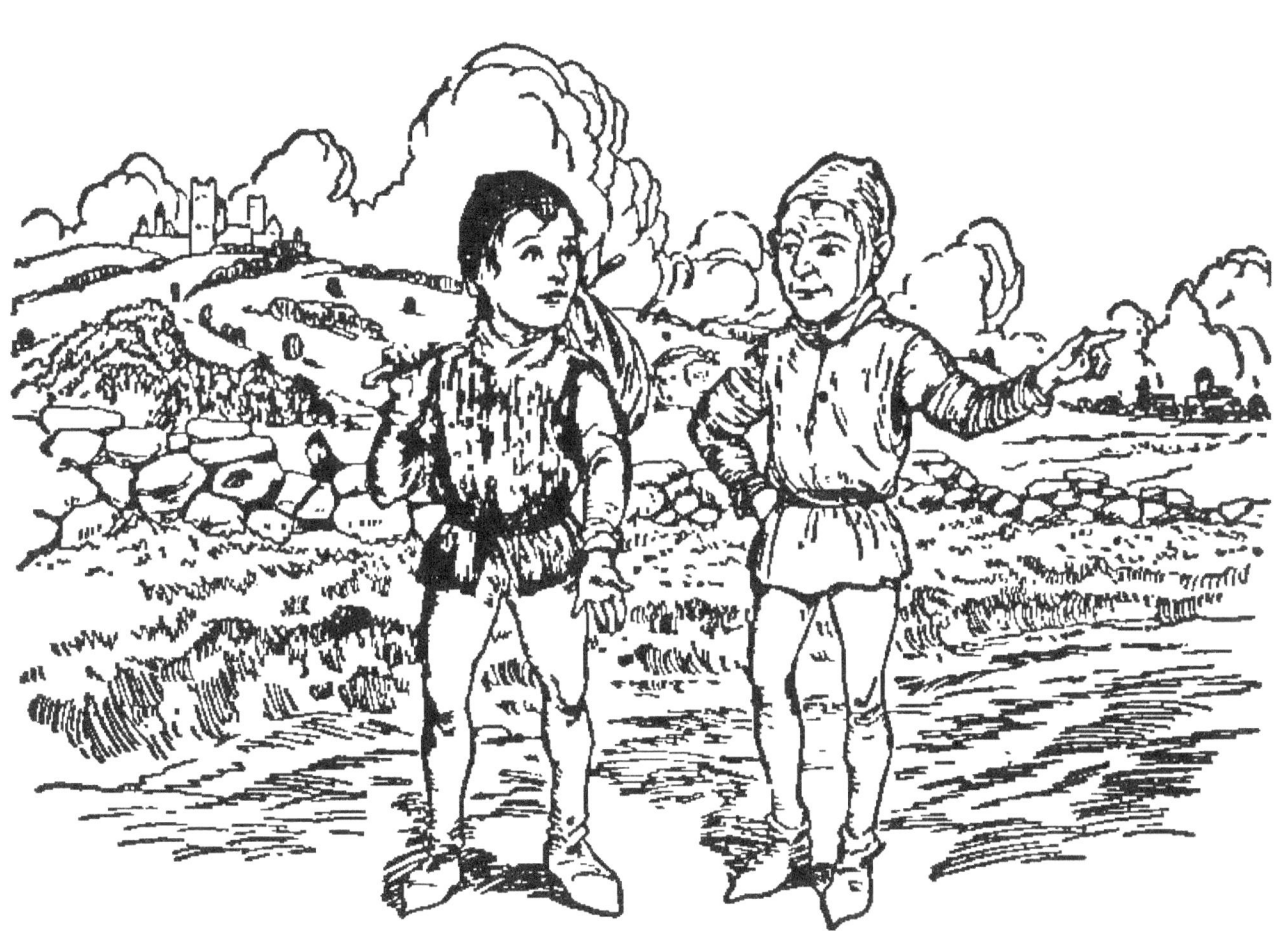

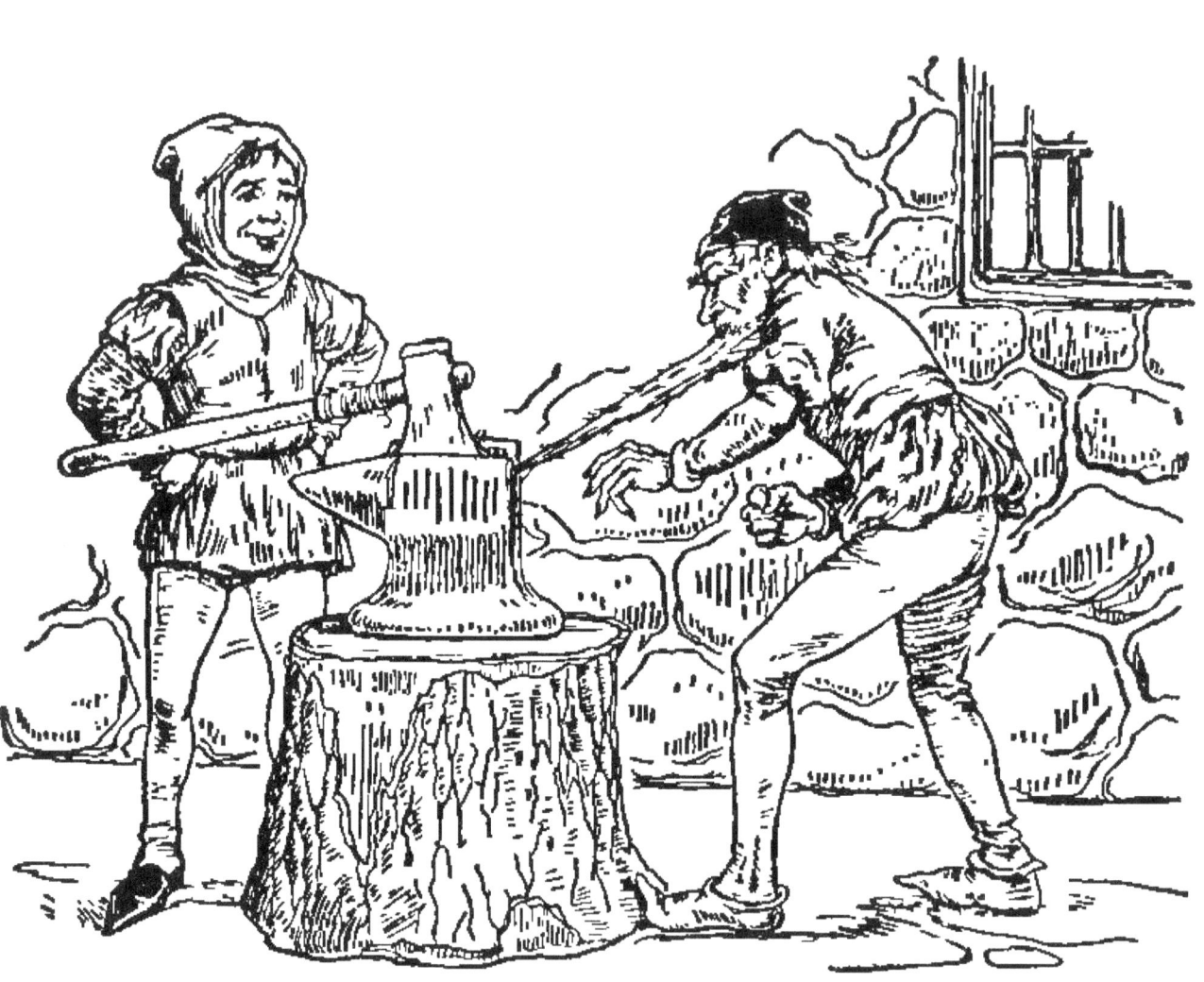

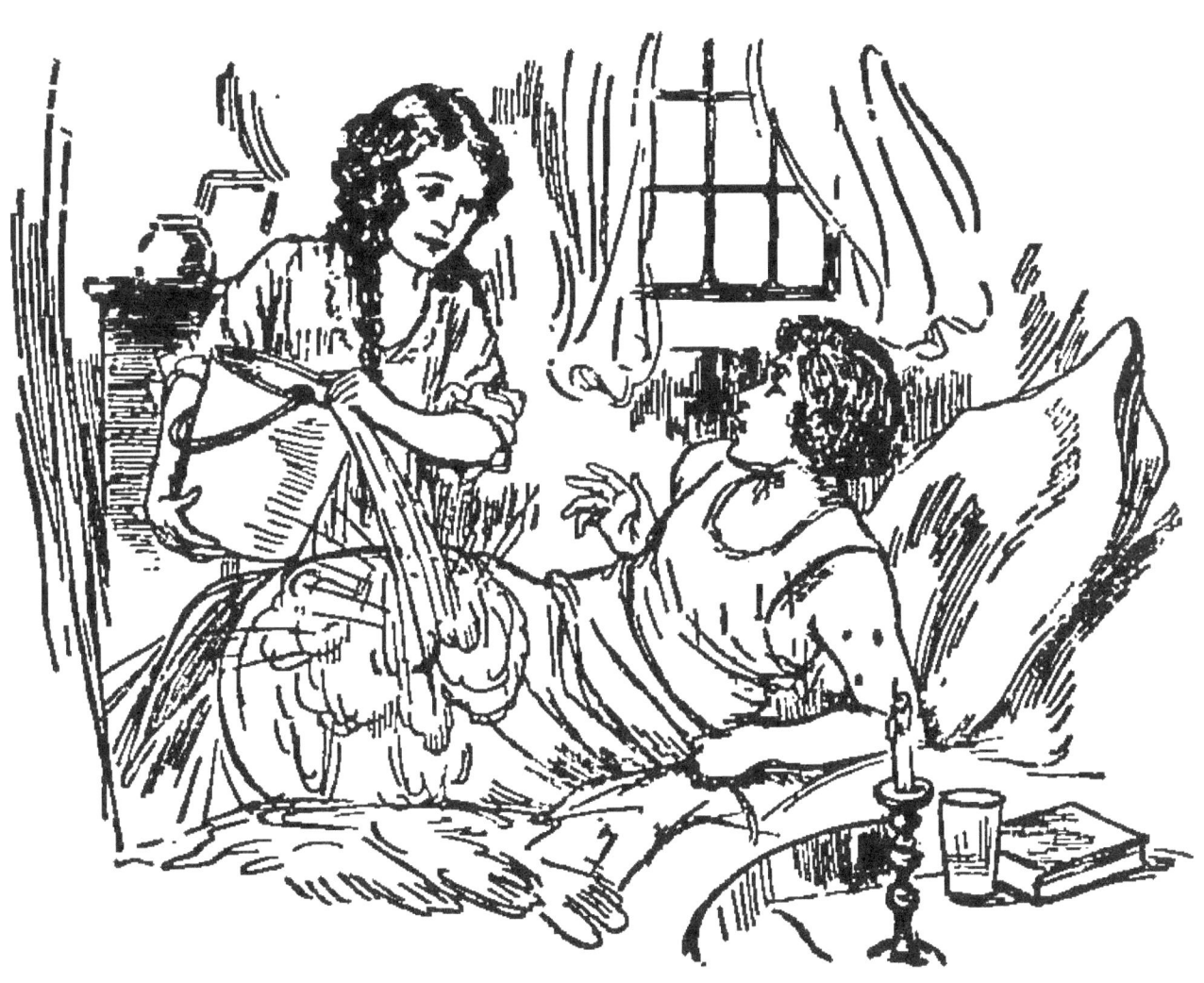

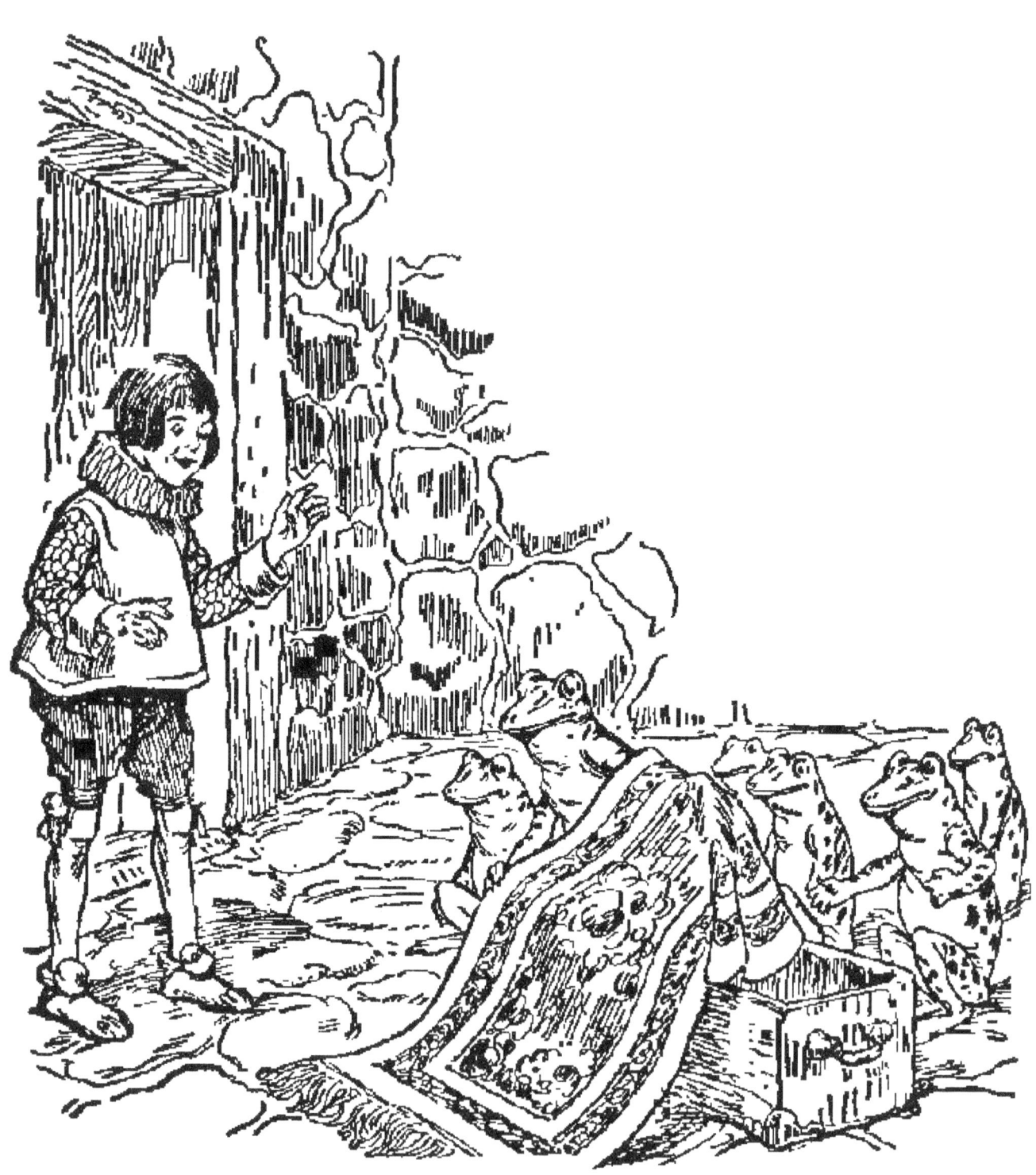

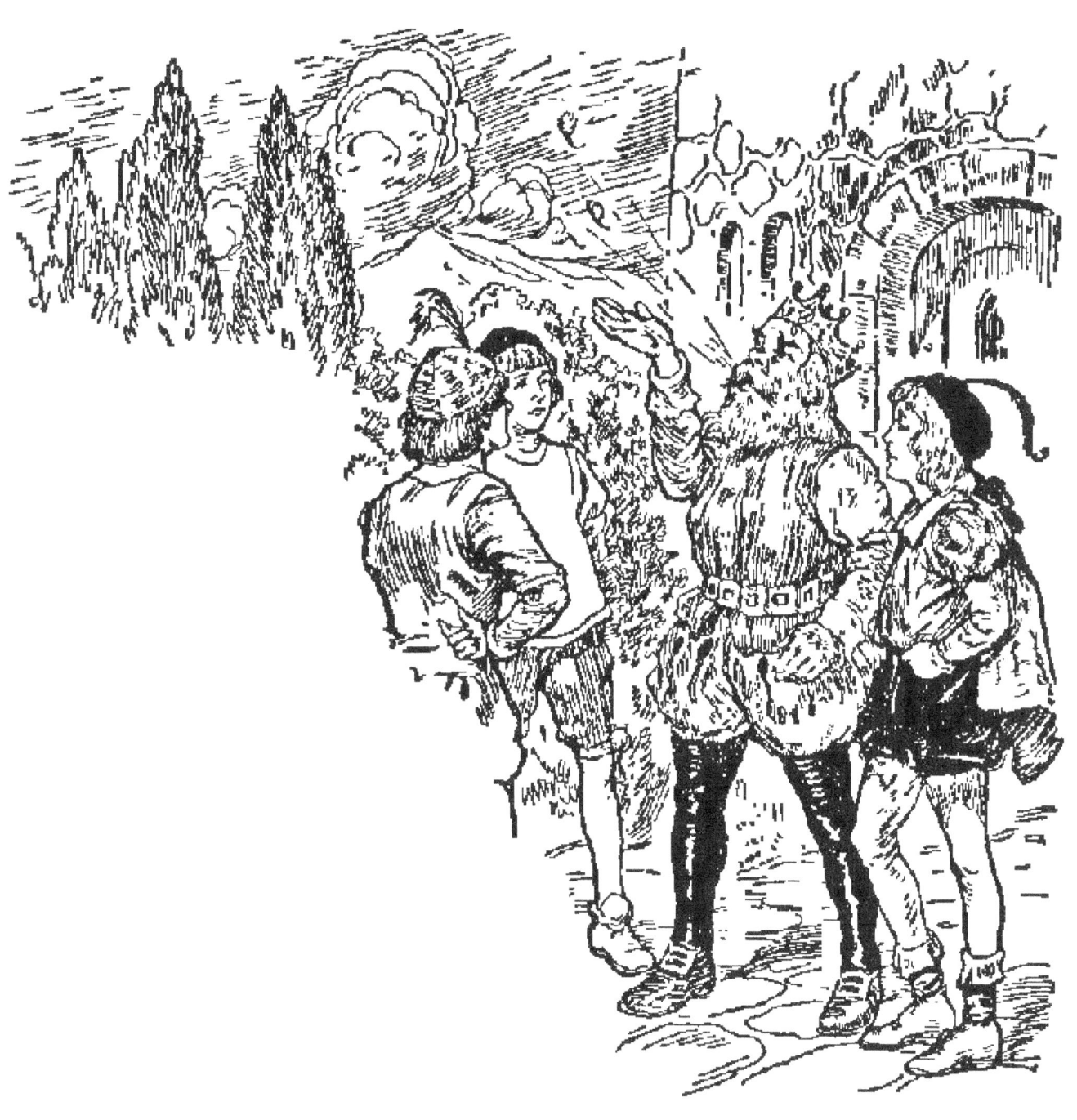

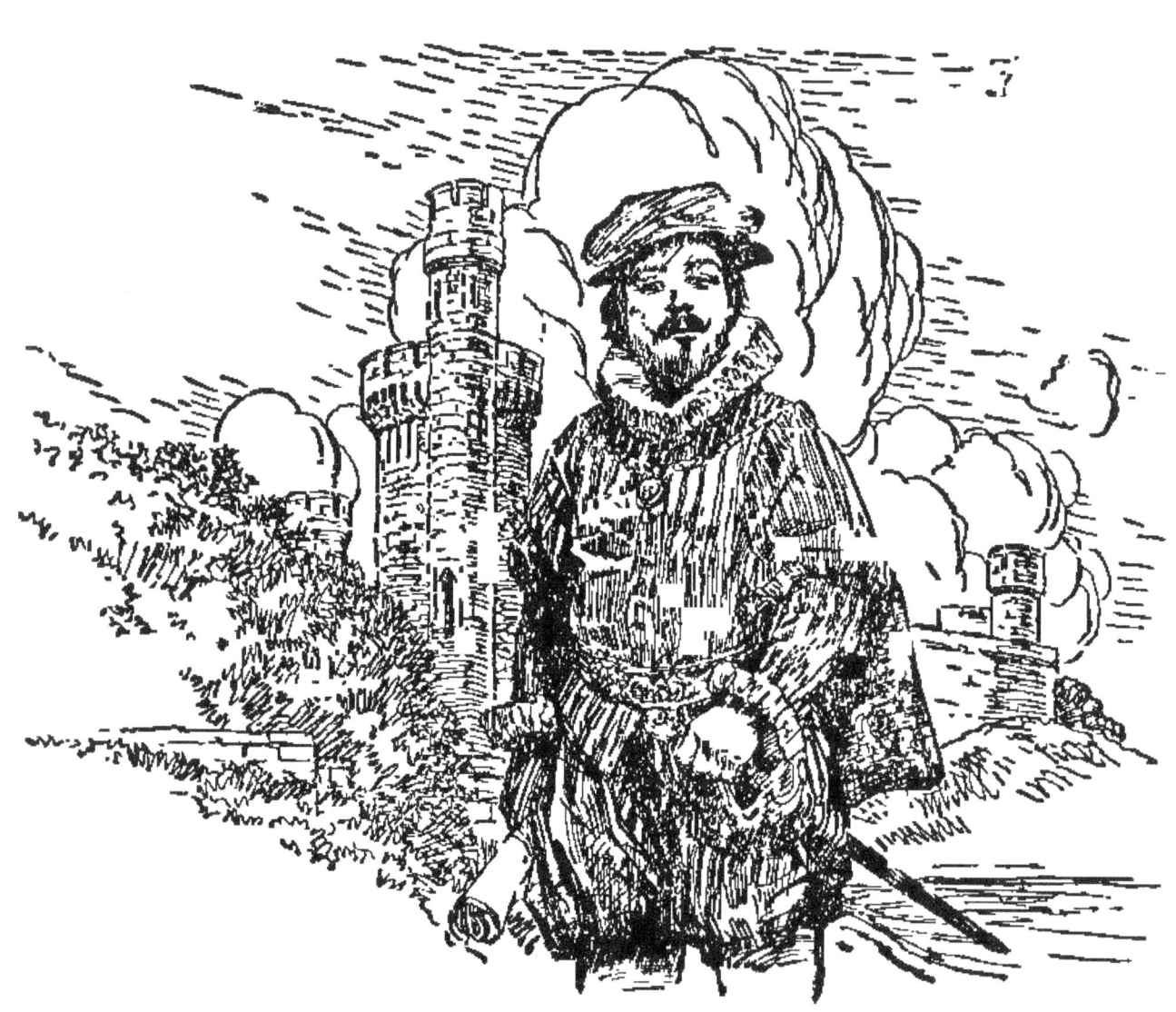

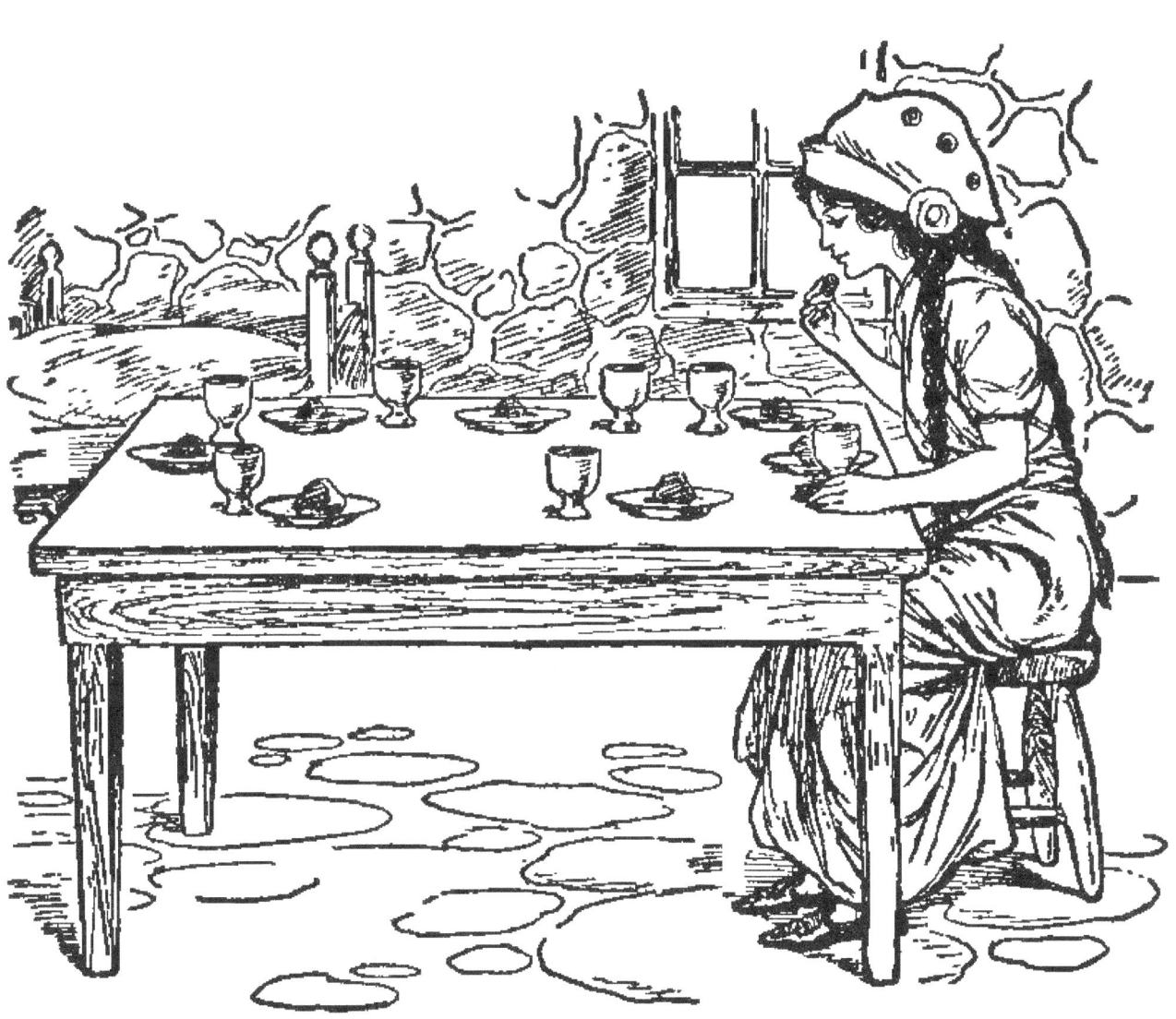

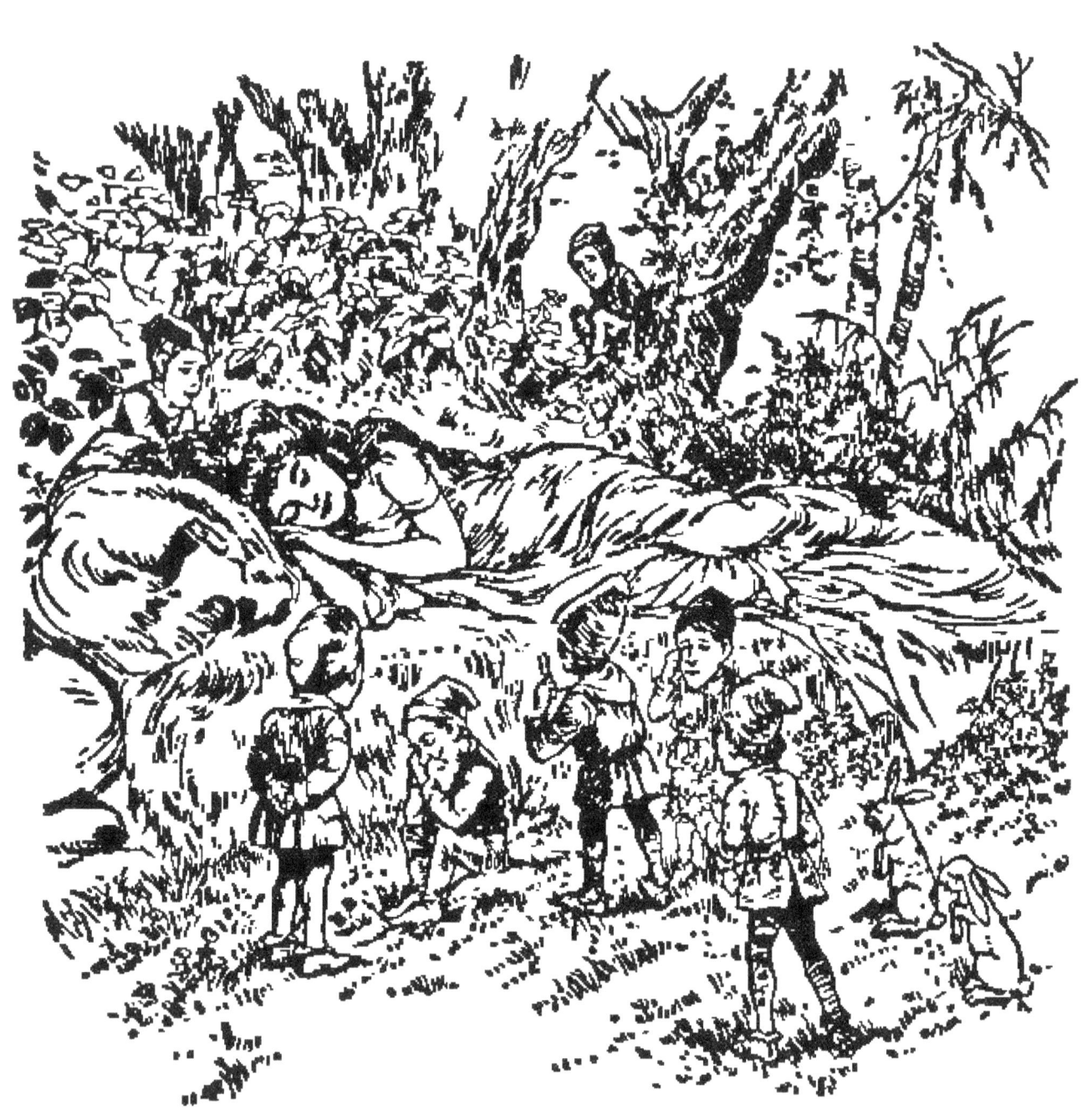

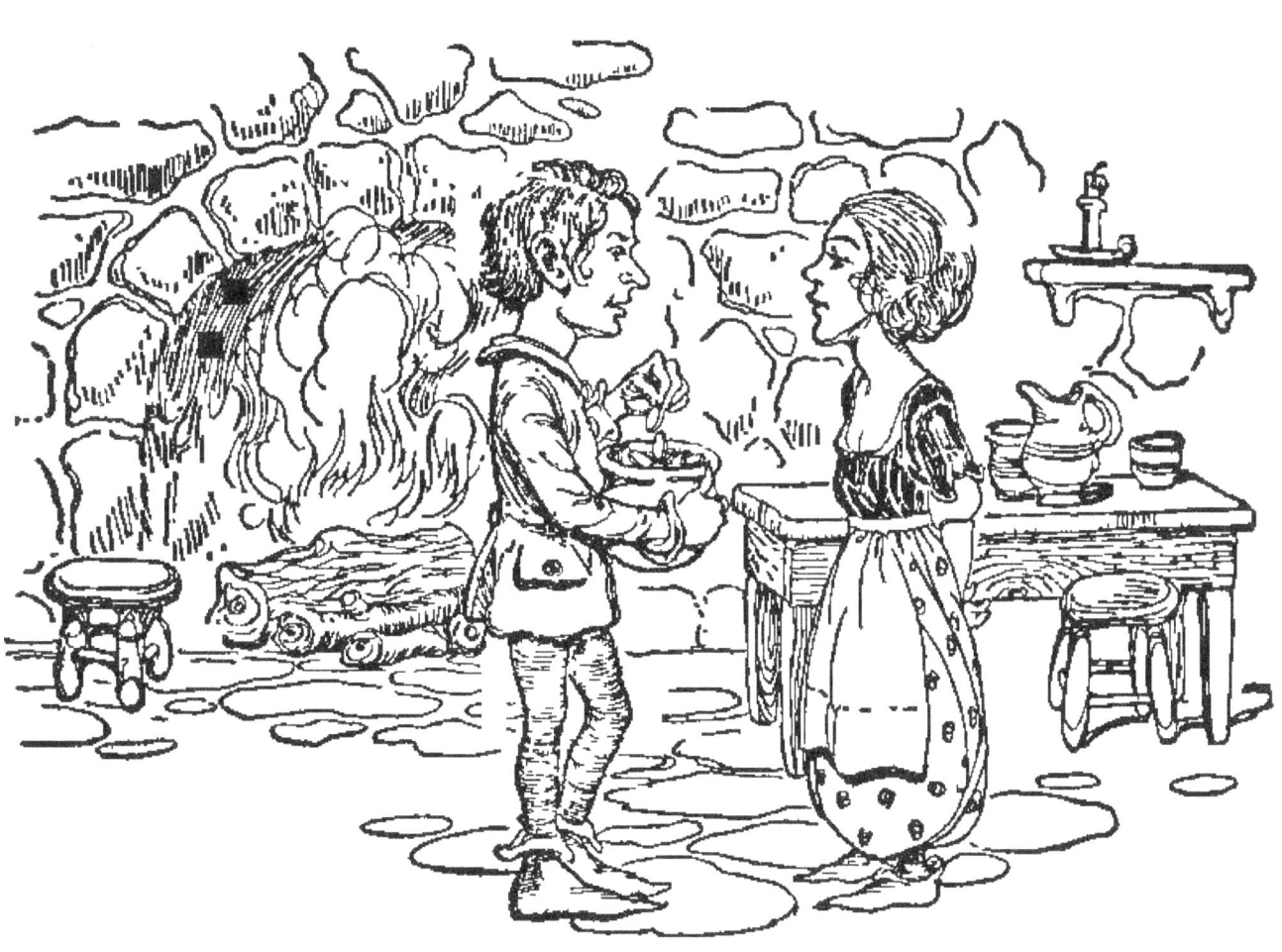

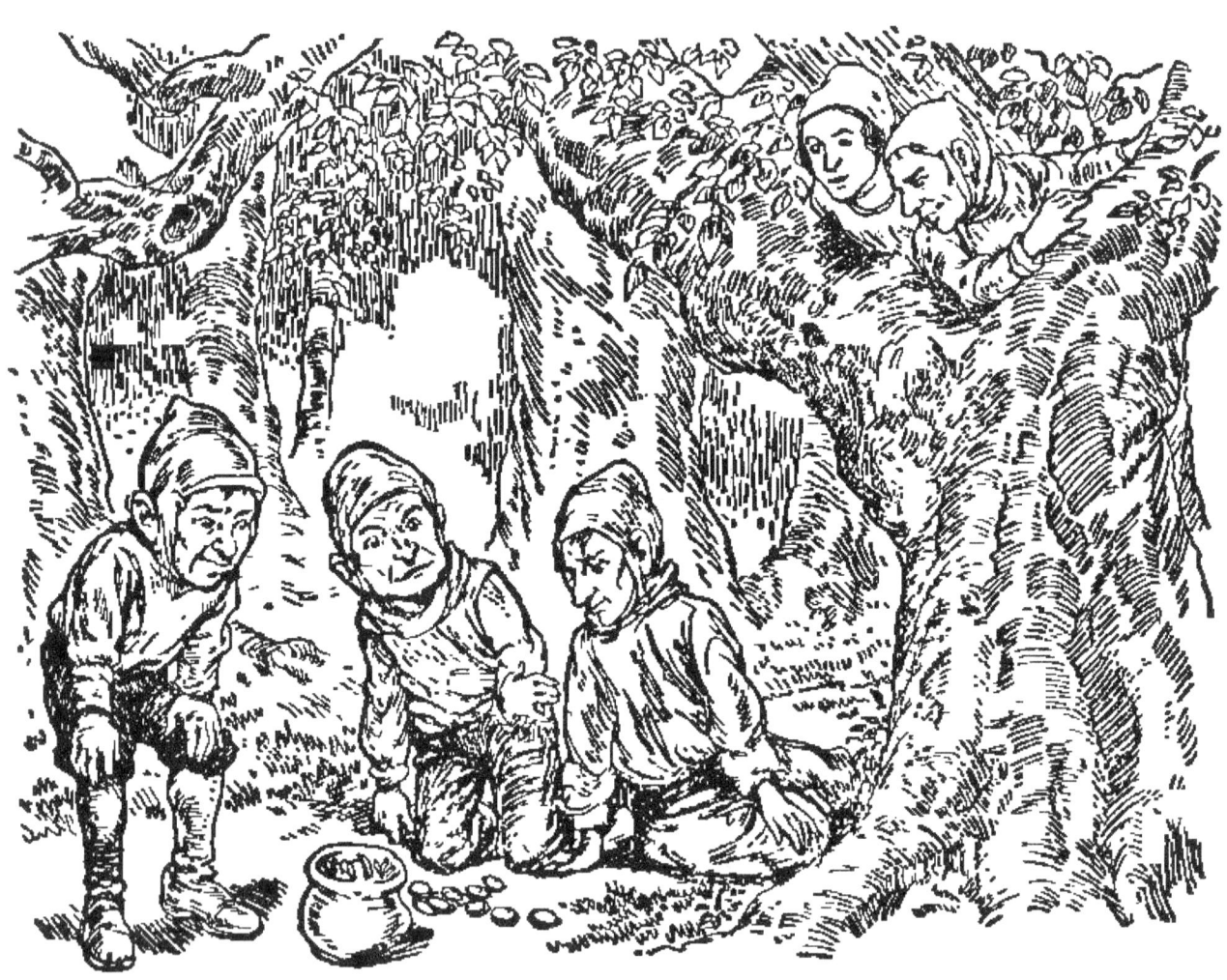

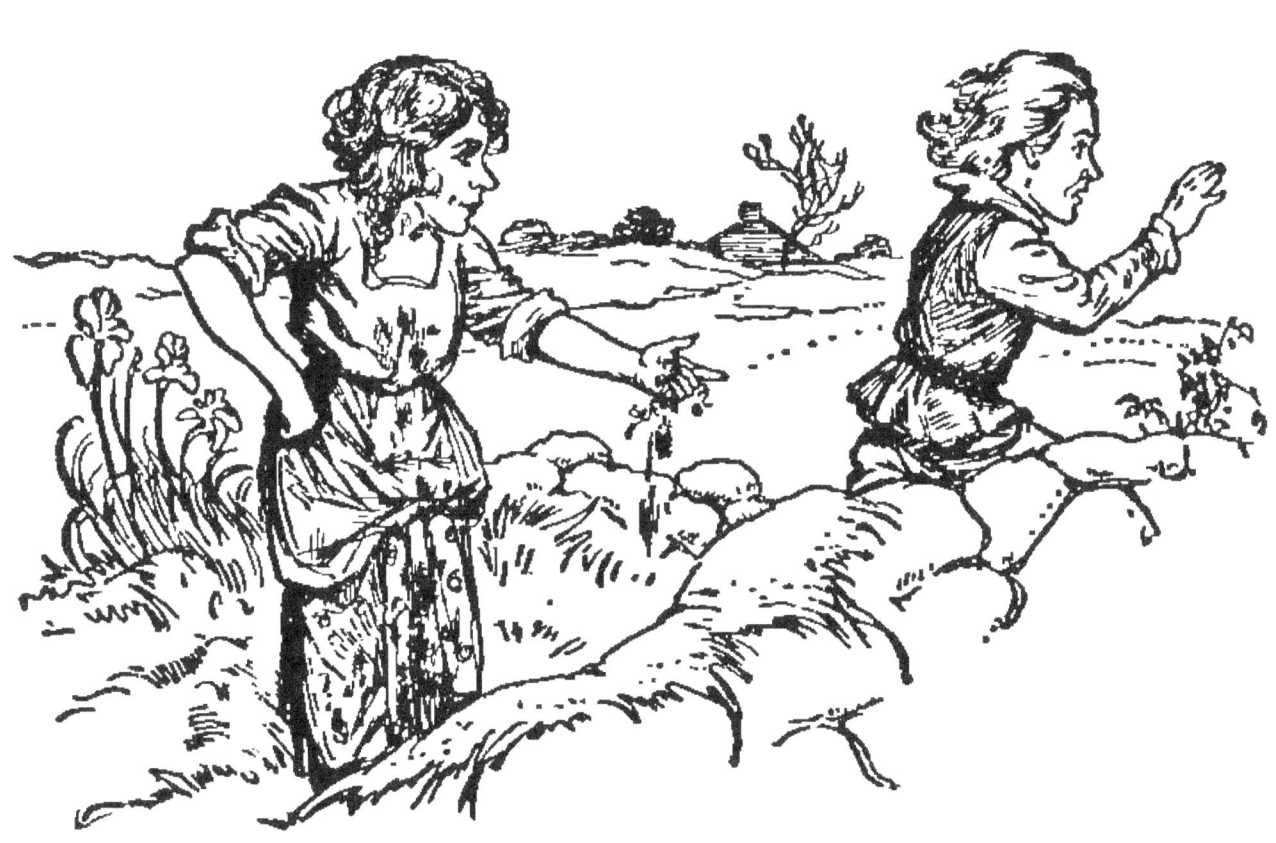

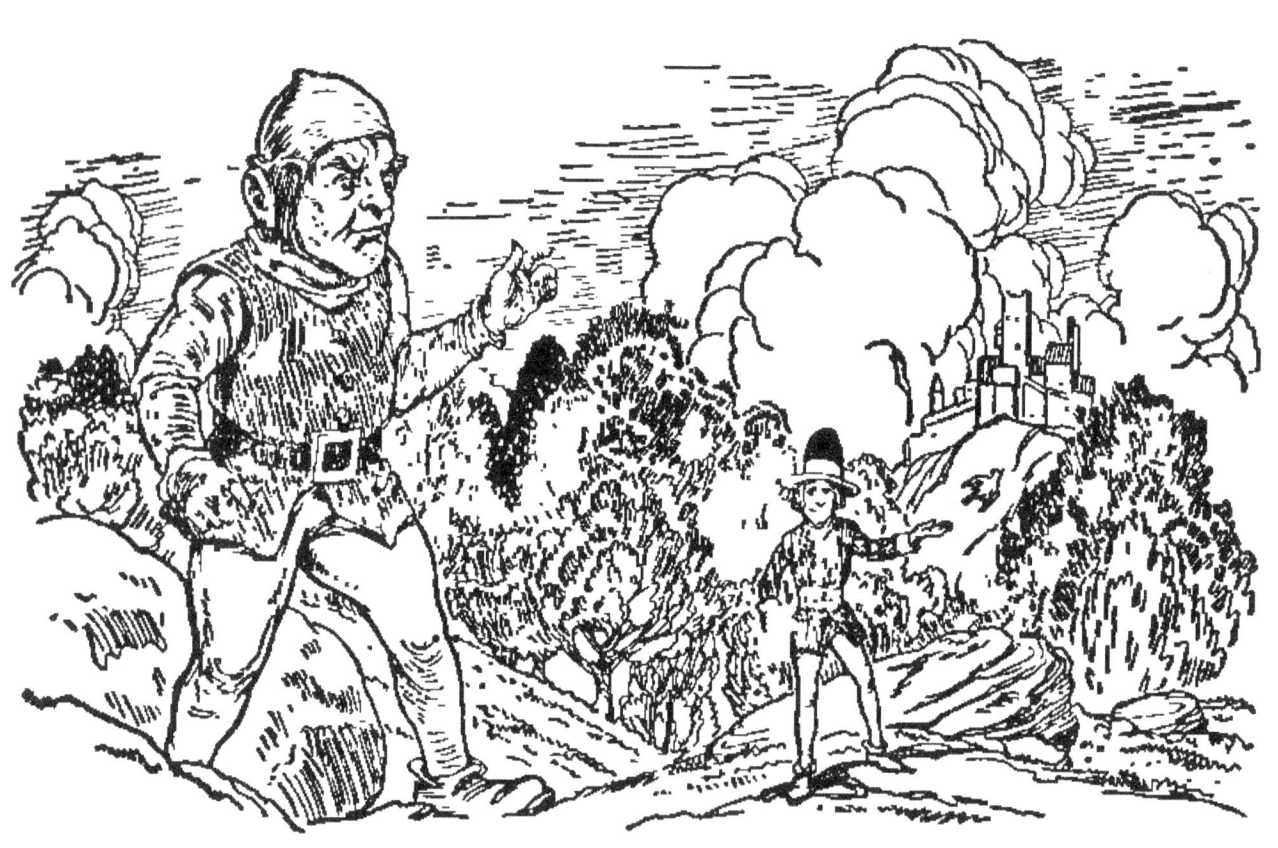

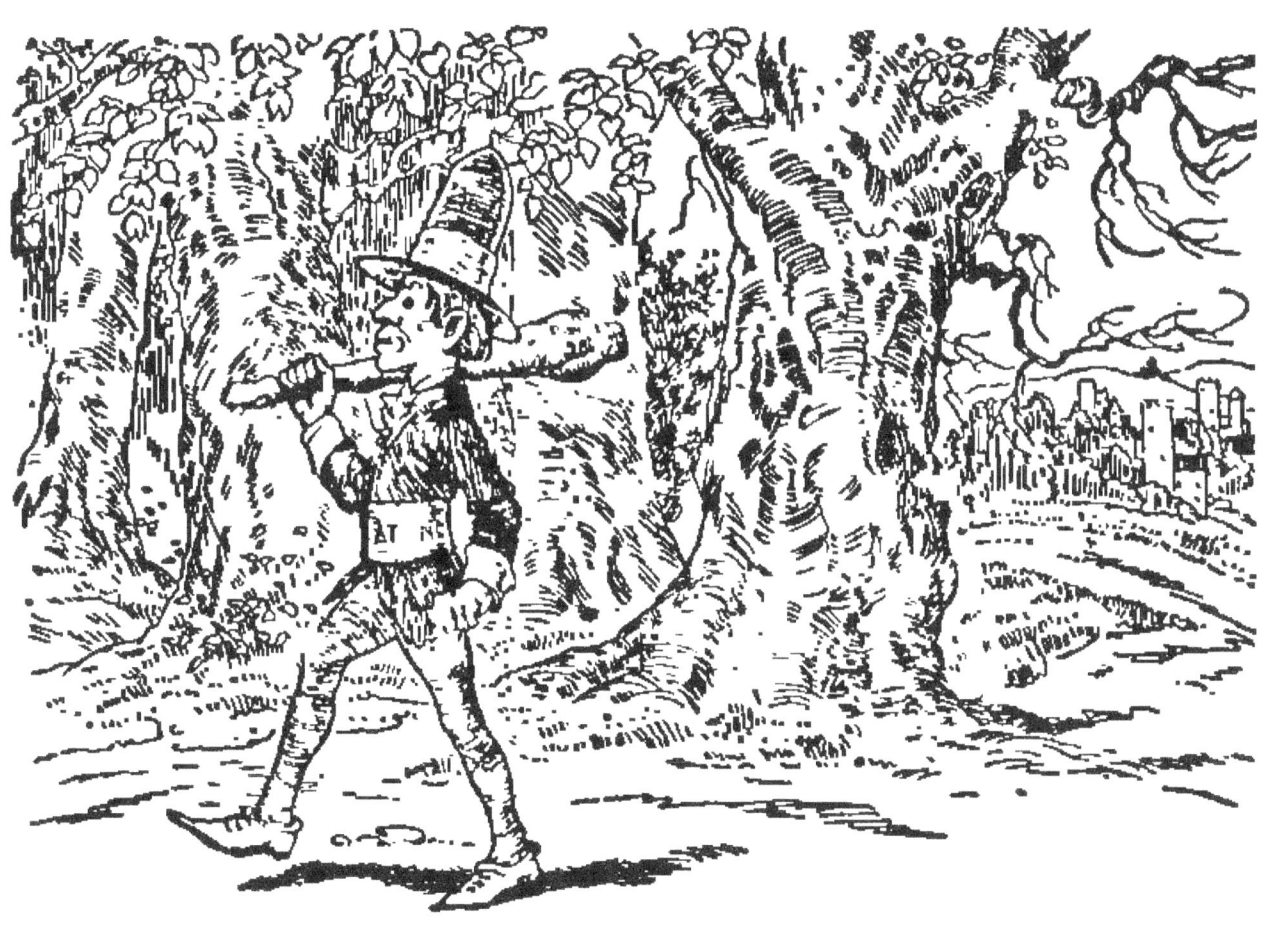

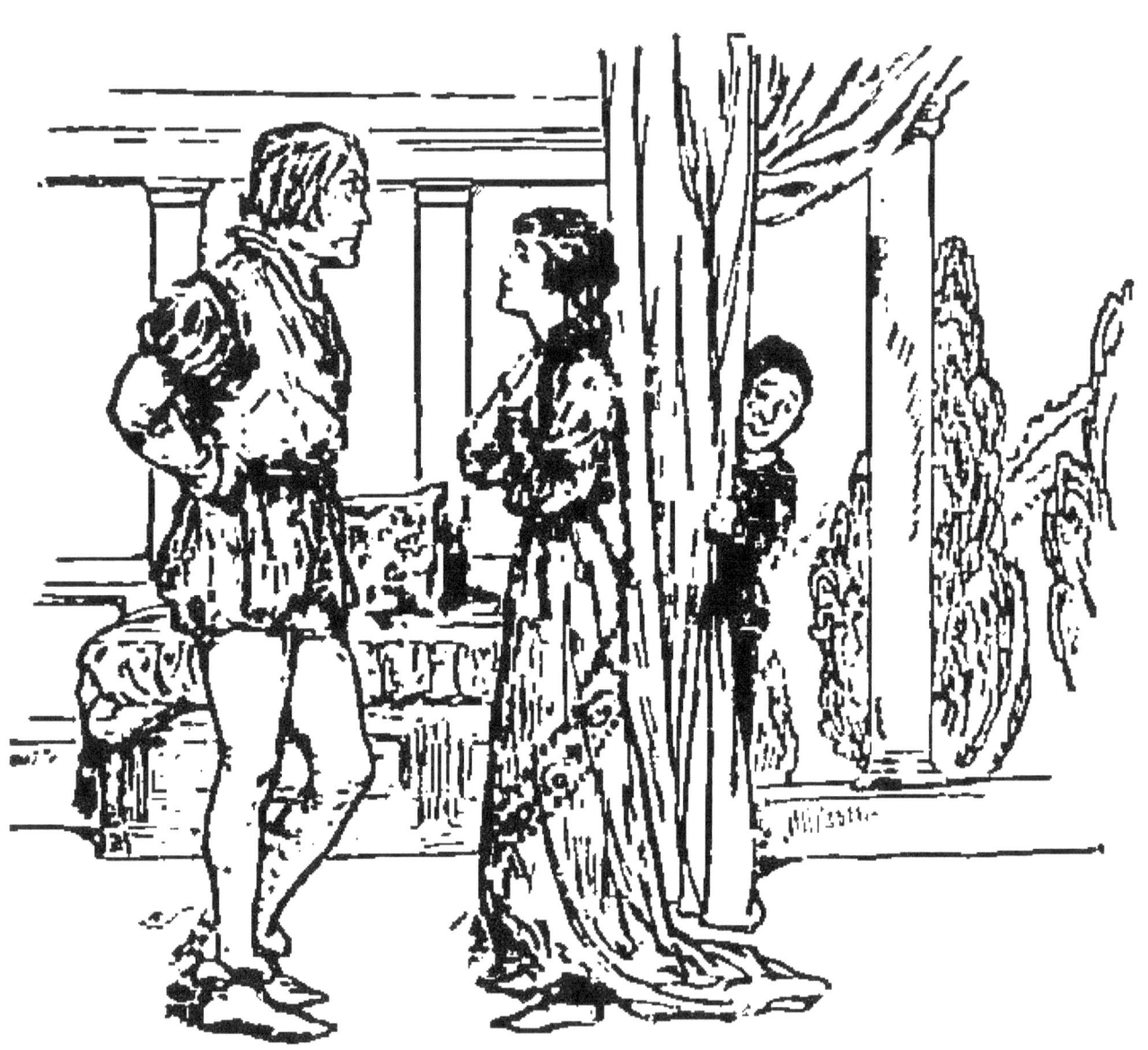

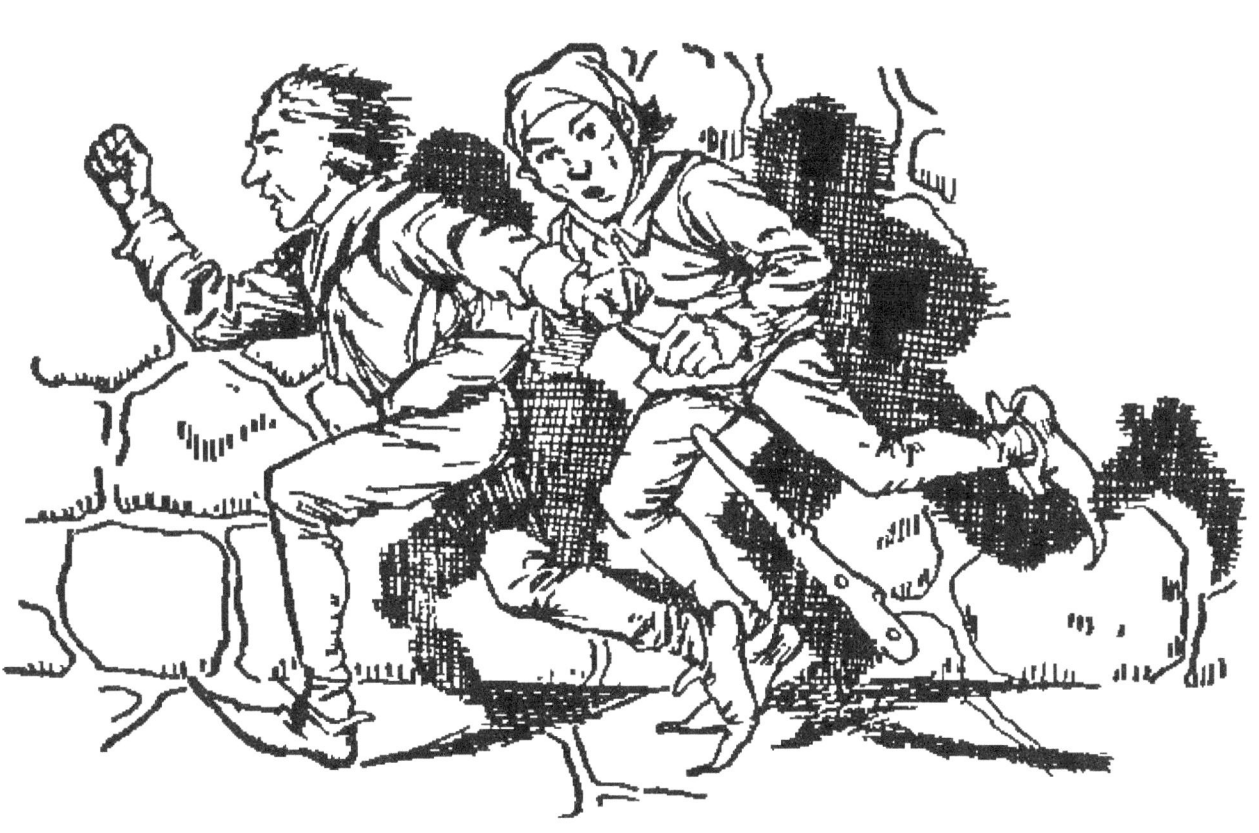

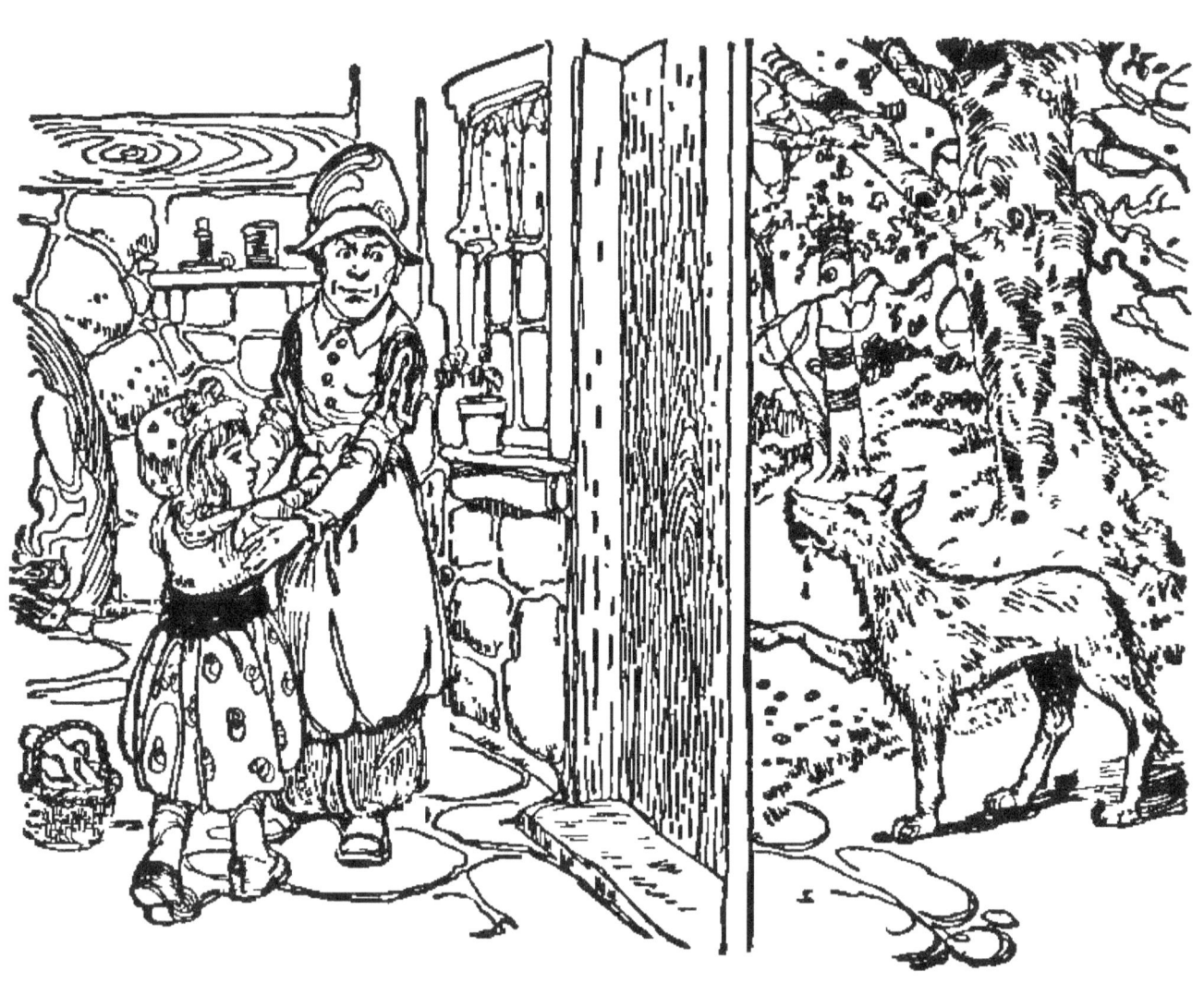

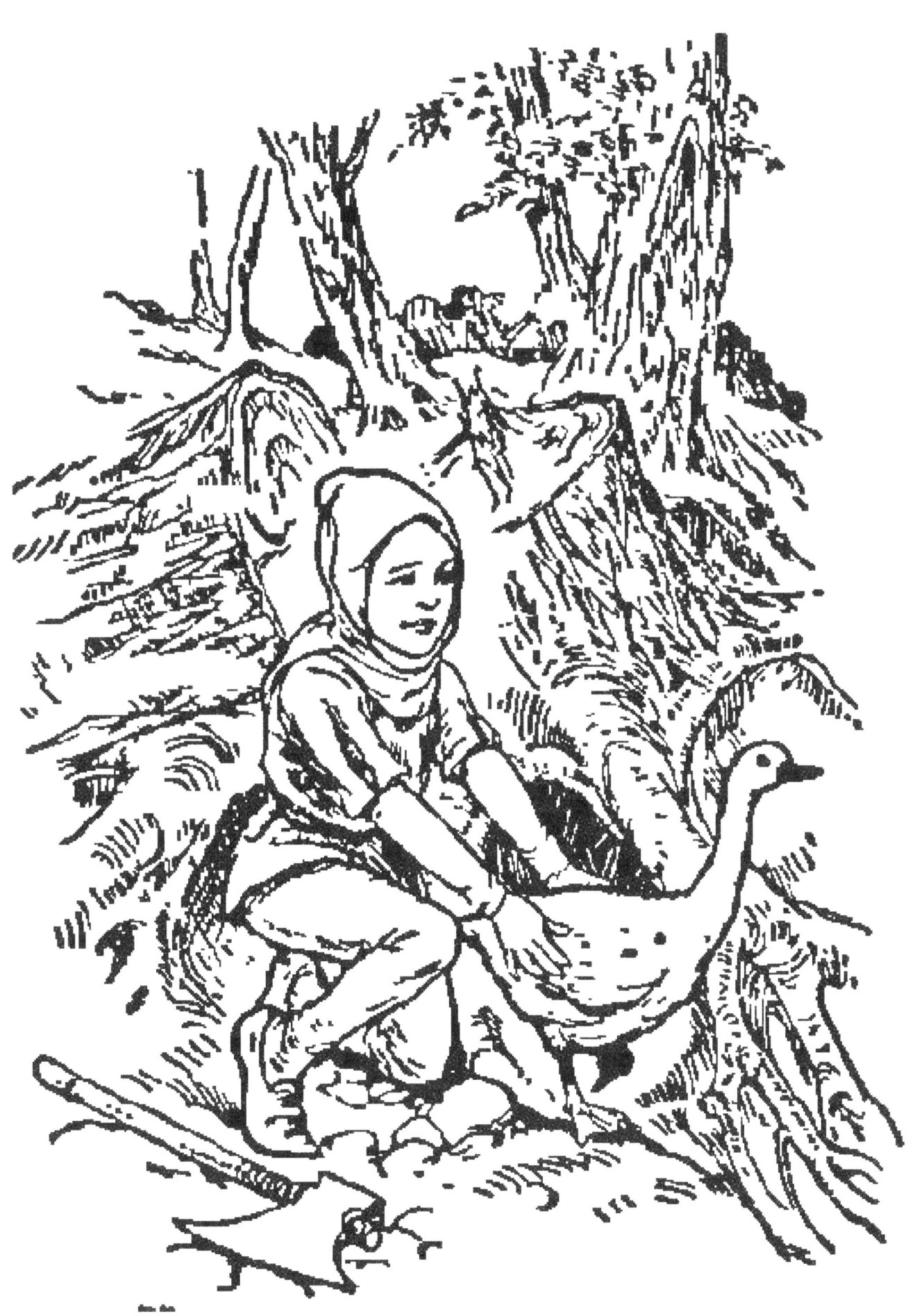

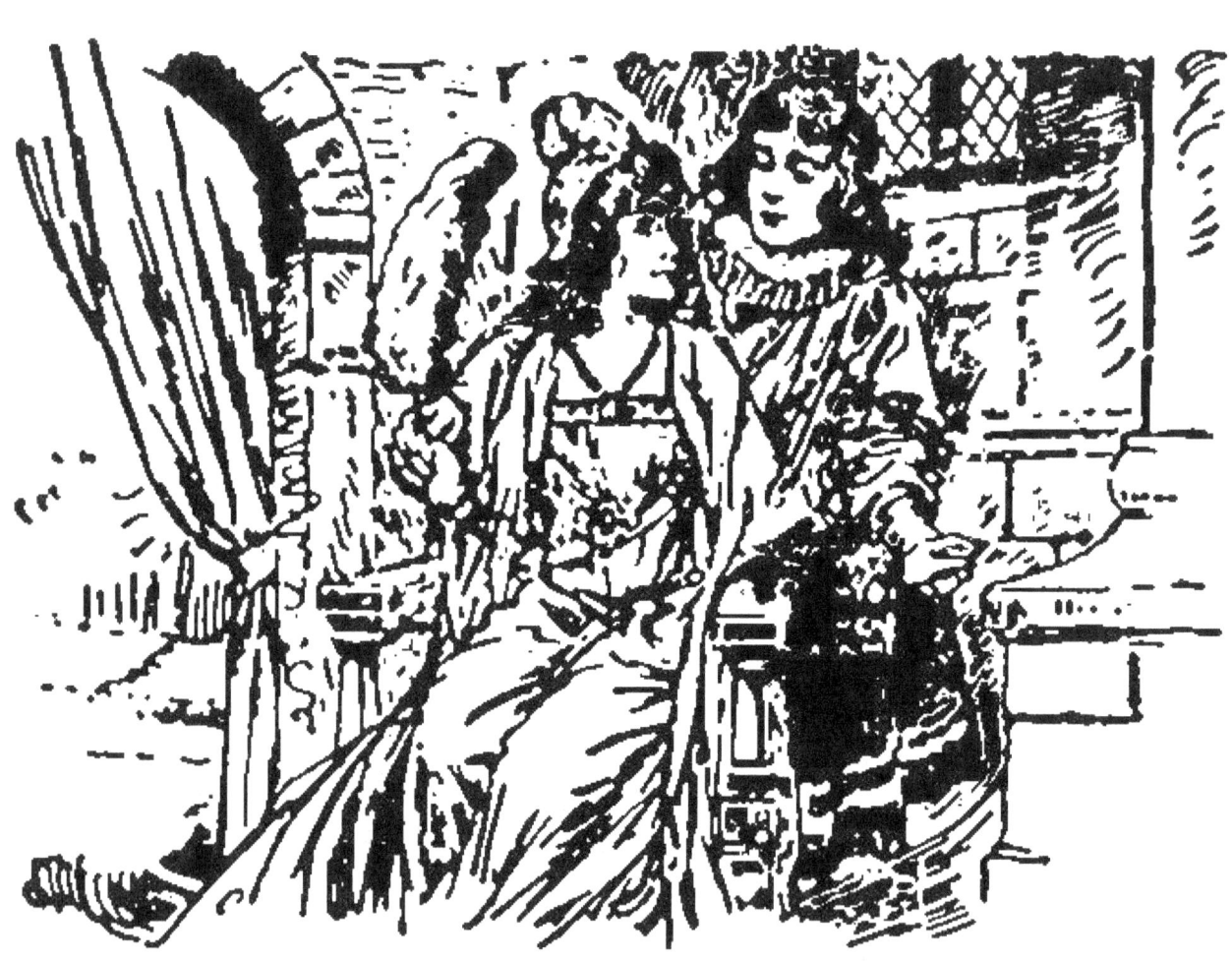

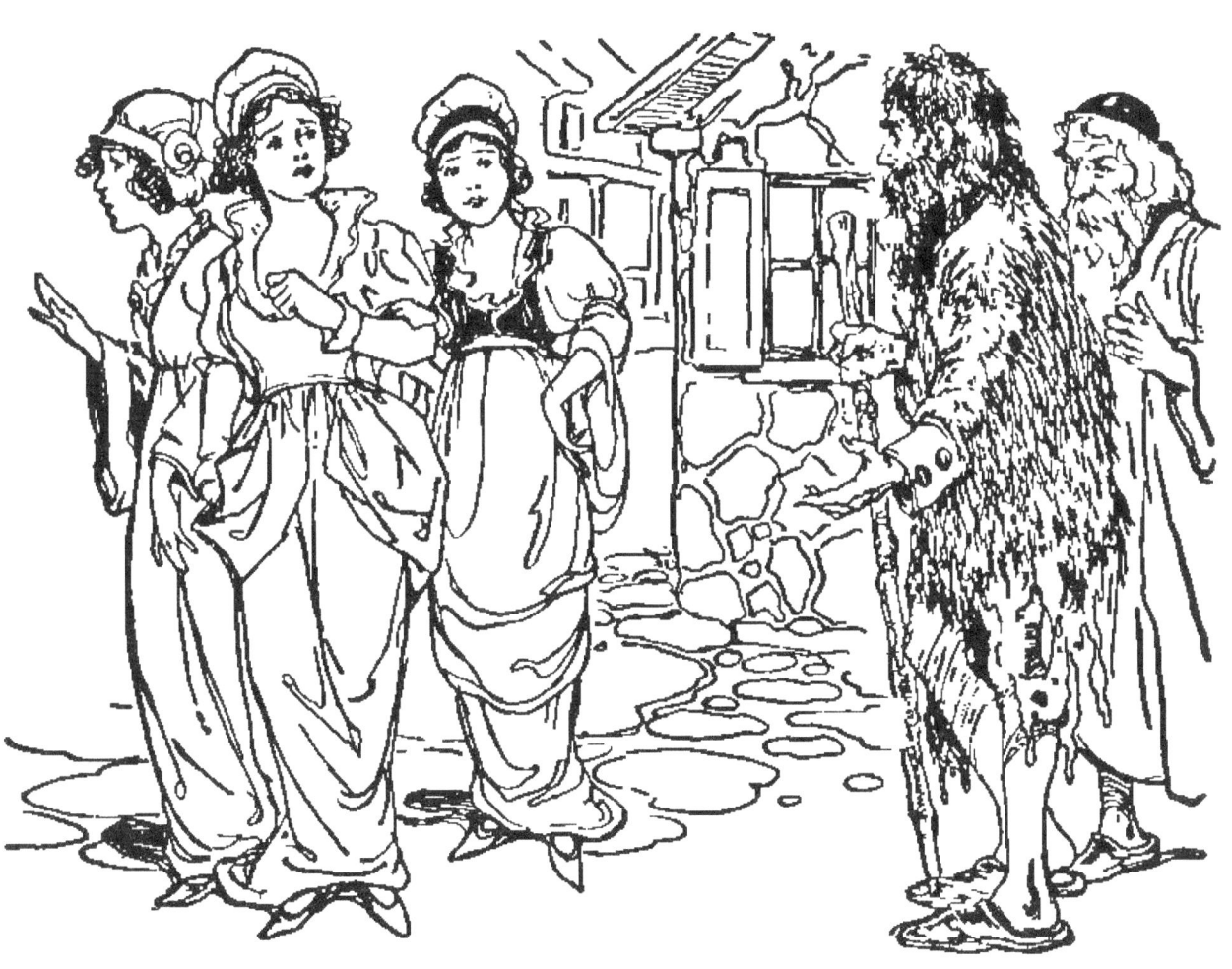

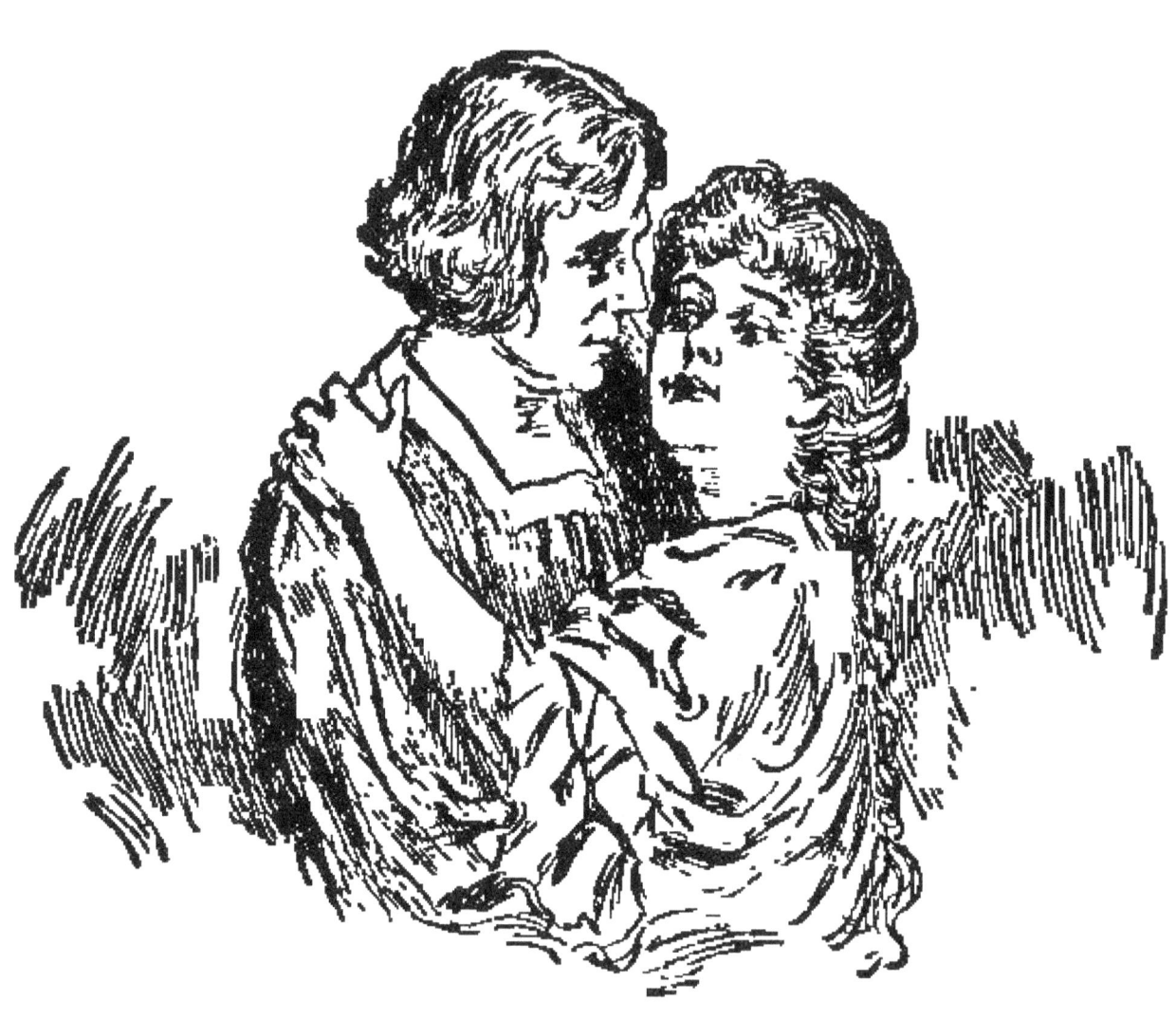

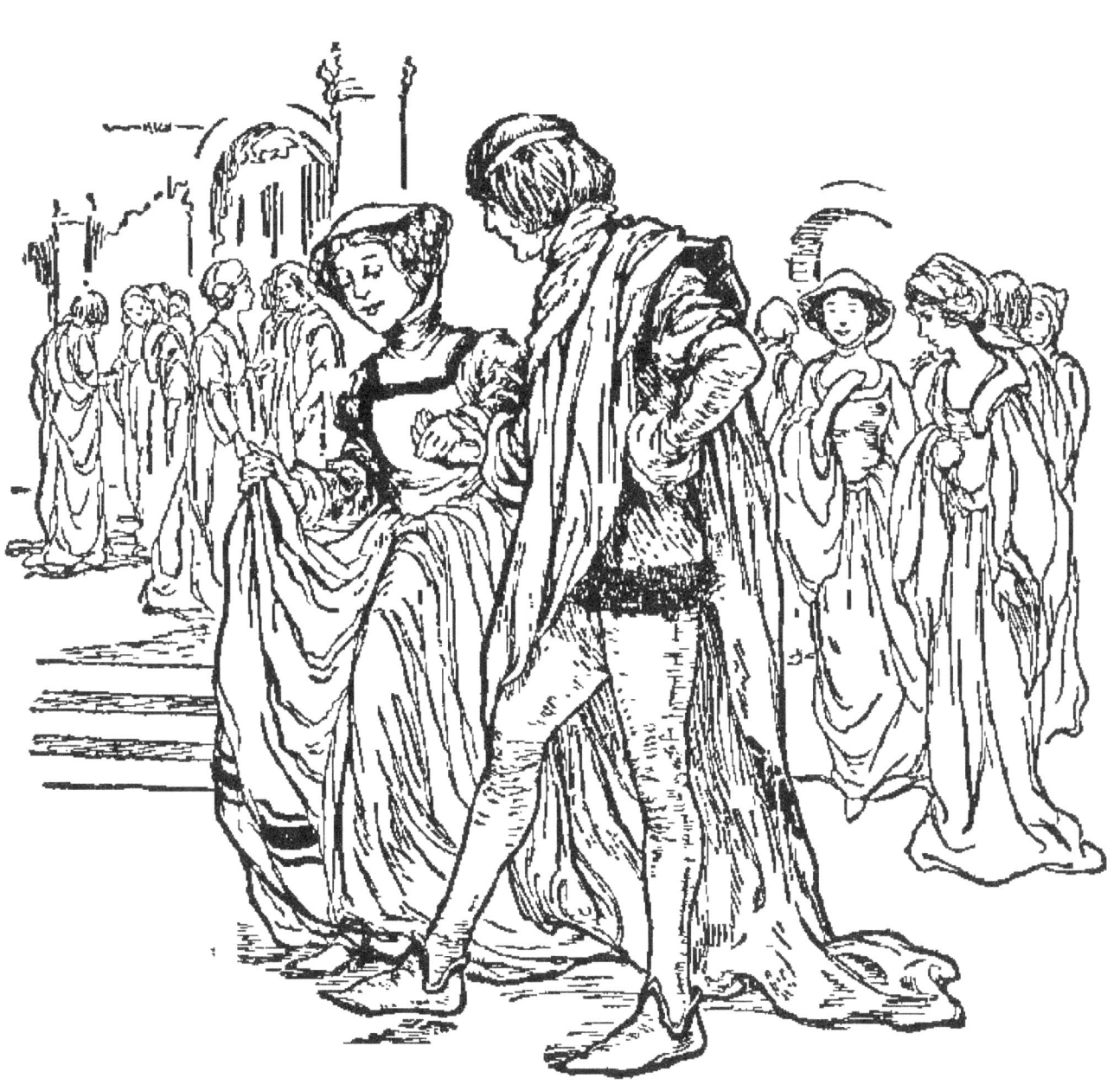

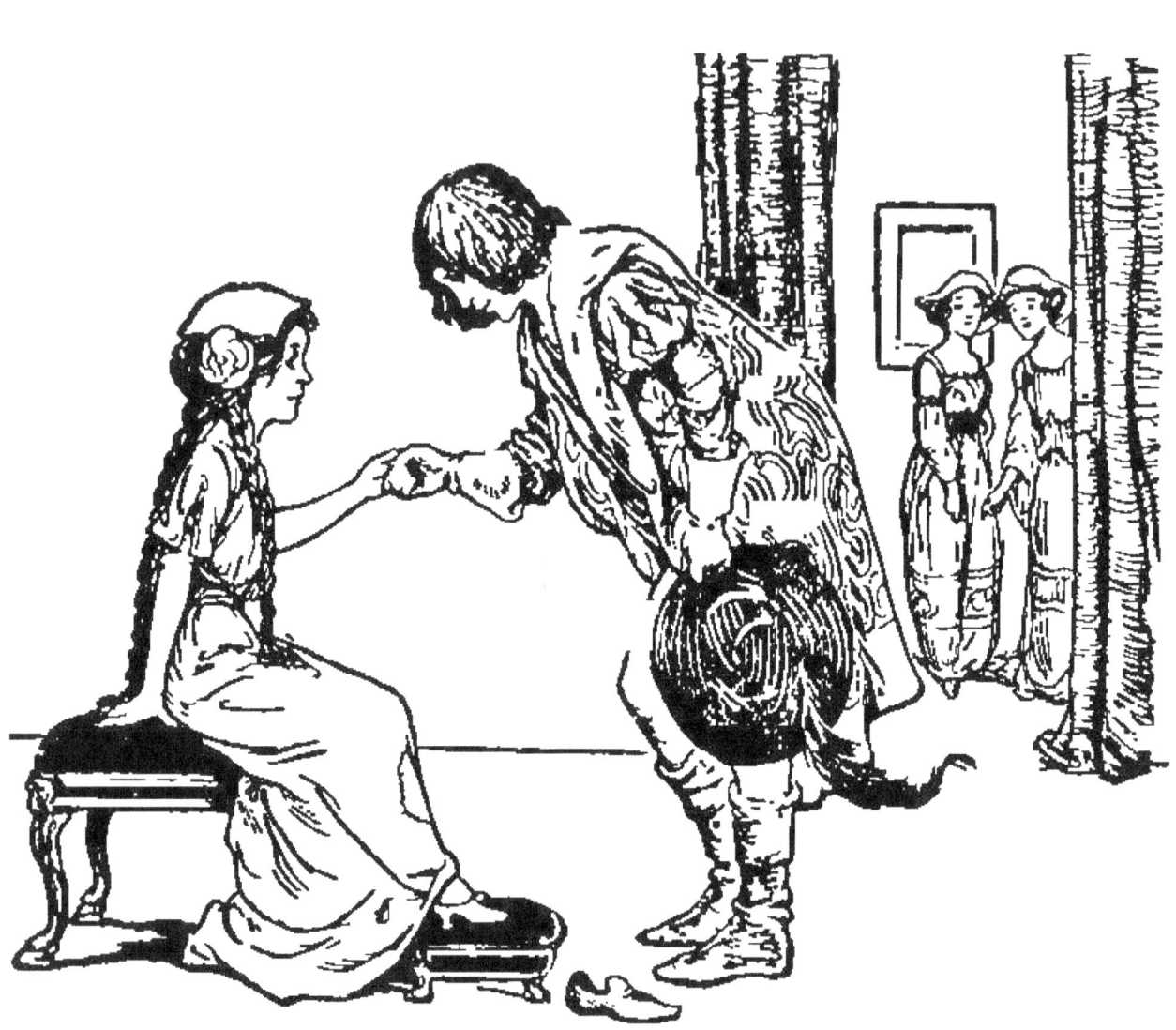

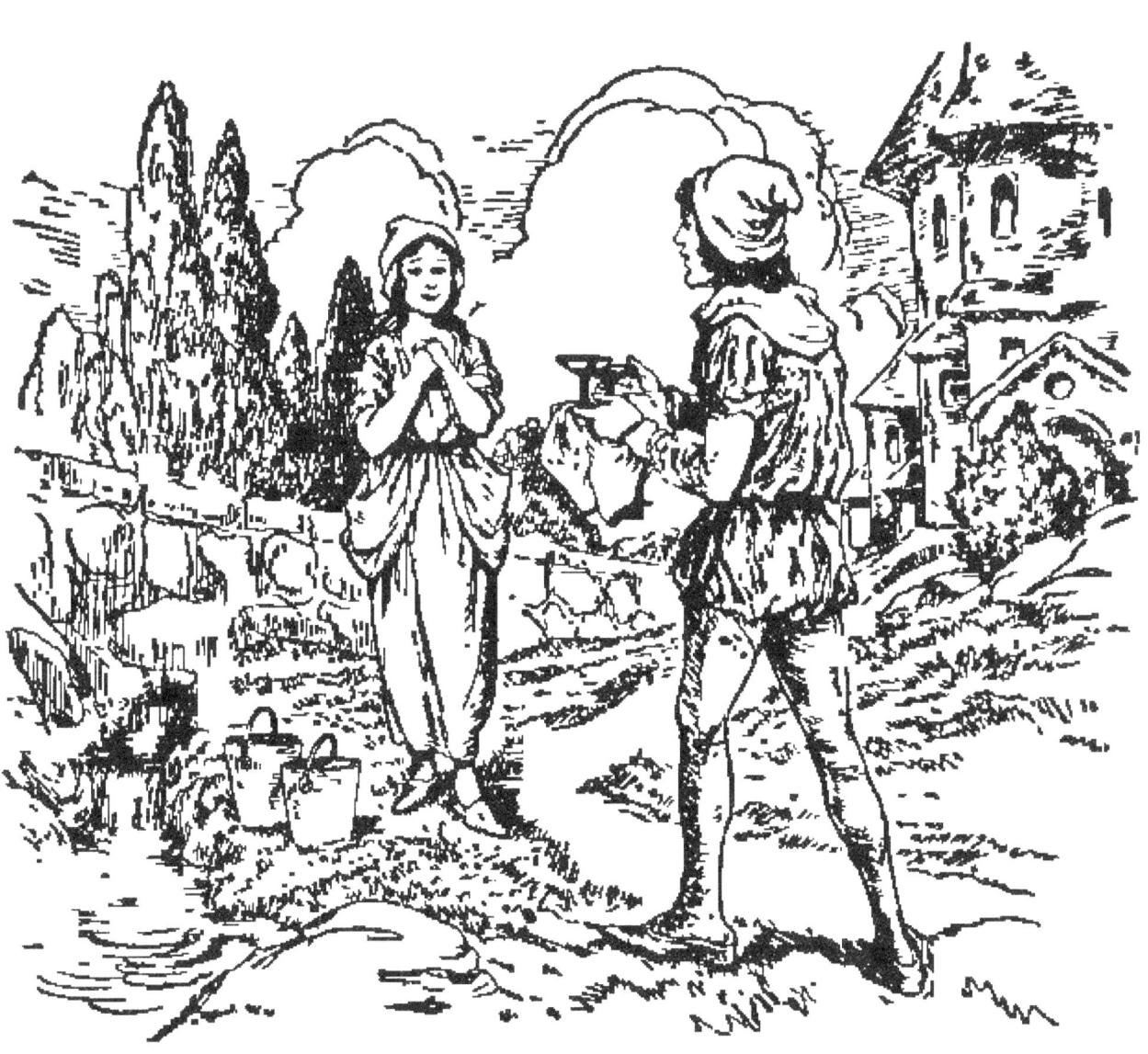

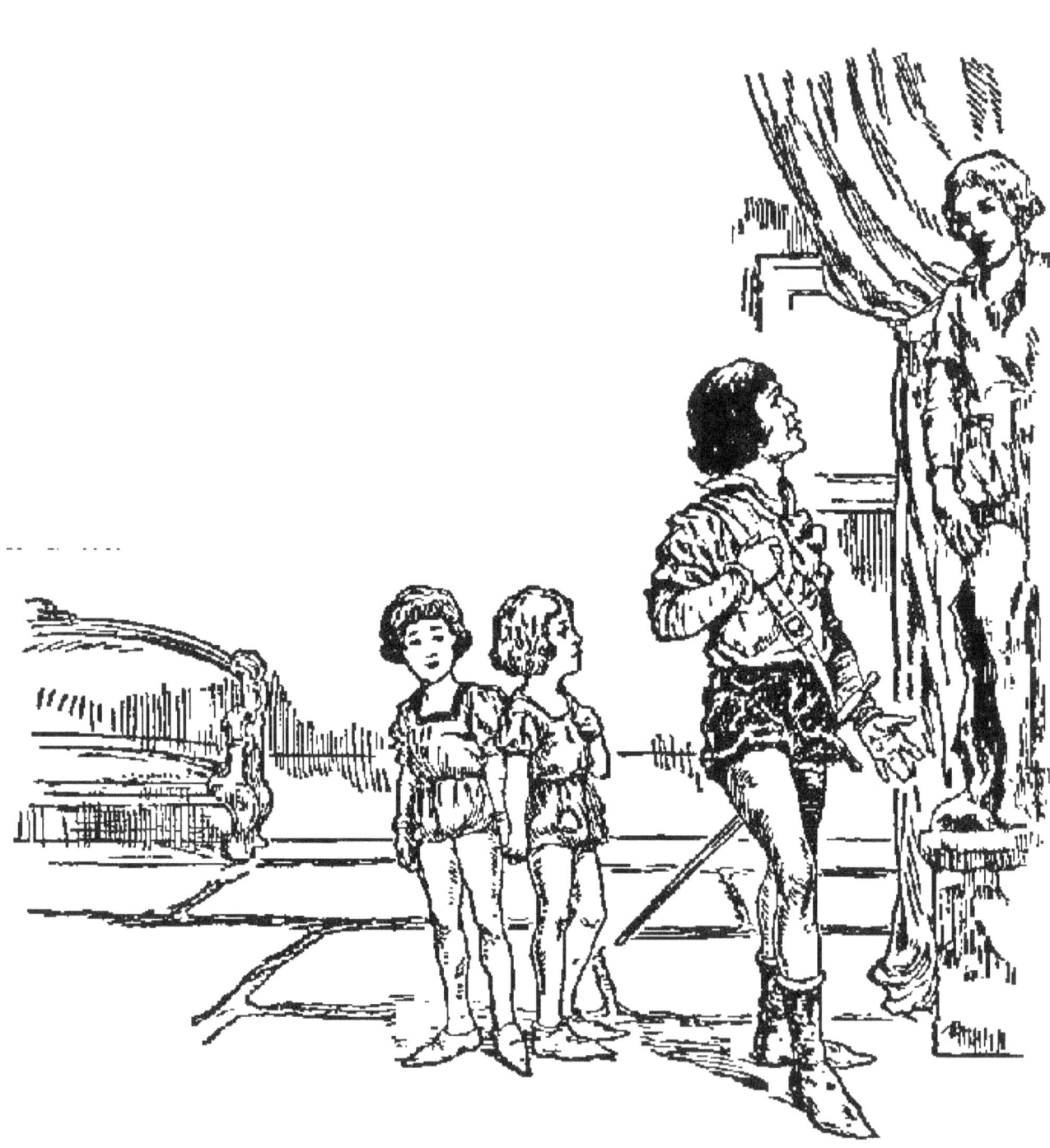

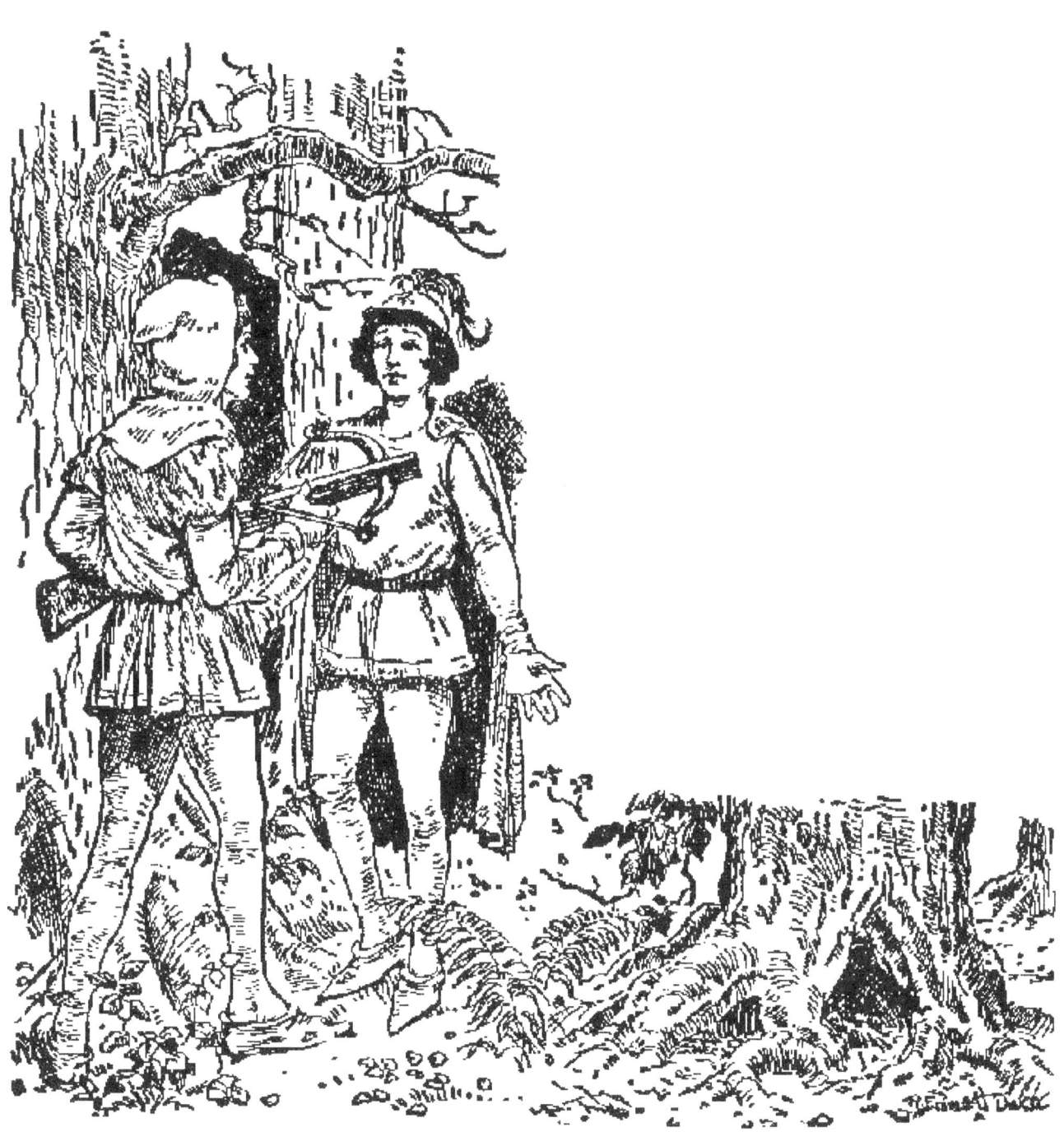

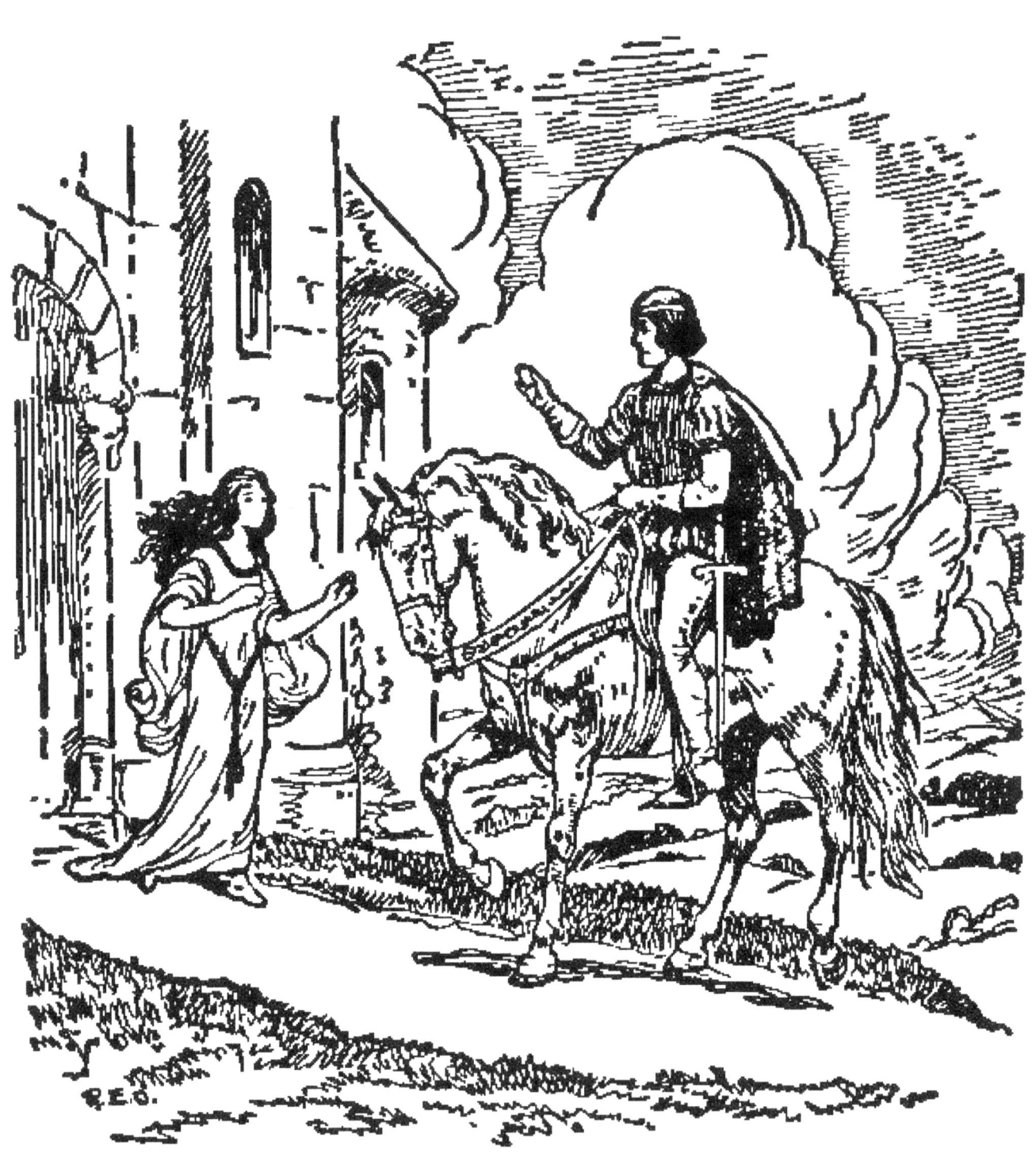

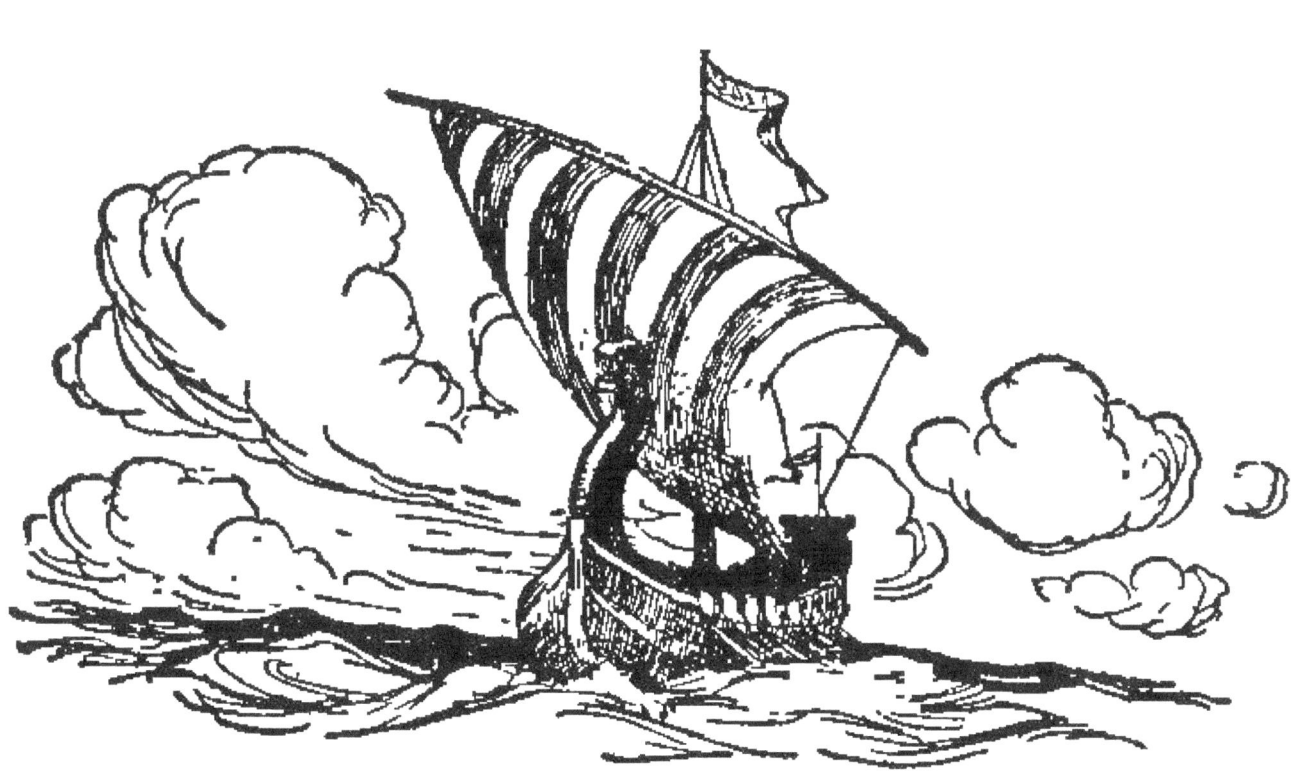

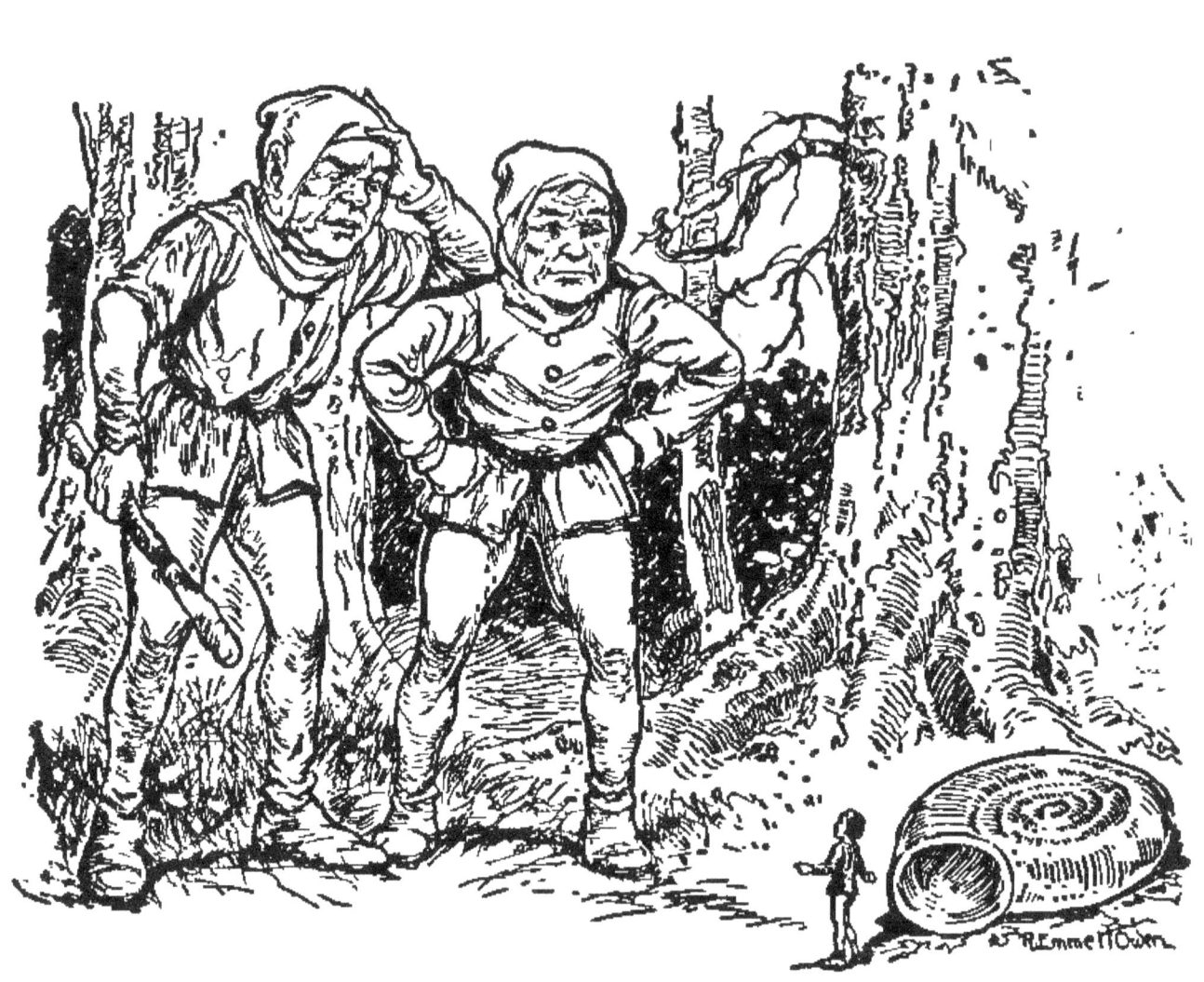

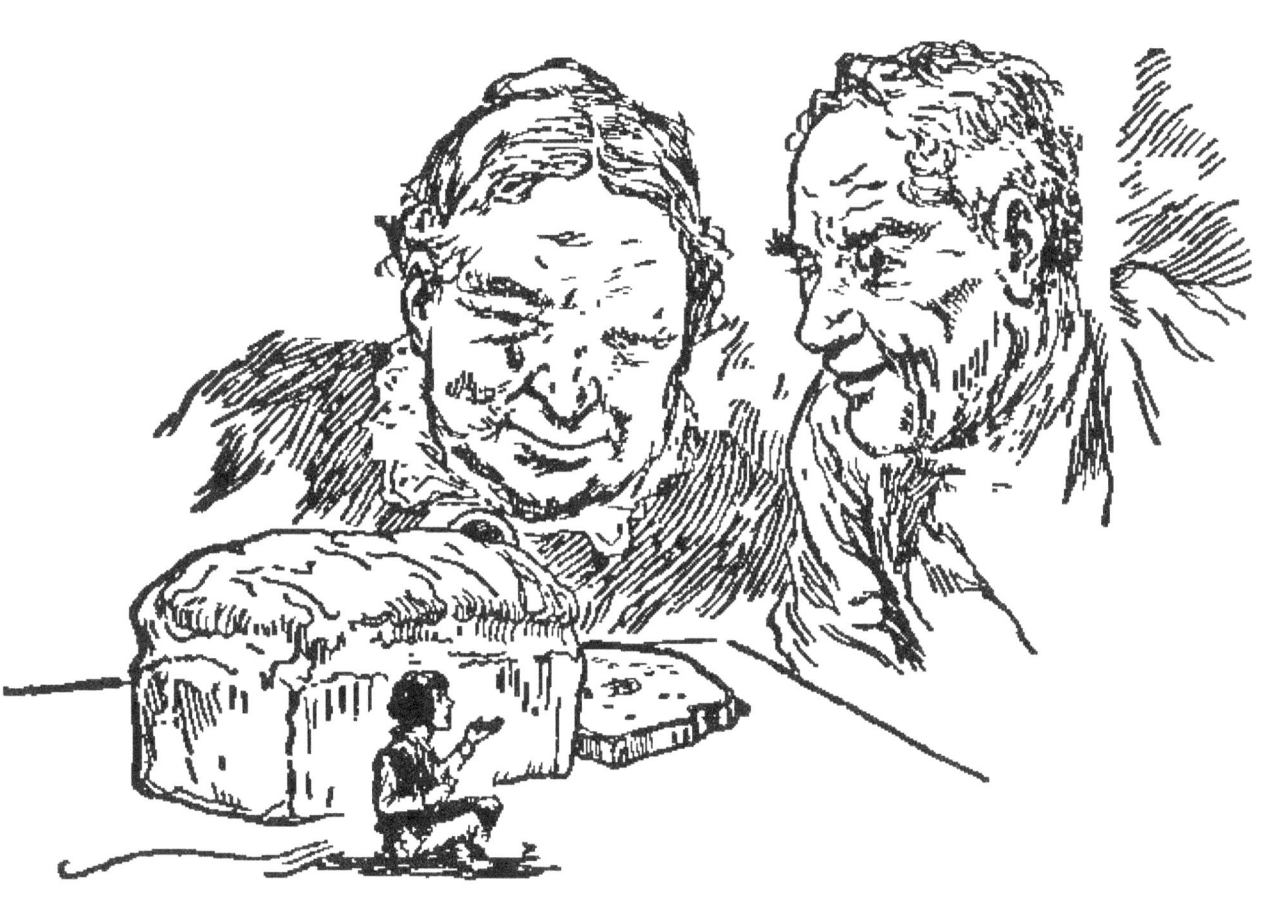

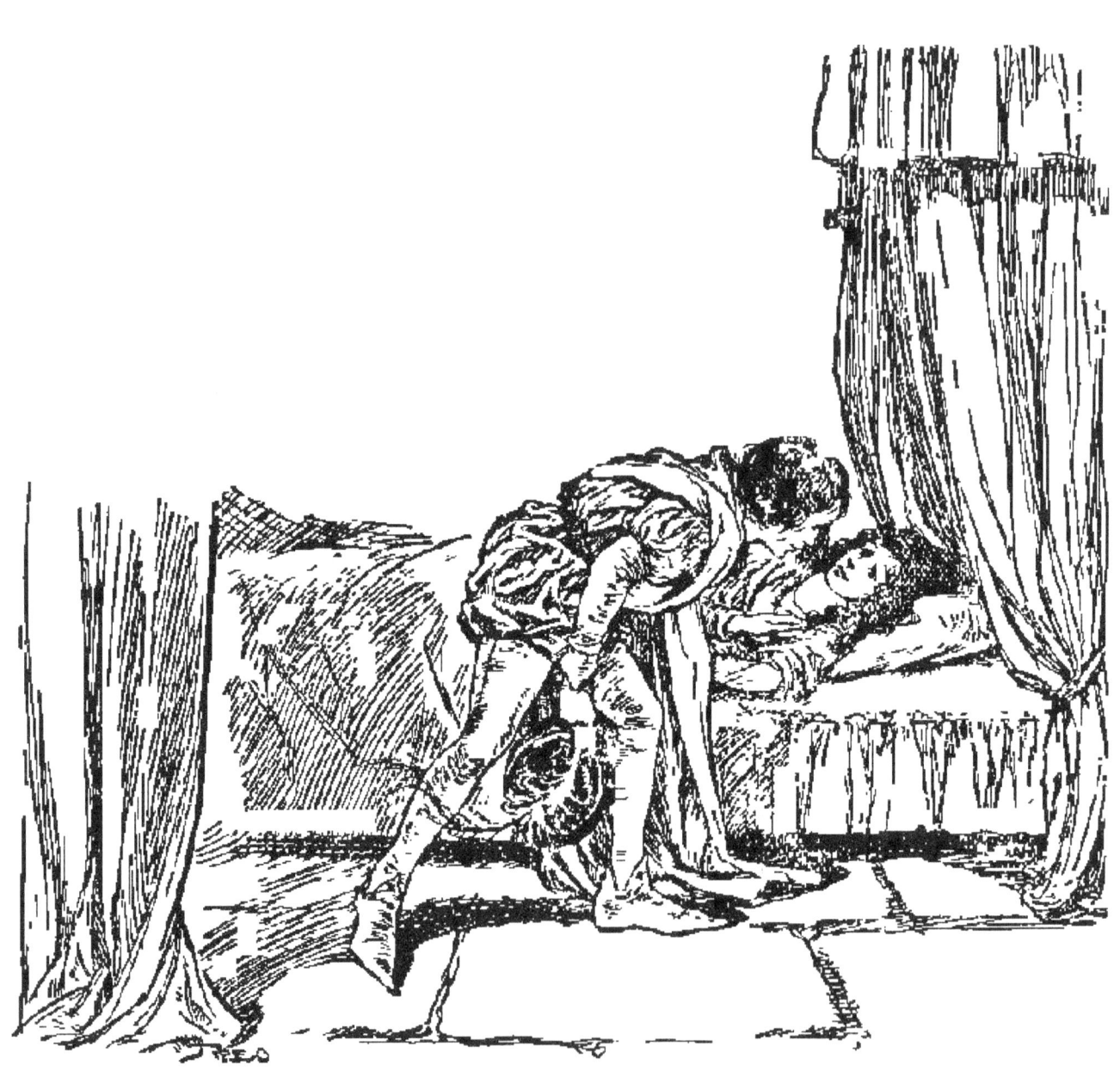

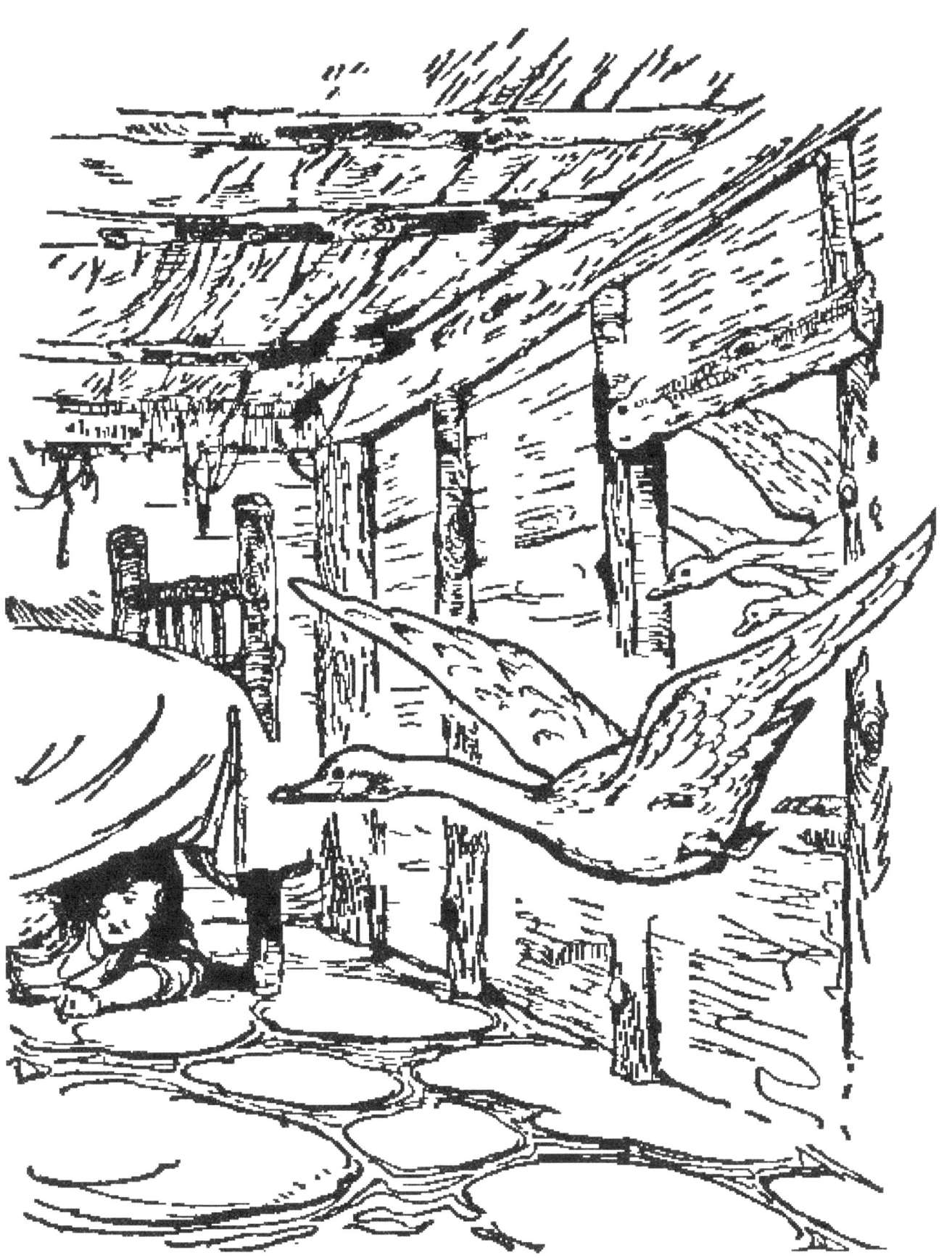

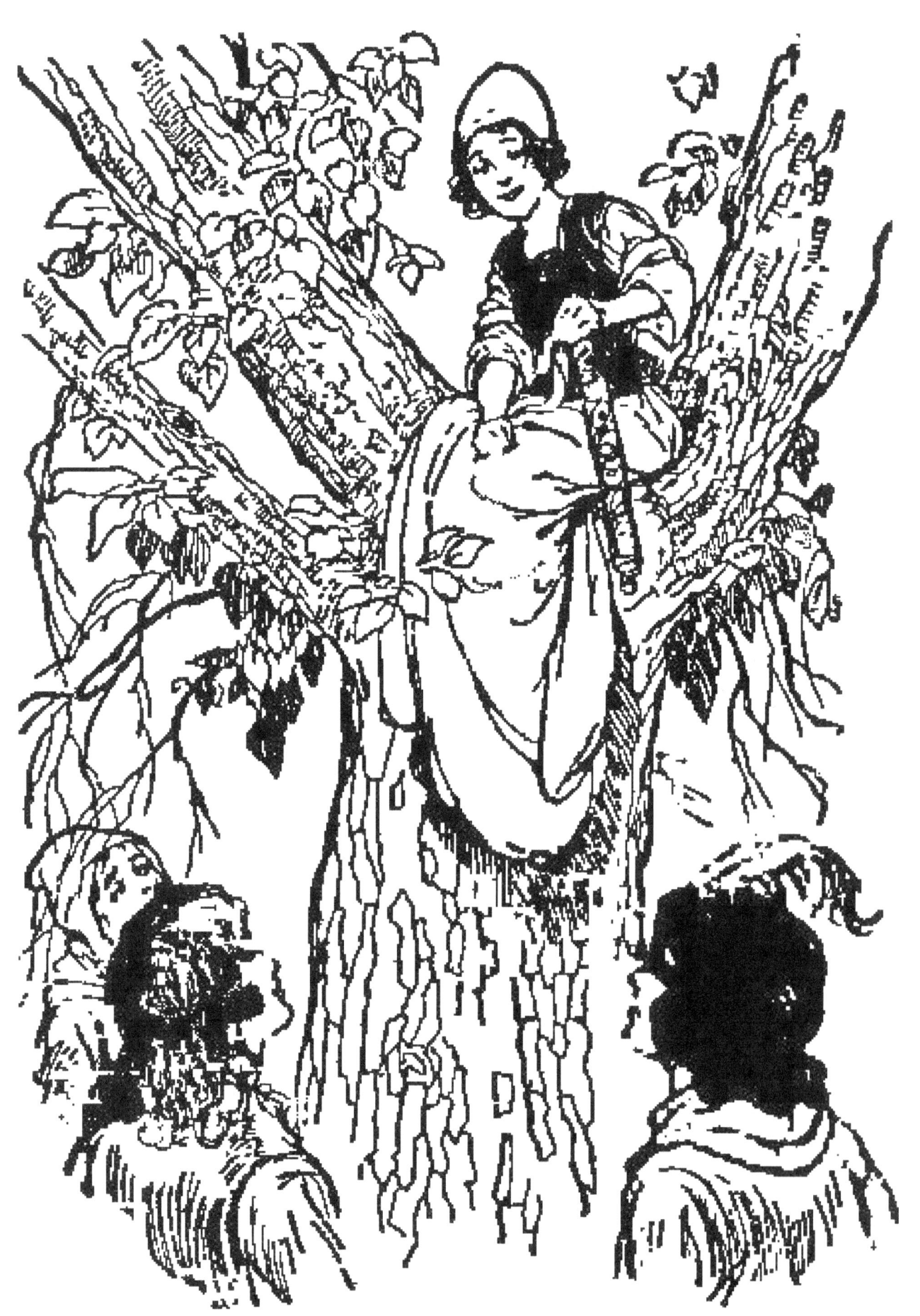

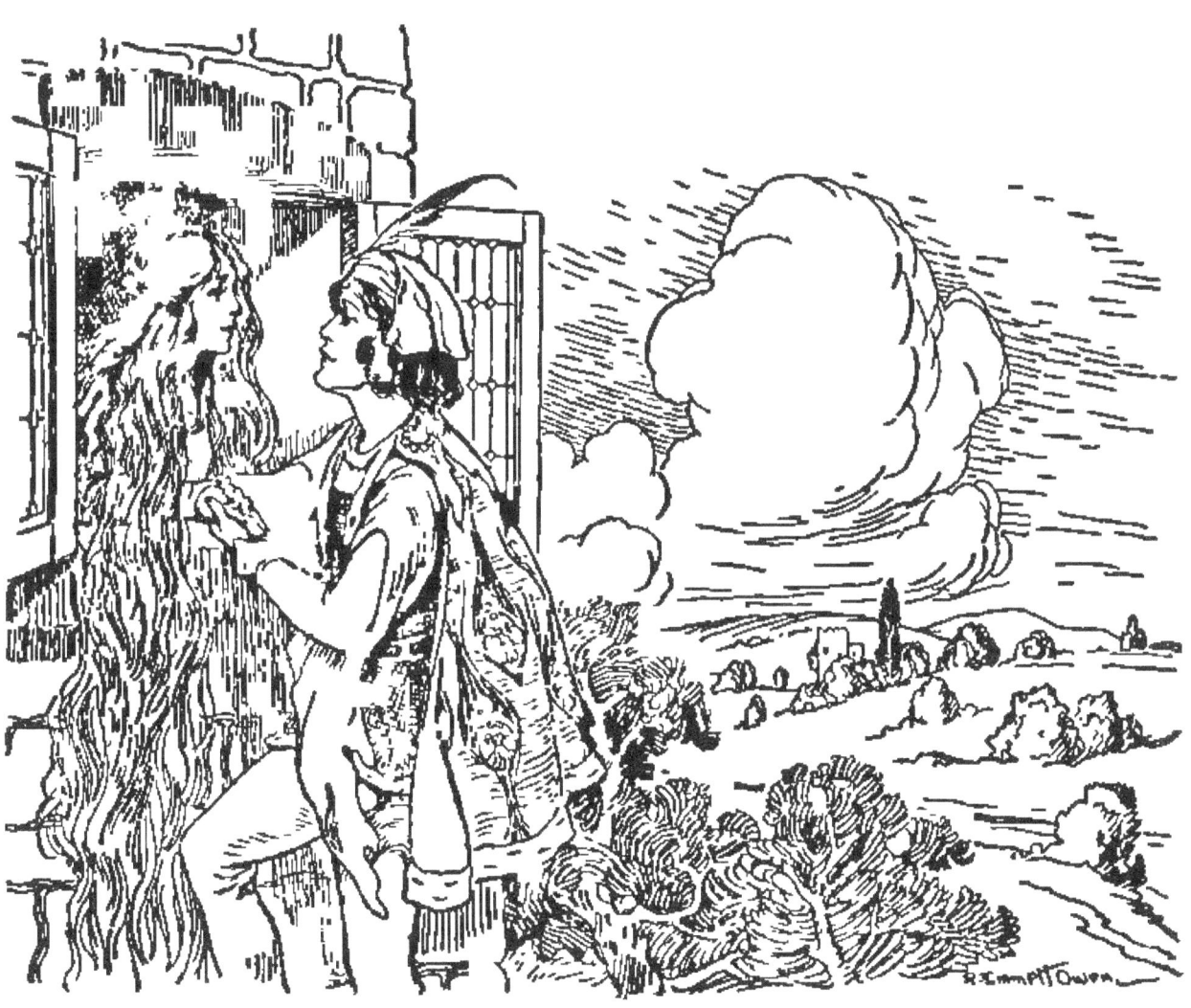

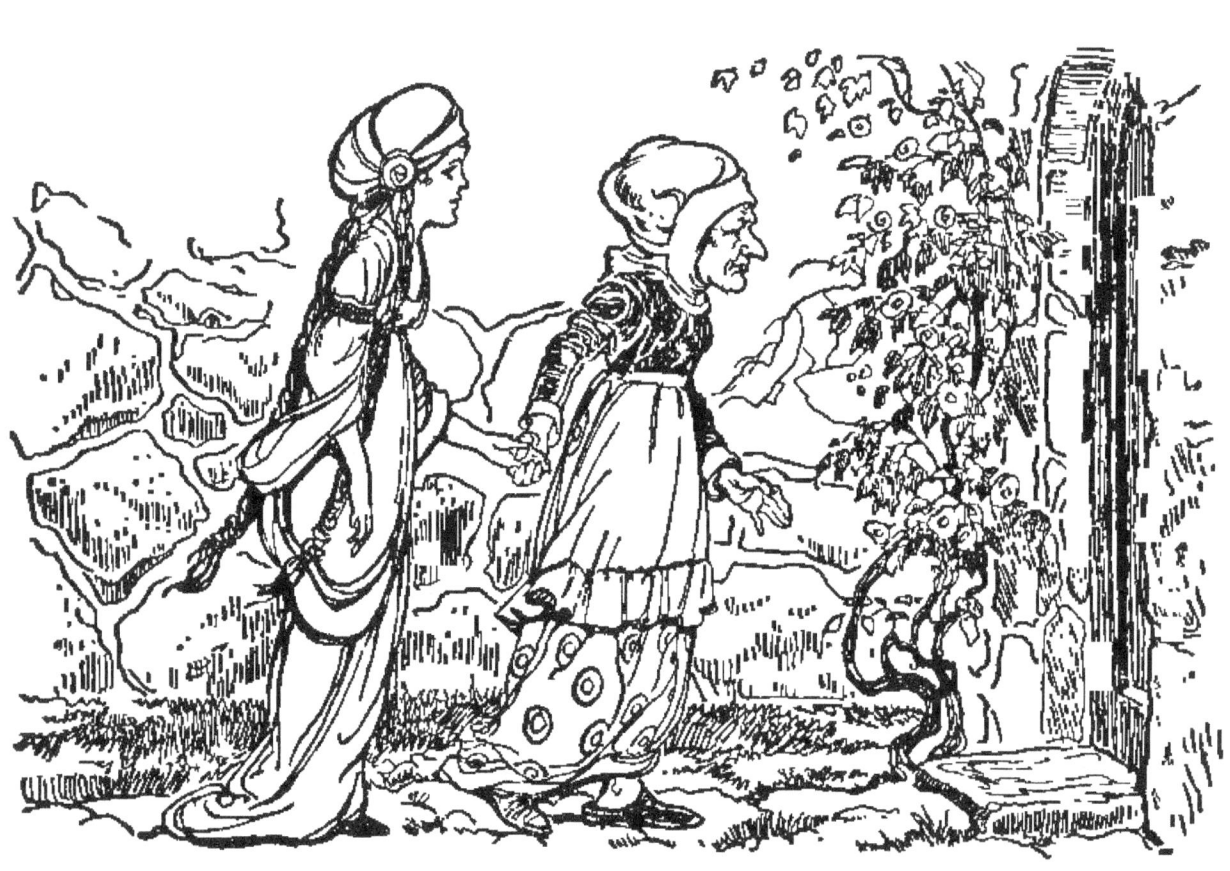

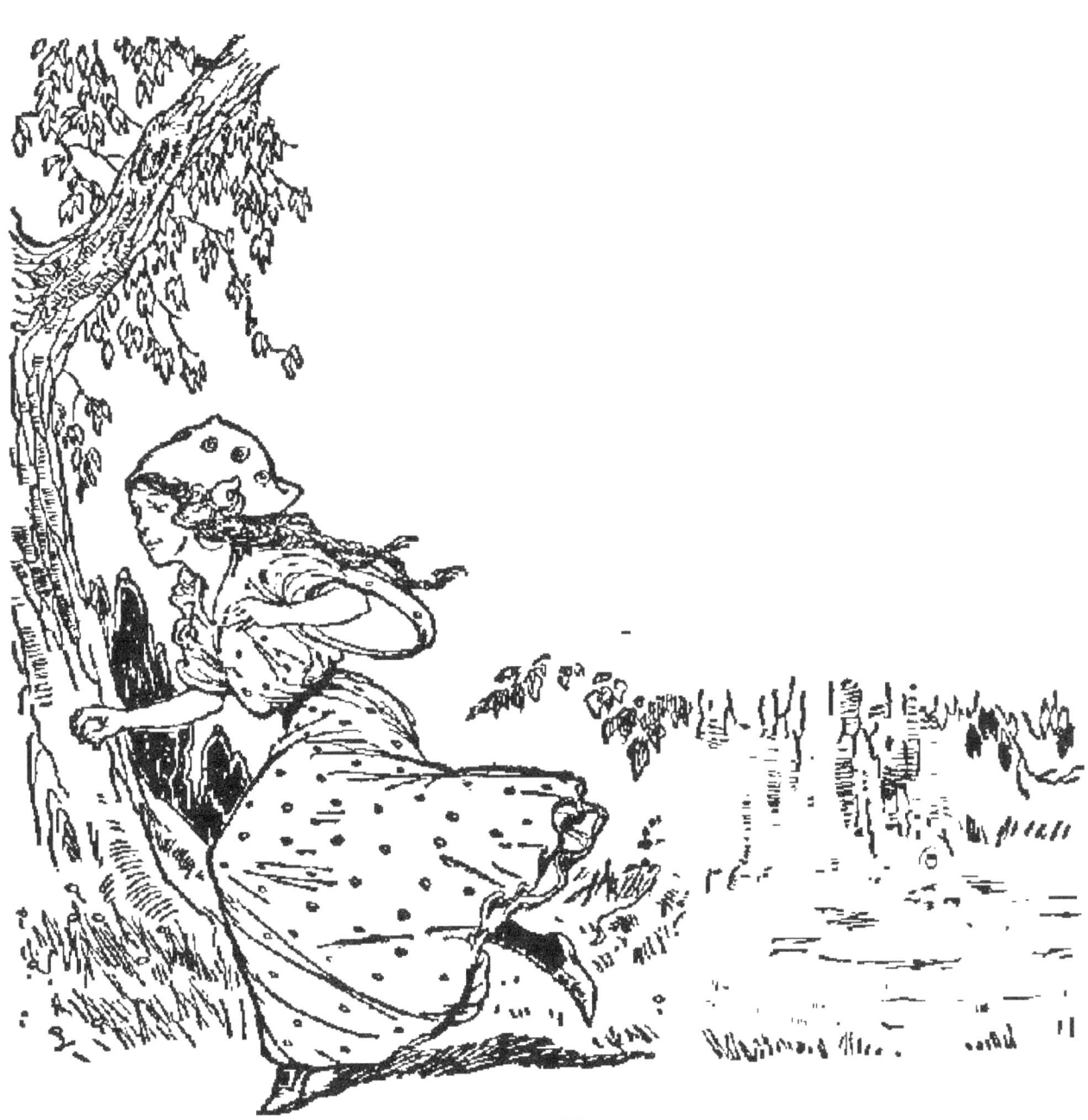

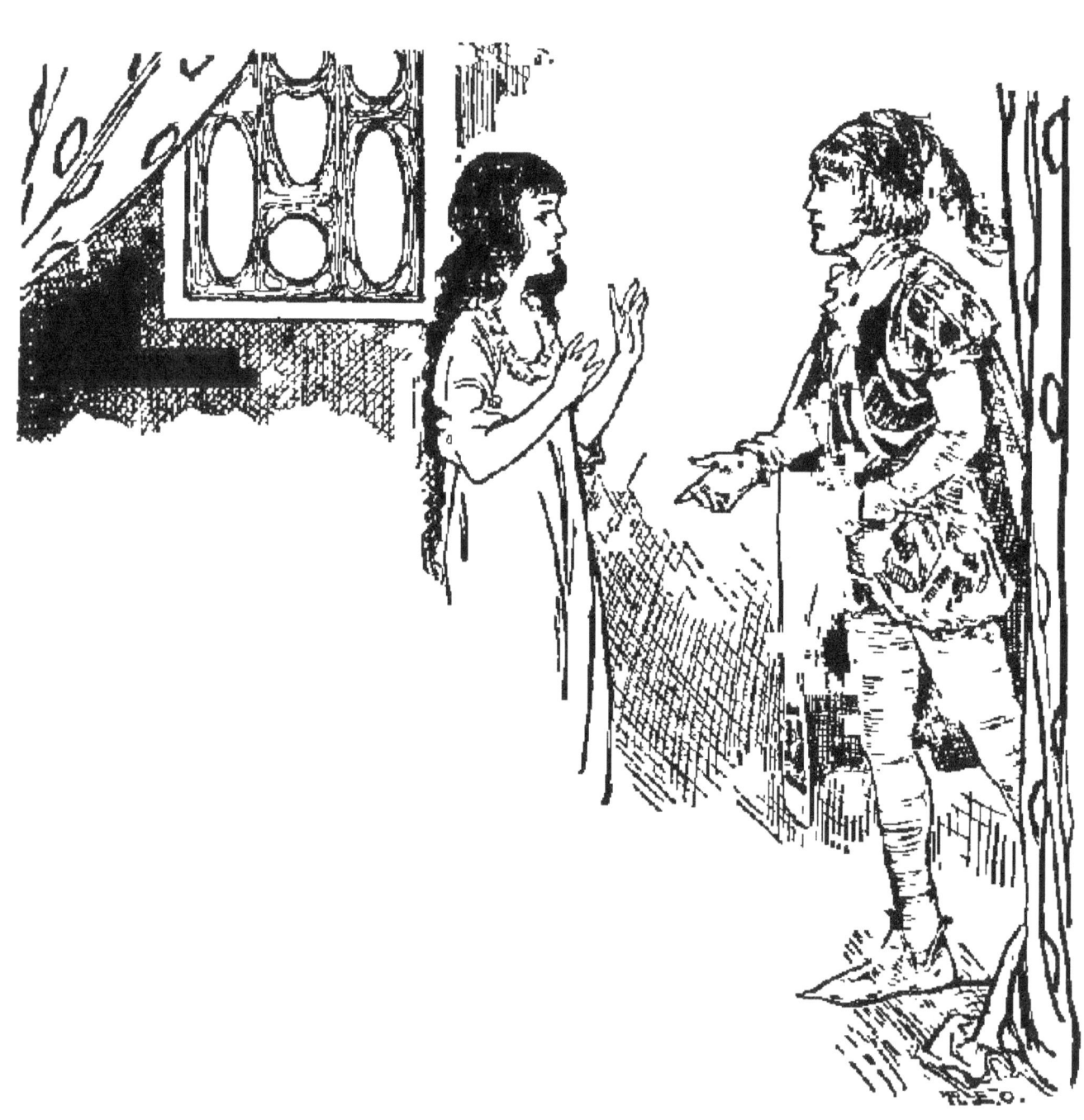

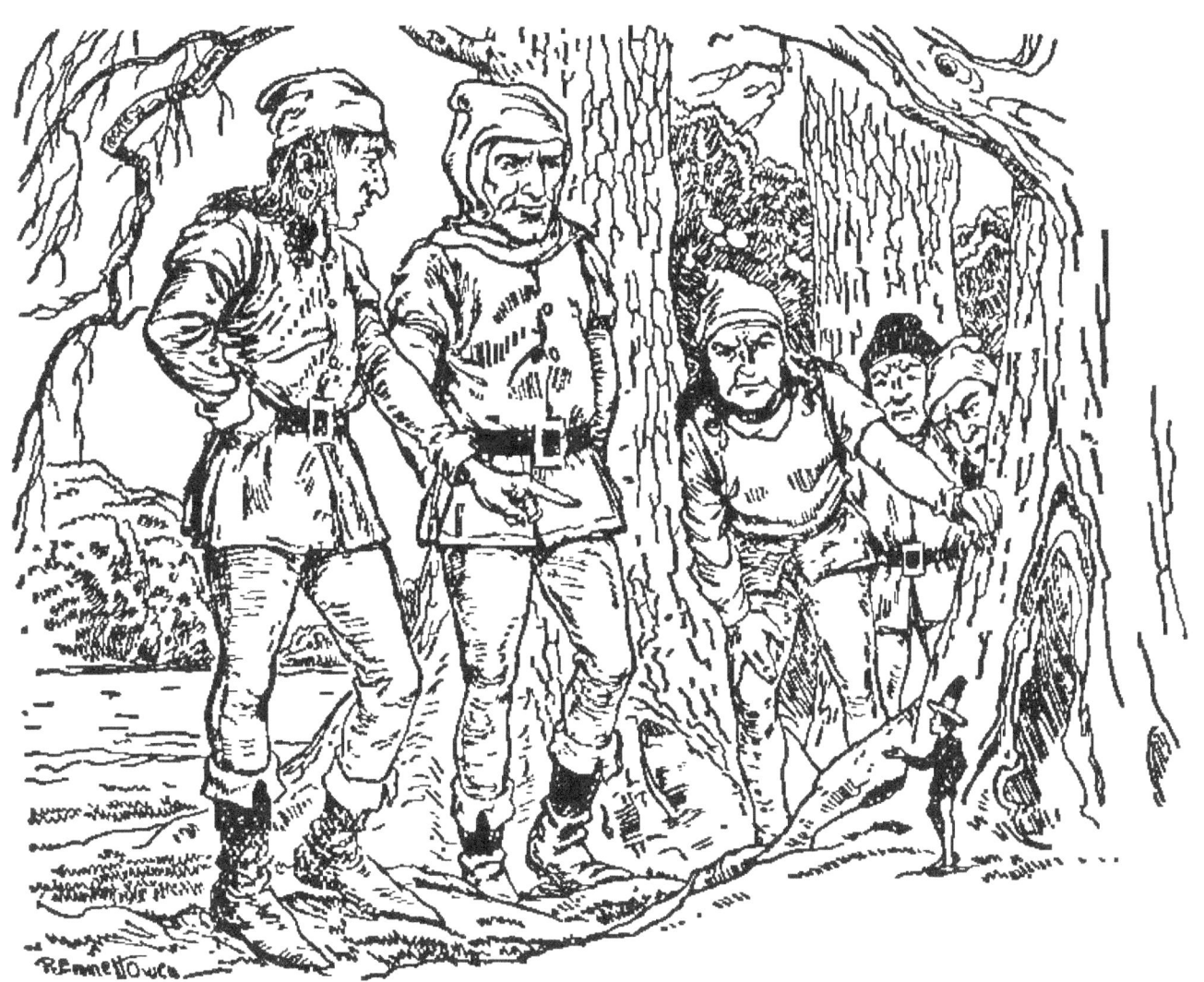

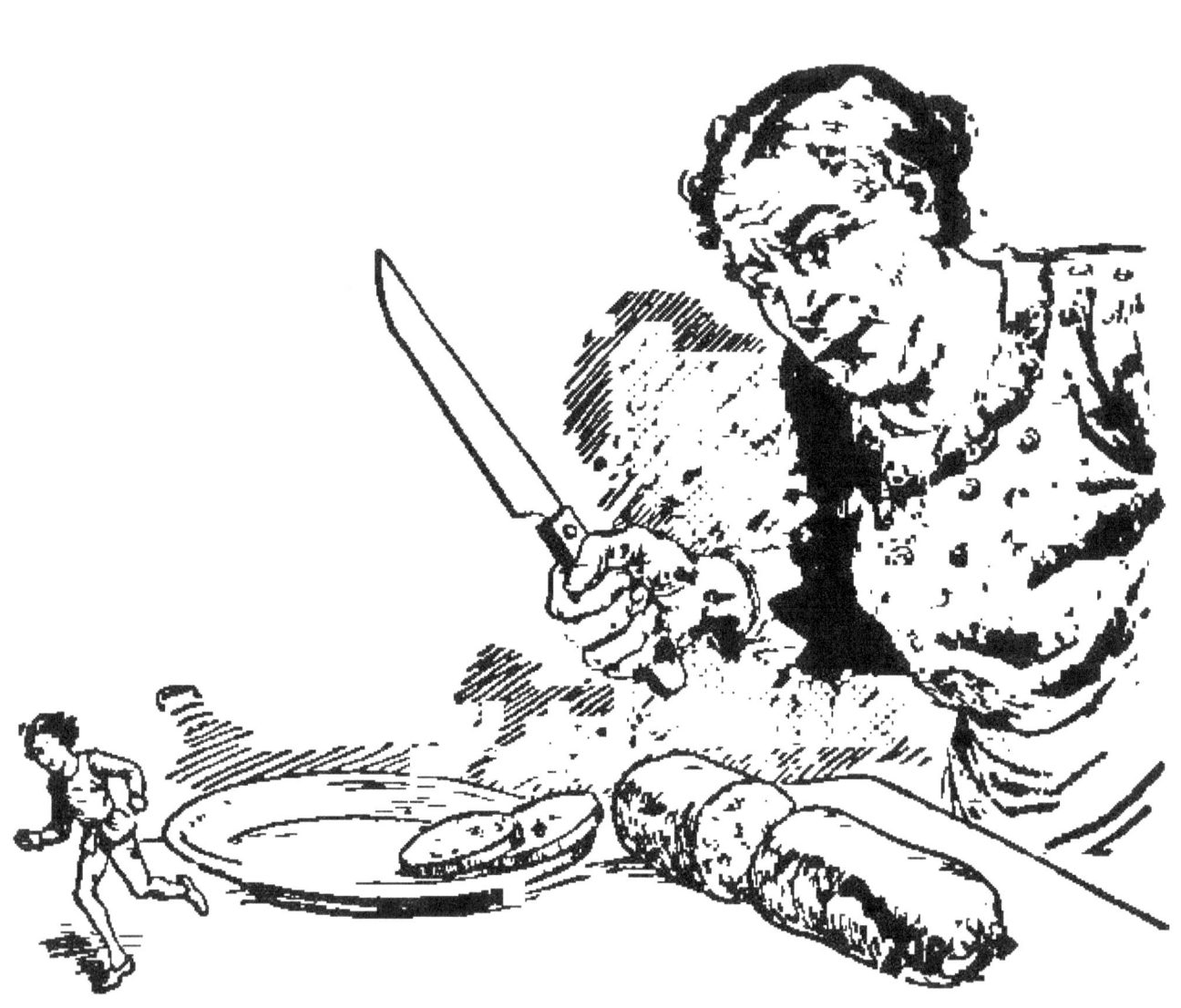

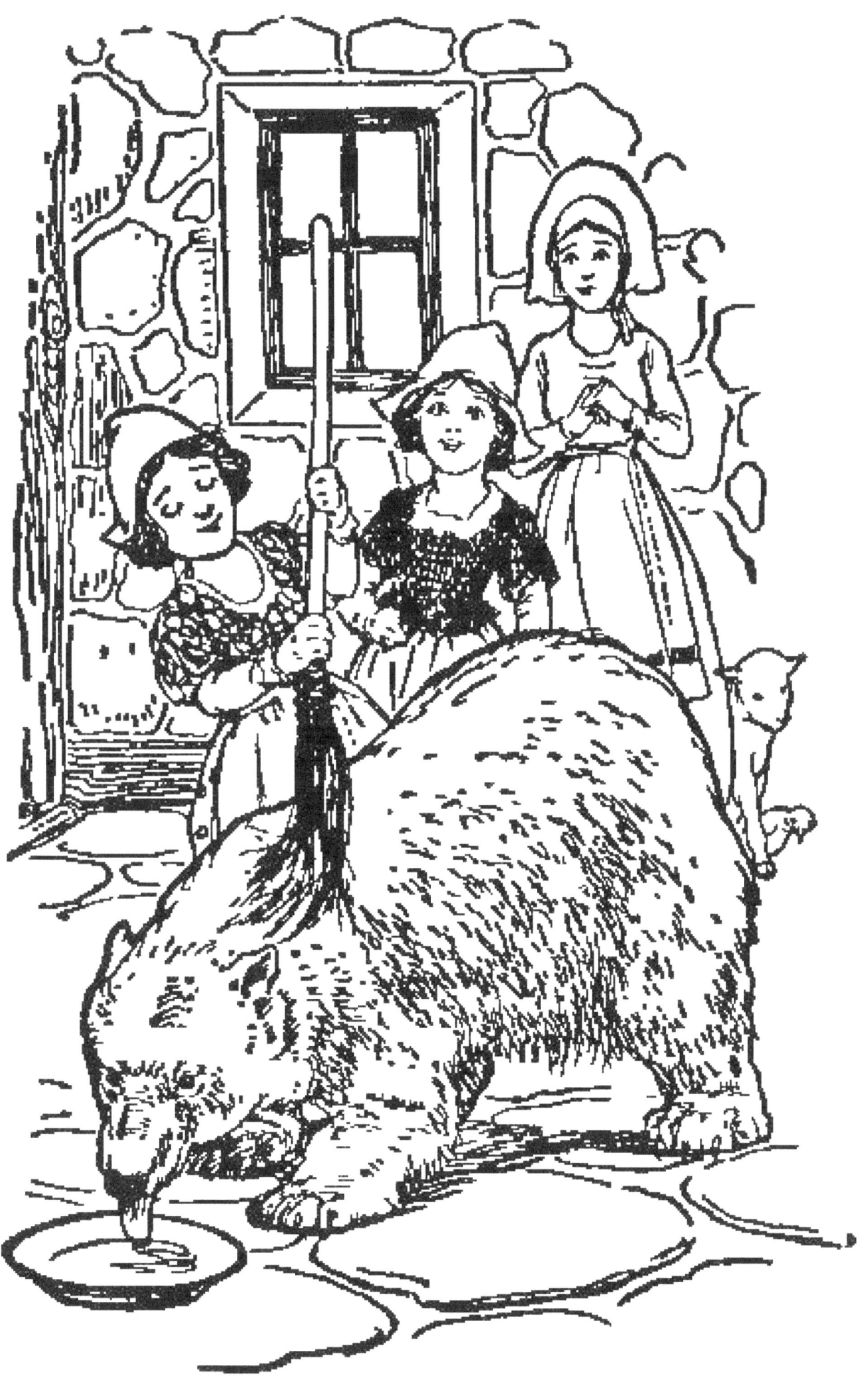

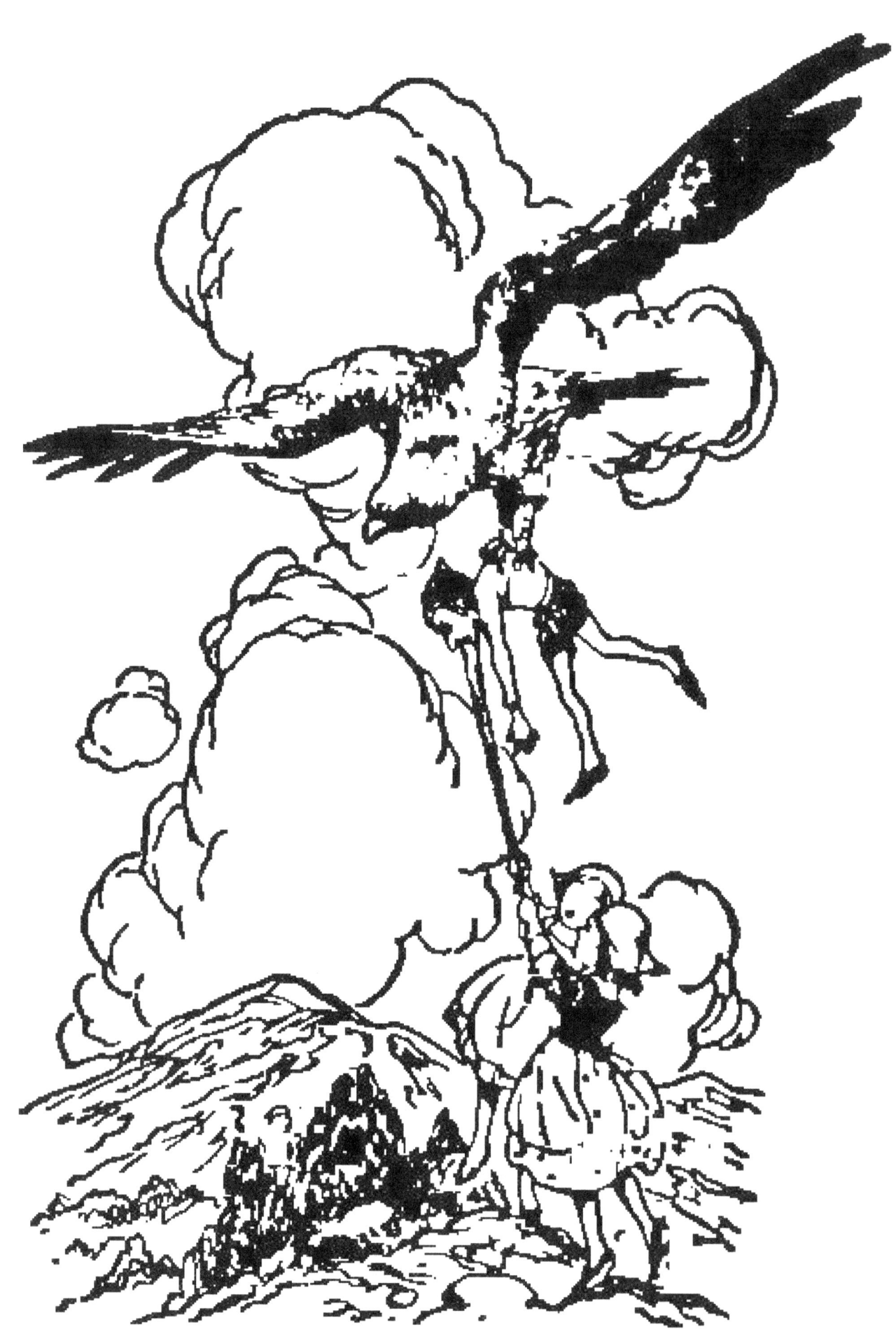

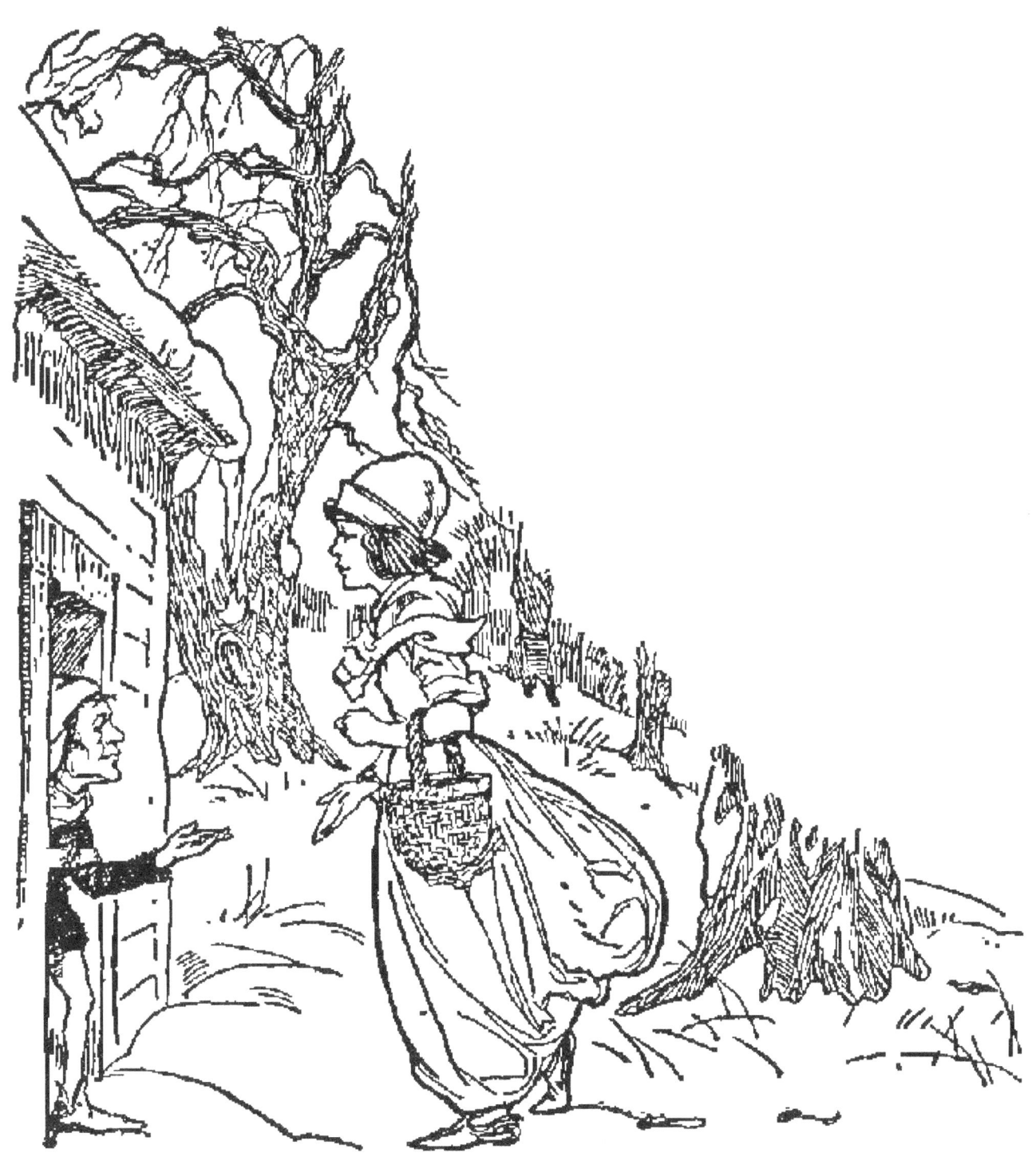

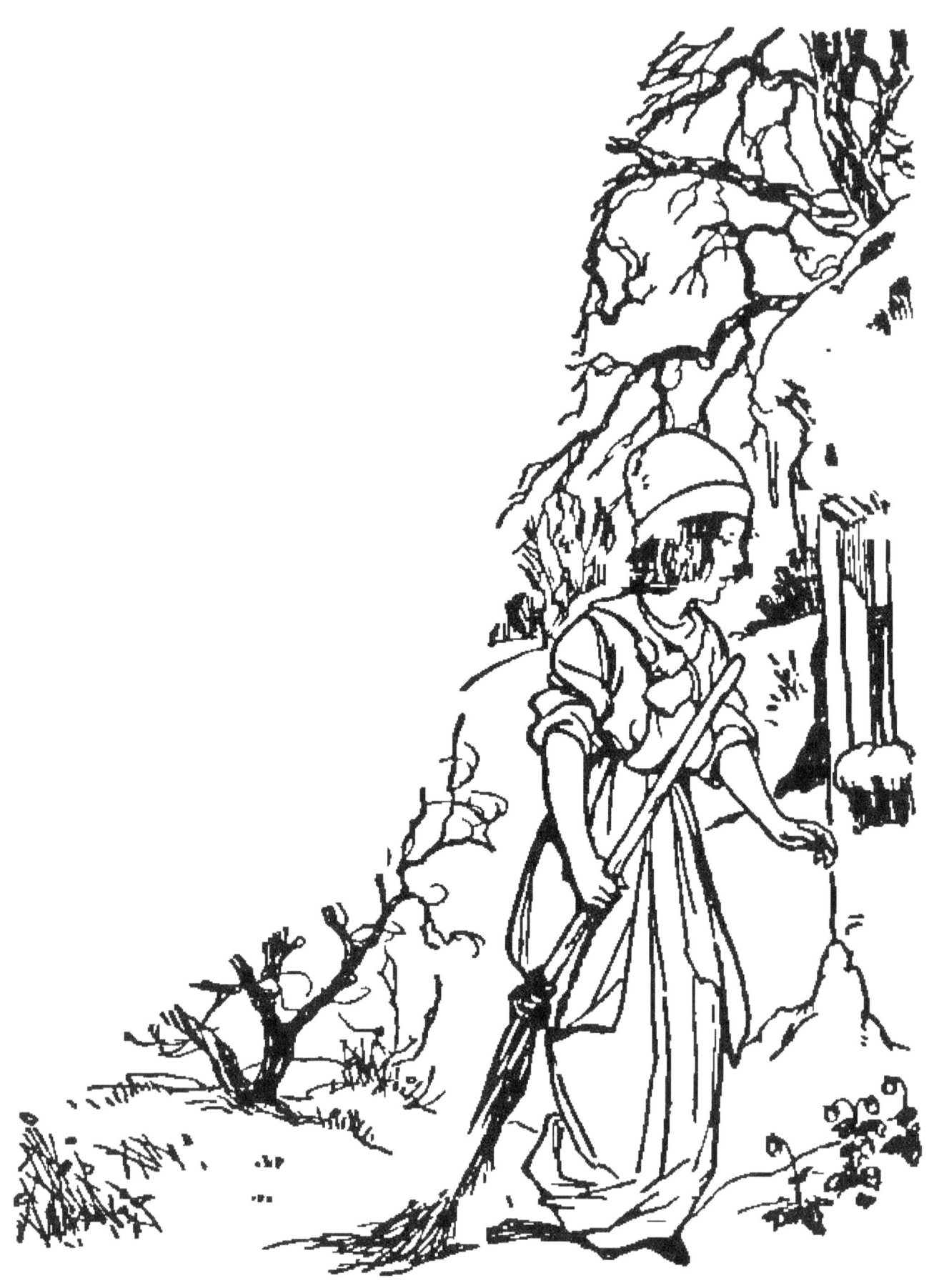

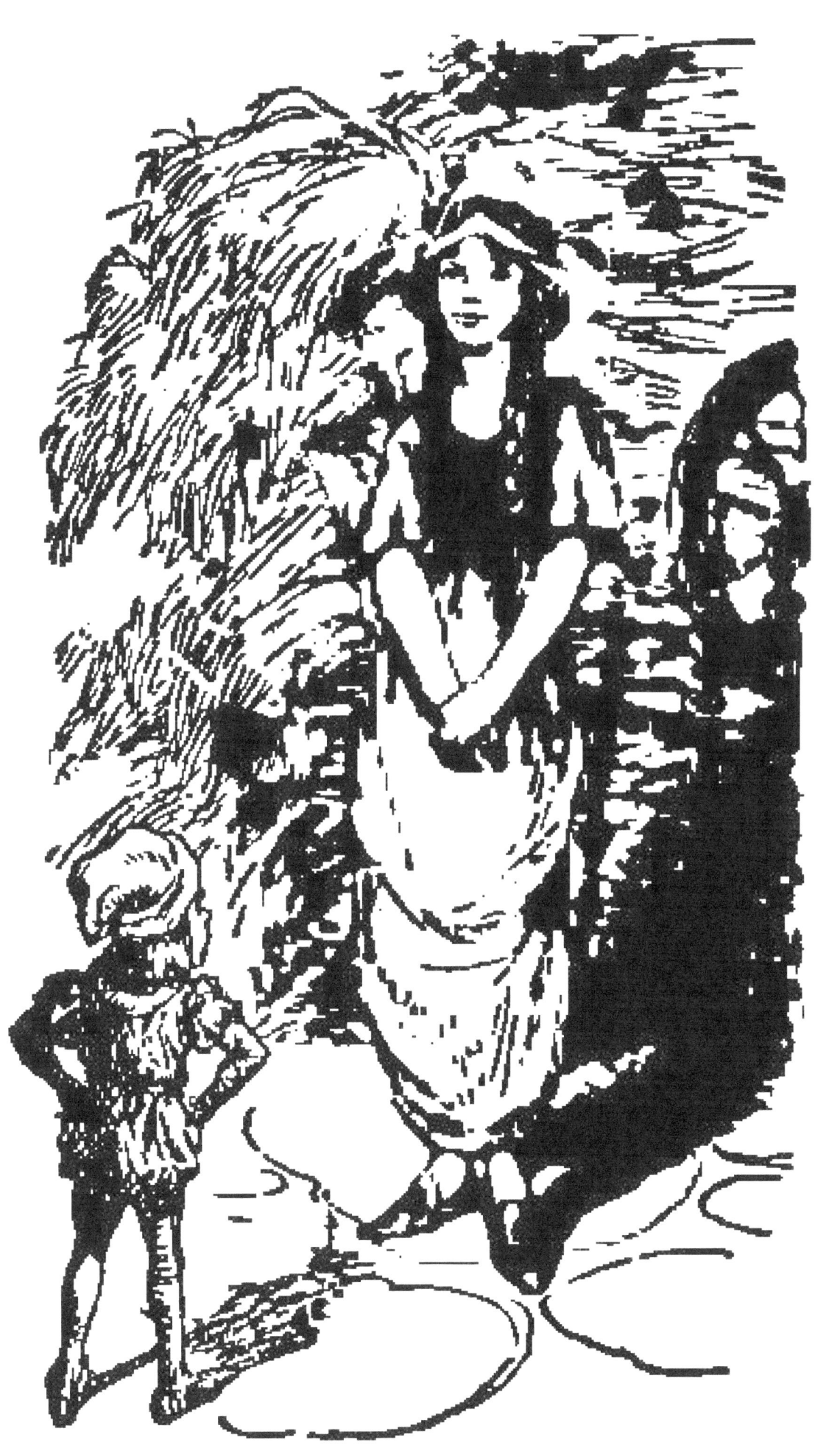

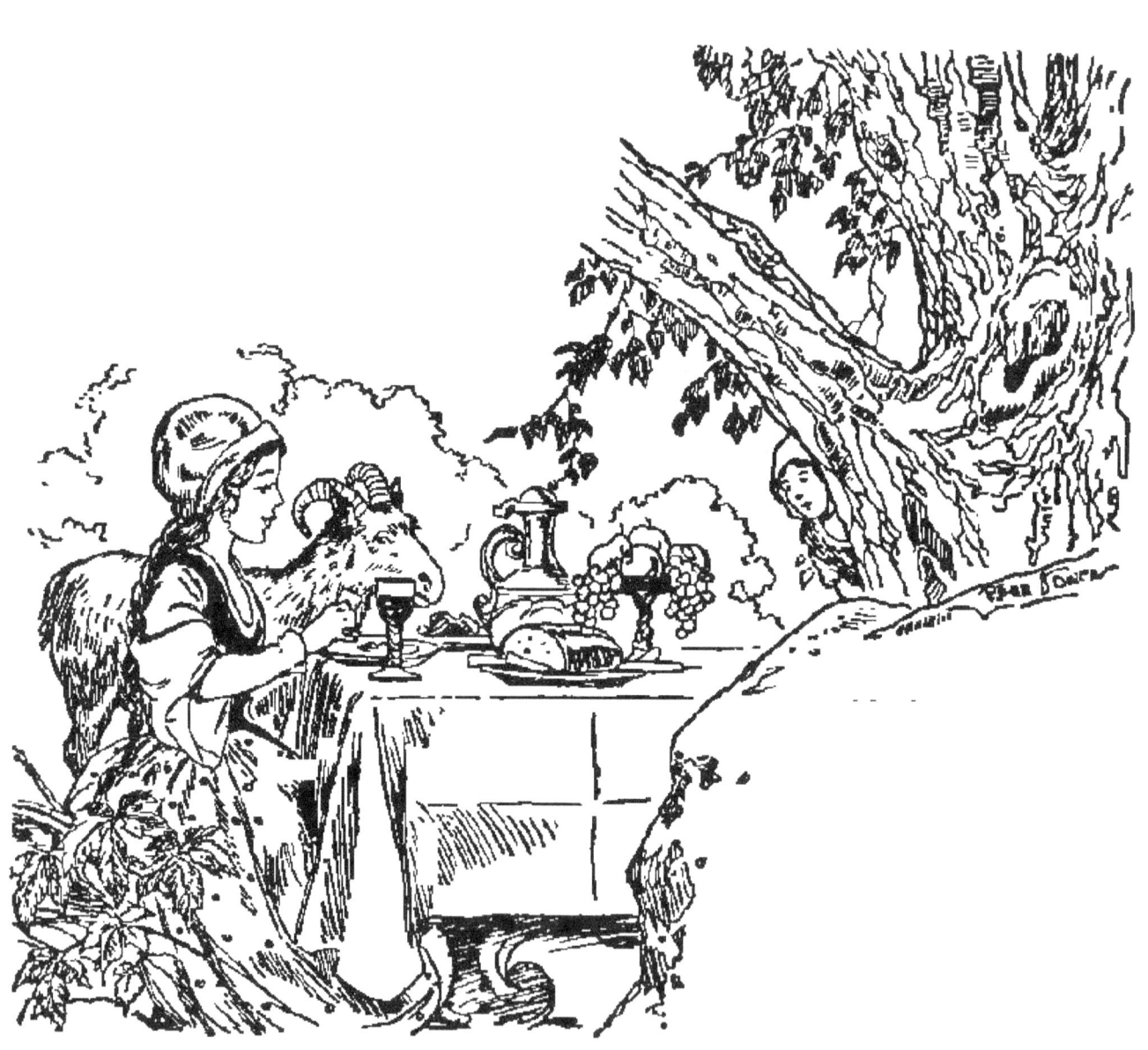

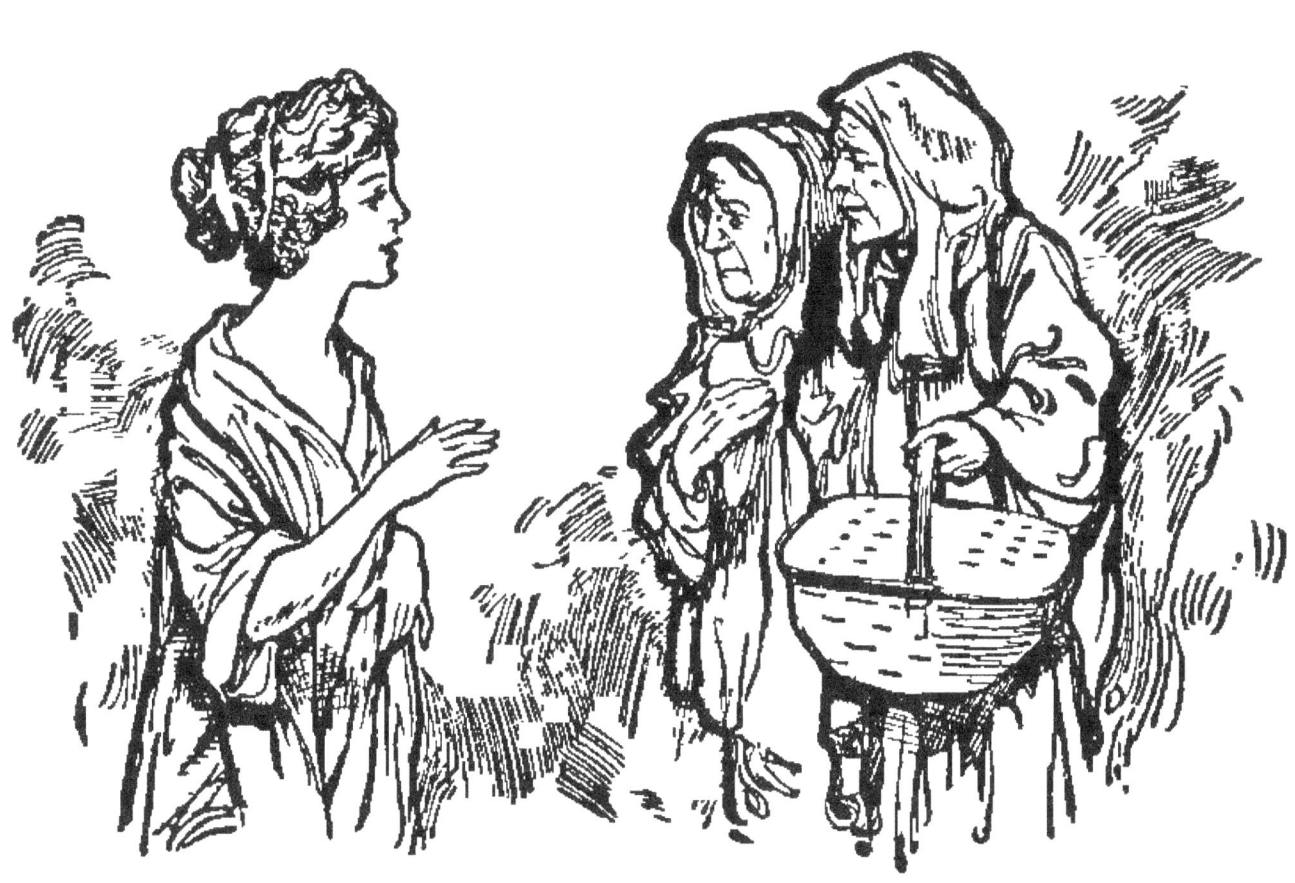

Johanna Berhardina
Midderigh-Bokhorst

Jean Jacques Midderigh

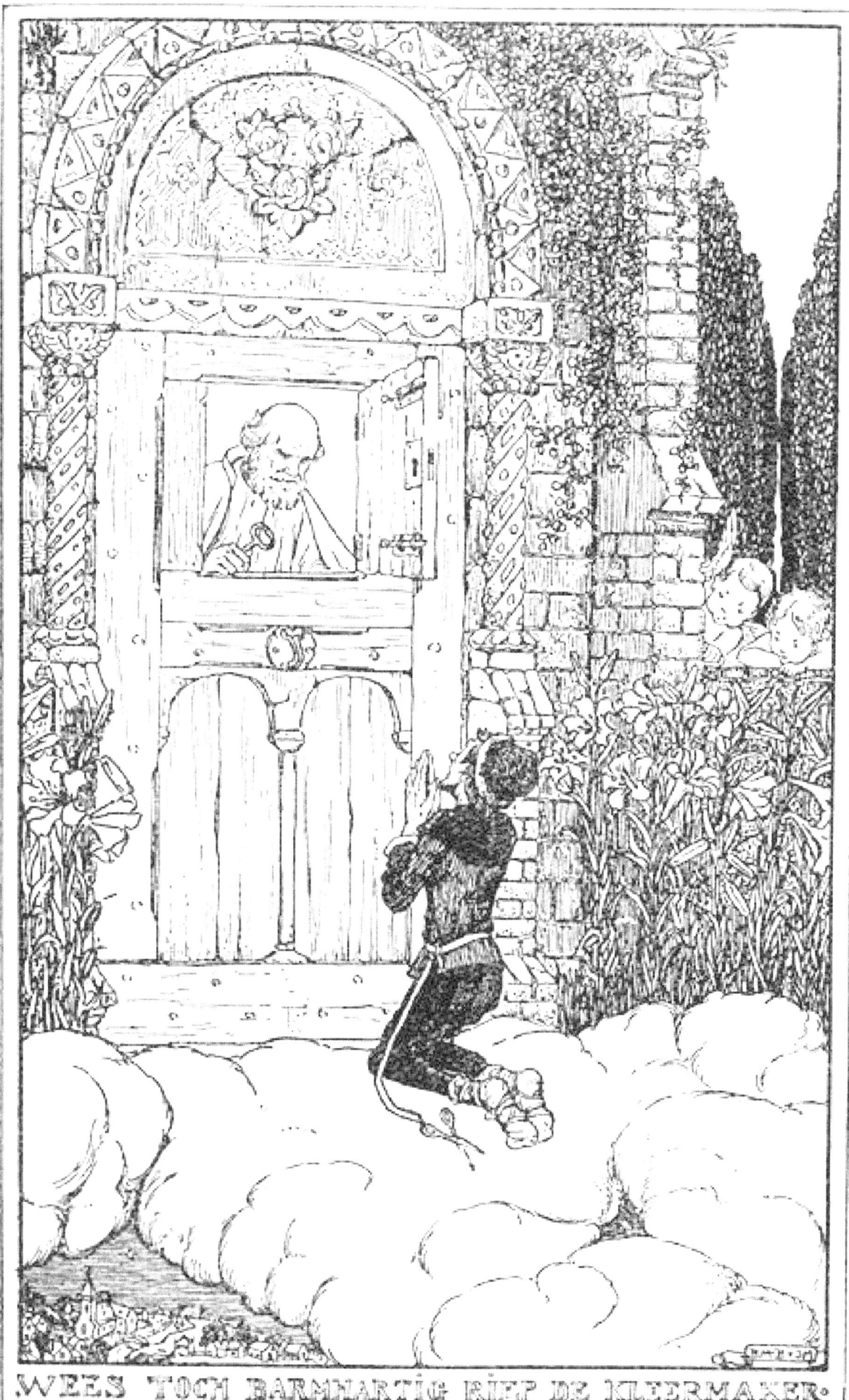

WEES TOCH BARMHARTIG RIEP DE KLEERMAKER.

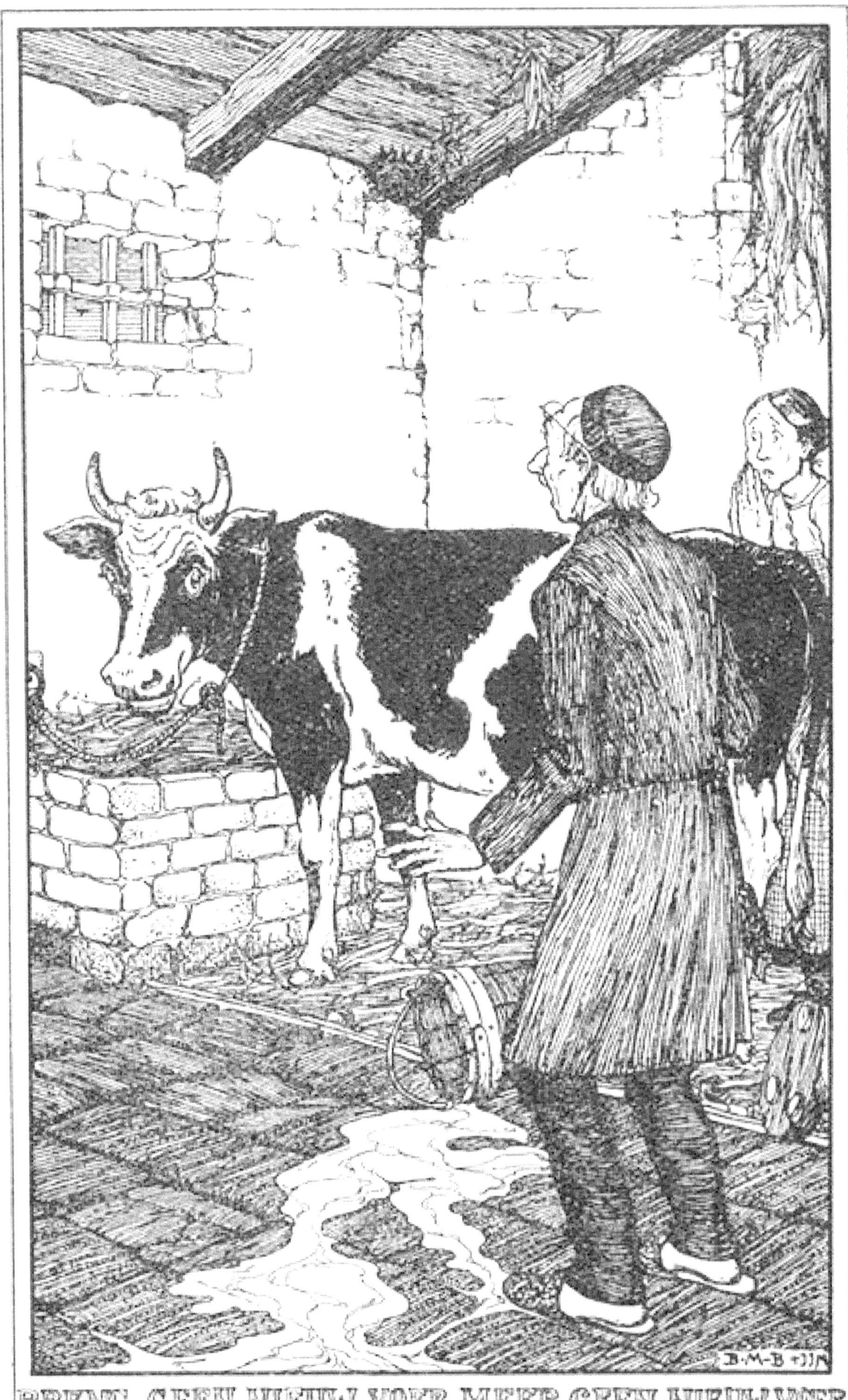

BRENG GEEN NIEUW VOER MEER, GEEN NIEUW VOER

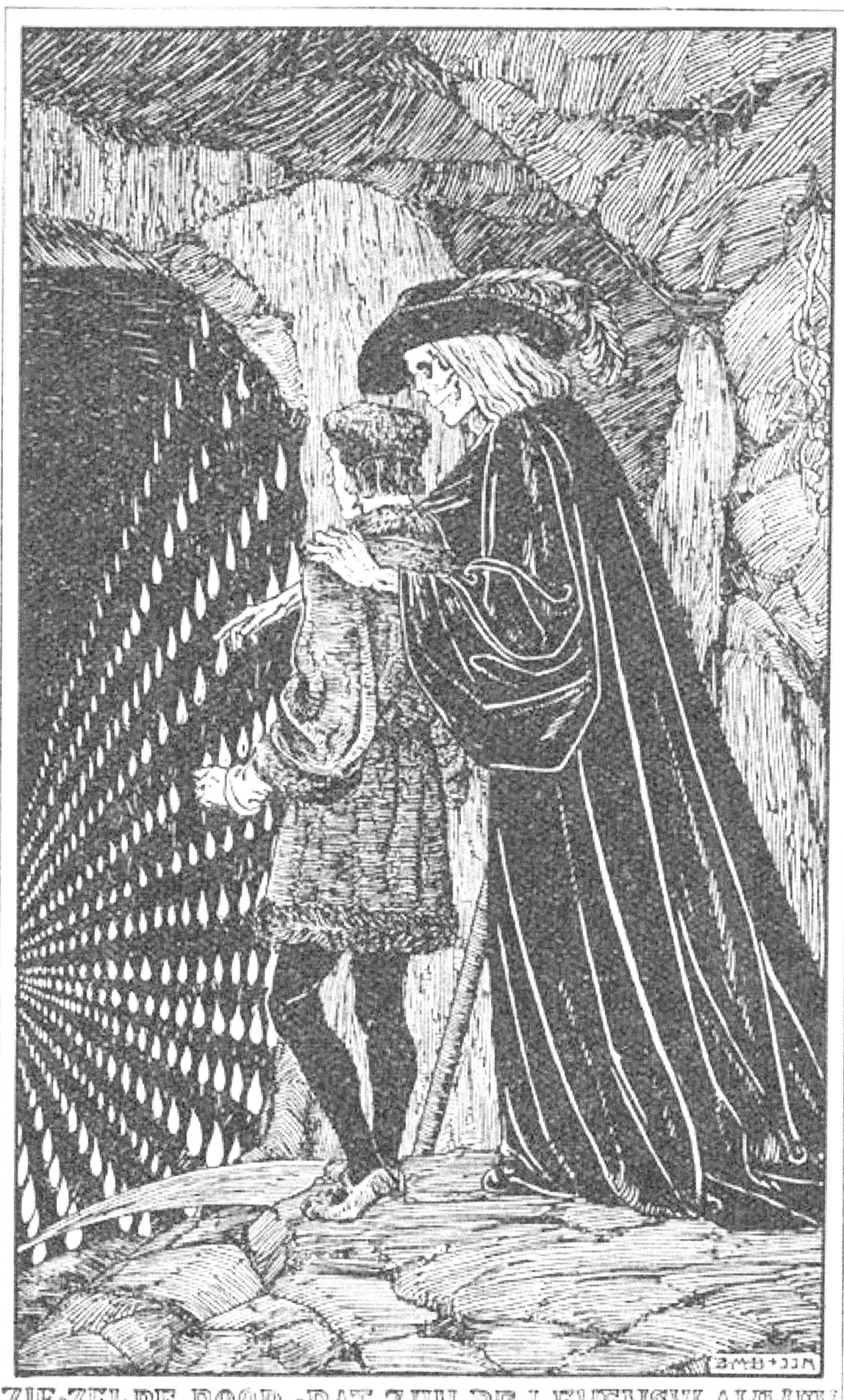

ZIE·ZEI·DE·DOOD·DAT·ZJN·DE·LEVENSVLAMMEN

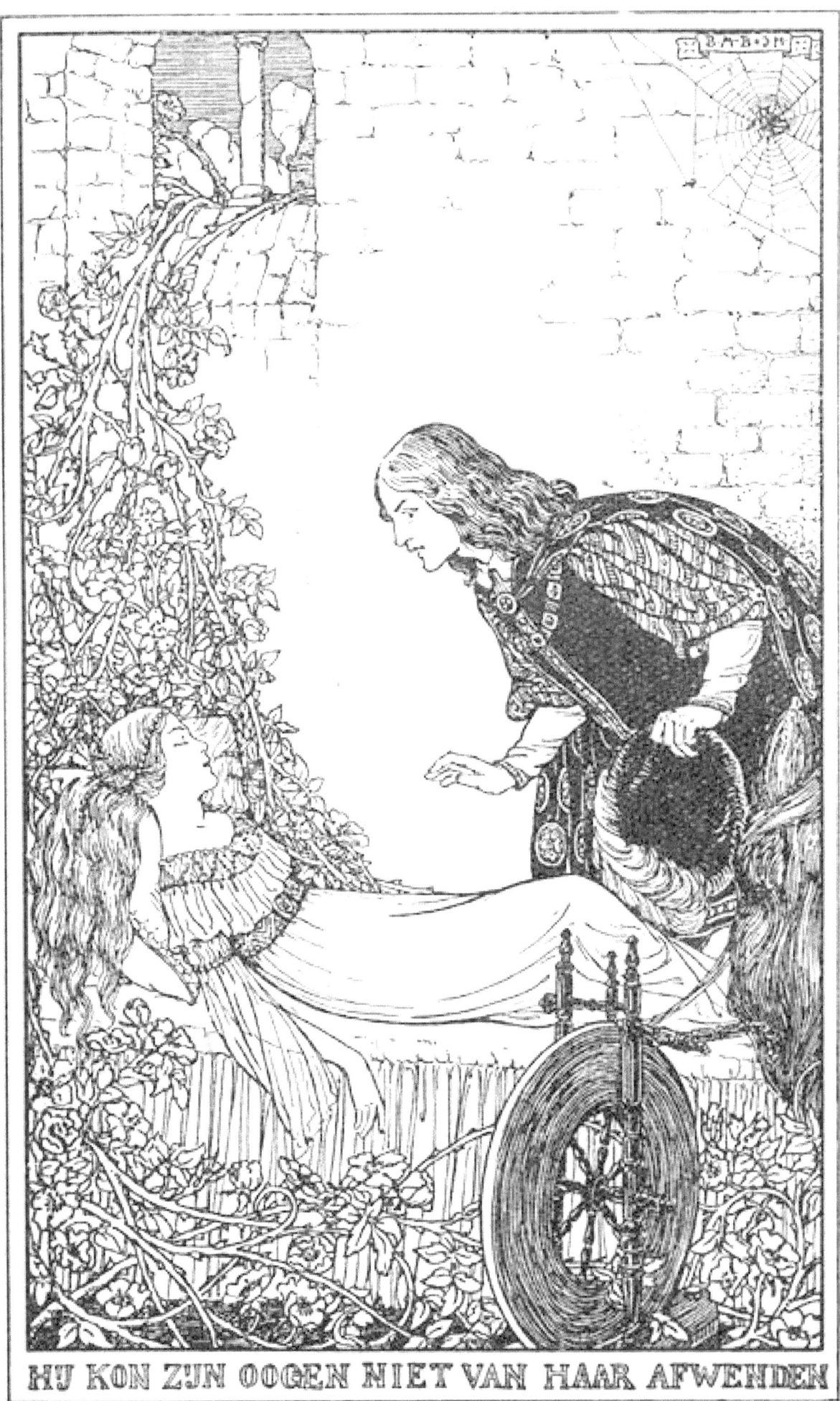

HIJ KON ZIJN OOGEN NIET VAN HAAR AFWENDEN

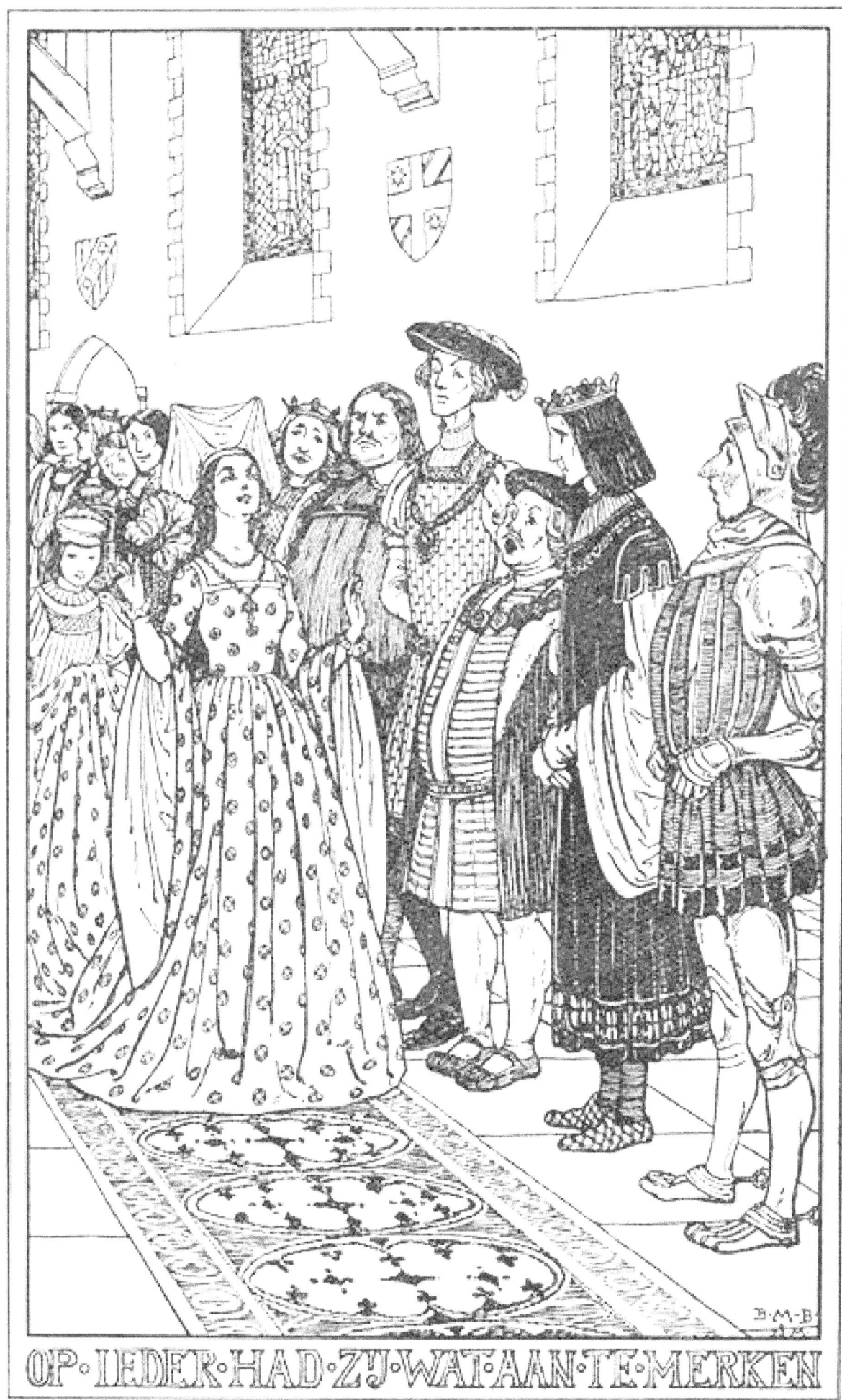

OP · IEDER · HAD · ZIJ · WAT · AAN · TE · MERKEN

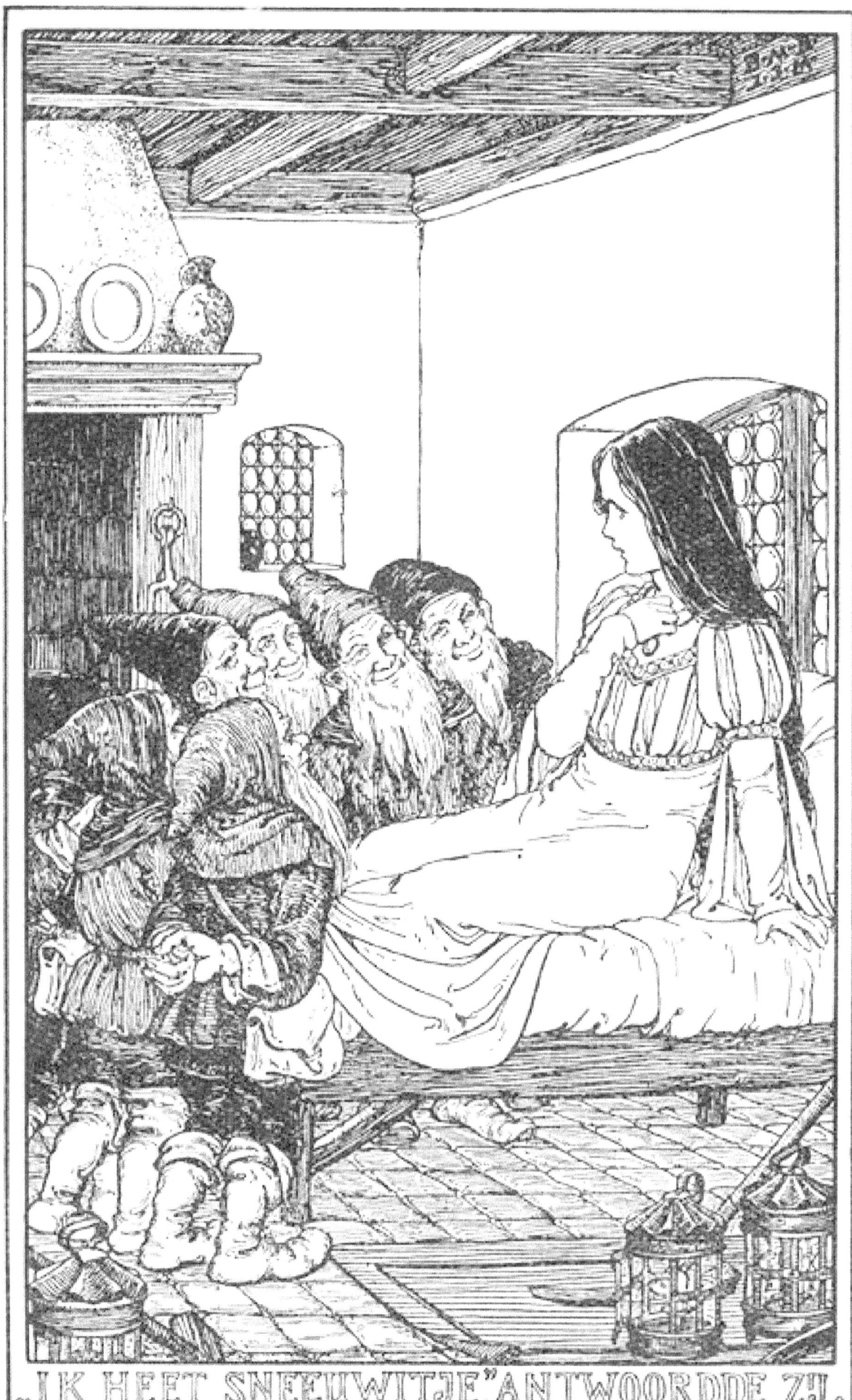

"IK HEET SNEEUWITJE" ANTWOORDDE ZIJ.

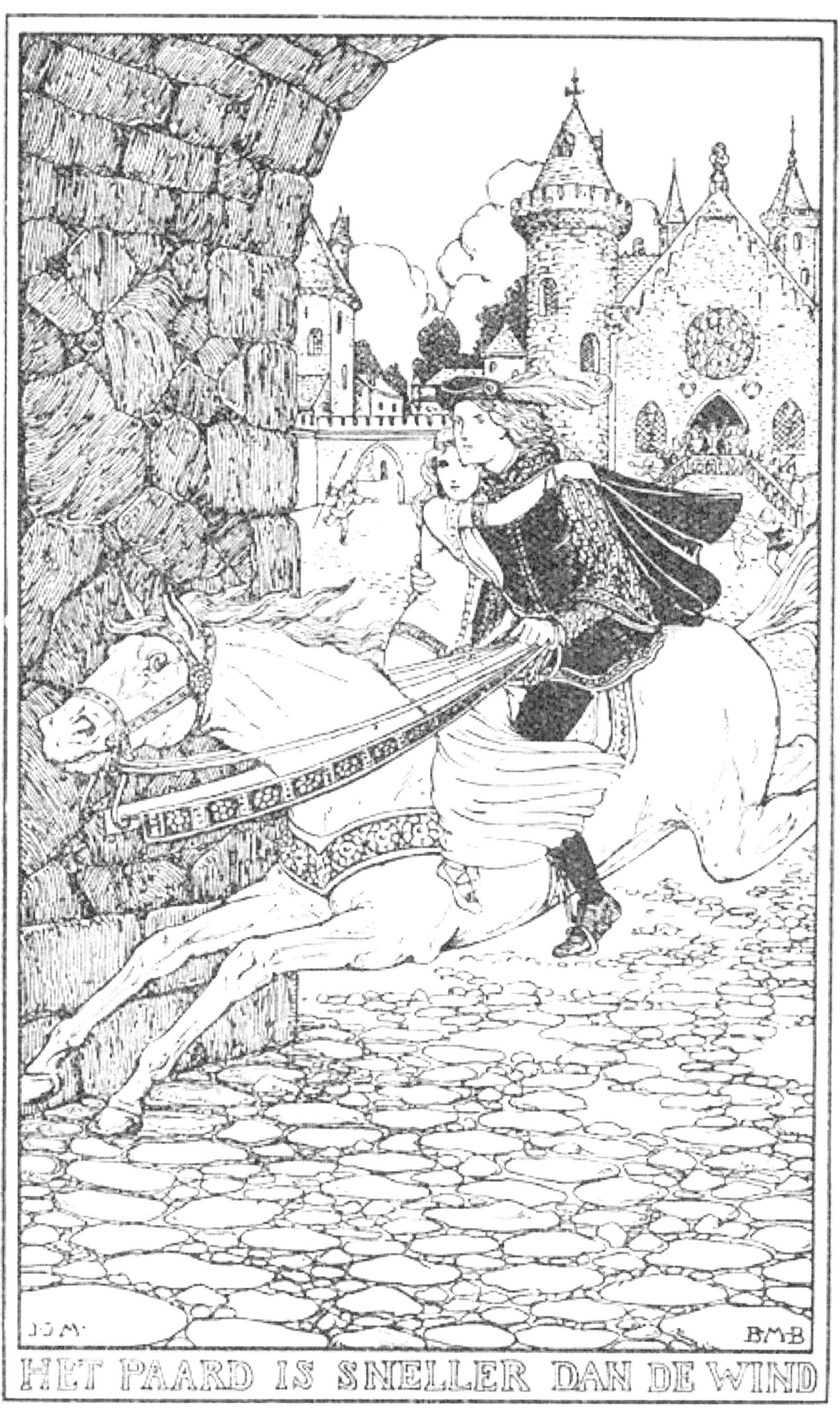

HET PAARD IS SNELLER DAN DE WIND

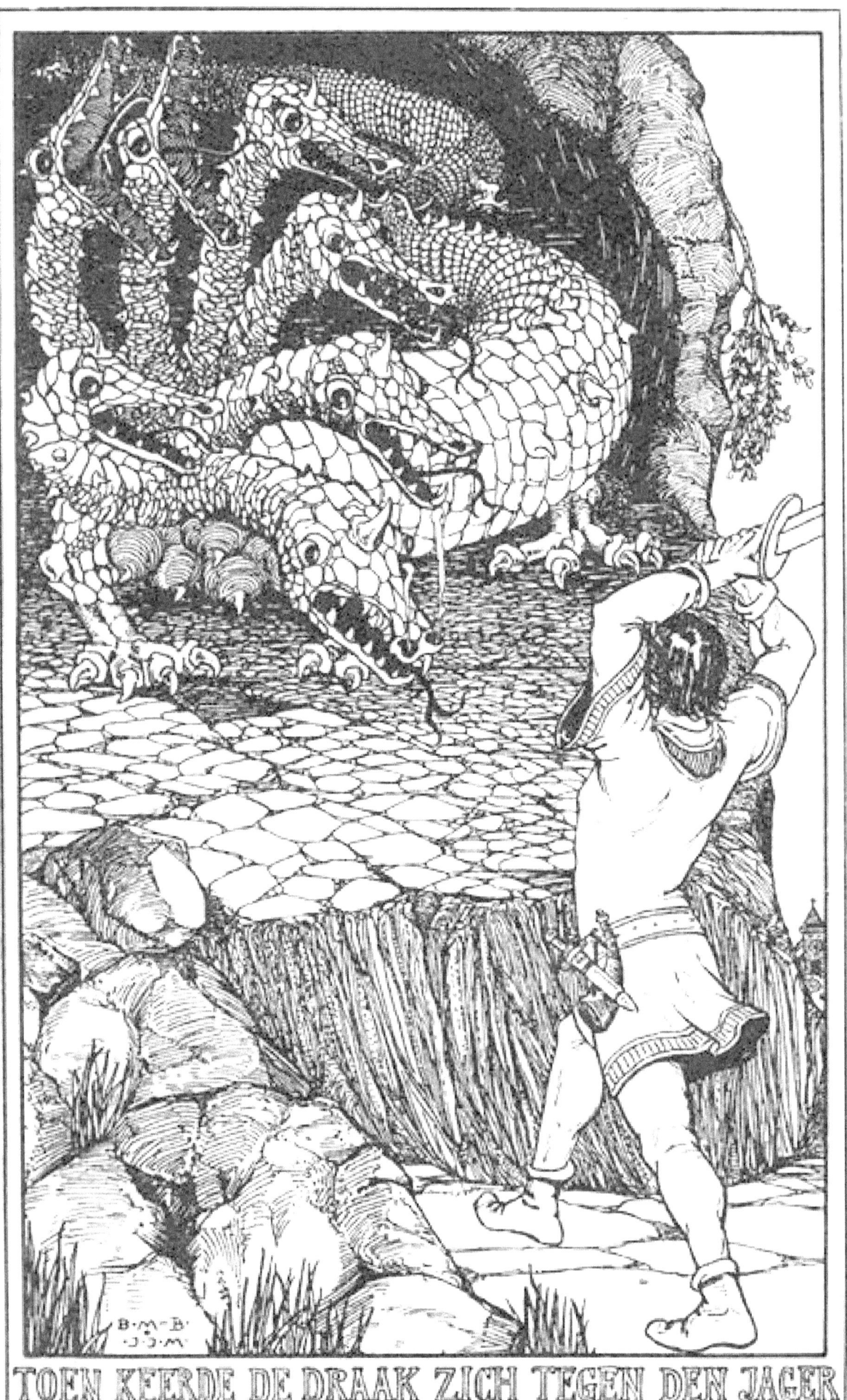

TOEN KEERDE DE DRAAK ZICH TEGEN DEN JAGER

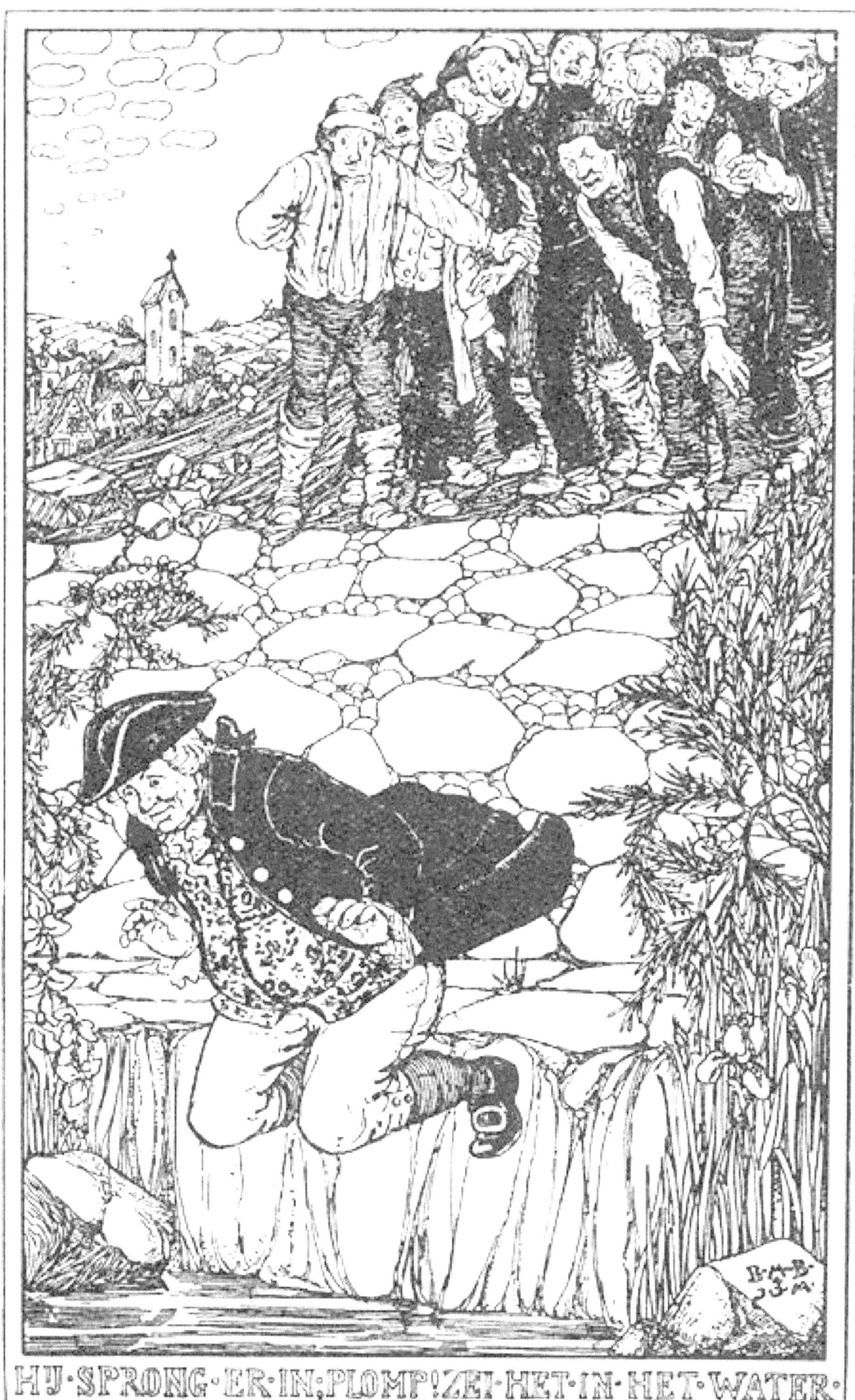

HIJ·SPRONG·ER·IN, PLOMP! ZEI·HET·IN·HET·WATER·

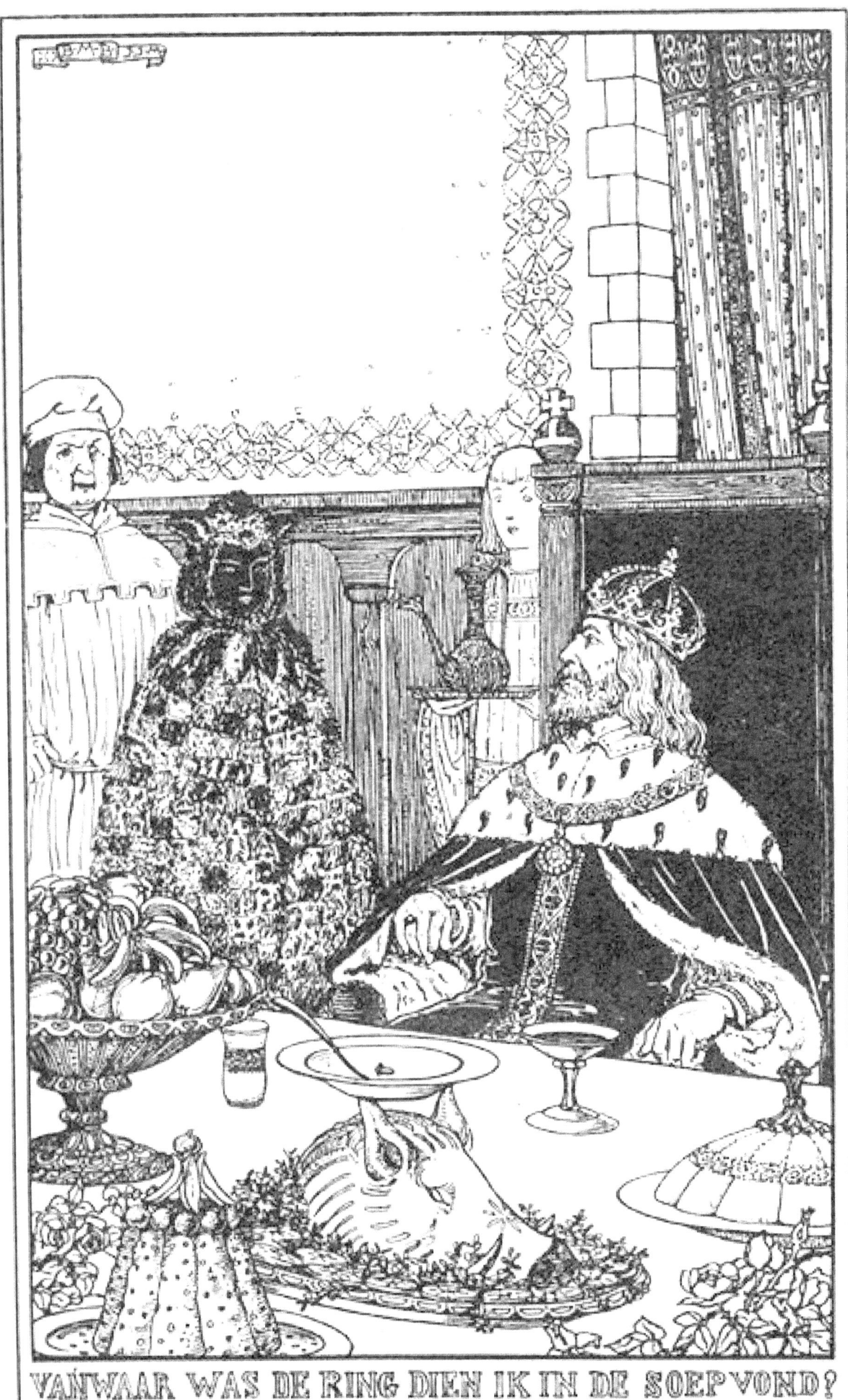

VANWAAR WAS DE RING DIEN IK IN DE SOEP VOND?

www.ingramcontent.com/pod-product-compliance
Lightning Source LLC
Chambersburg PA
CBHW081112180526
45170CB00008B/2810